ABSOLUTE PERSON AND MORAL EXPERIENCE

T&T Clark Enquiries in Theological Ethics

Series Editors
Brian Brock
Susan F. Parsons

ABSOLUTE PERSON AND MORAL EXPERIENCE

A Study in Neo-Calvinism

Nathan D. Shannon

LONDON • NEW YORK • OXFORD • NEW DELHI • SYDNEY

T&T CLARK
Bloomsbury Publishing Plc
50 Bedford Square, London, WC1B 3DP, UK
1385 Broadway, New York, NY 10018, USA
29 Earlsfort Terrace, Dublin 2, Ireland

BLOOMSBURY, T&T CLARK and the T&T Clark logo are trademarks of
Bloomsbury Publishing Plc

First published in Great Britain 2022
Paperback edition published 2024

Copyright © Nathan D. Shannon, 2022

Nathan D. Shannon has asserted his right under the Copyright, Designs and Patents Act, 1988, to be identified as Author of this work.

For legal purposes the Acknowledgments on p. xiv constitute an extension of this copyright page.

All rights reserved. No part of this publication may be reproduced or transmitted in any form or by any means, electronic or mechanical, including photocopying, recording, or any information storage or retrieval system, without prior permission in writing from the publishers.

Bloomsbury Publishing Plc does not have any control over, or responsibility for, any third-party websites referred to or in this book. All internet addresses given in this book were correct at the time of going to press. The author and publisher regret any inconvenience caused if addresses have changed or sites have ceased to exist, but can accept no responsibility for any such changes.

A catalogue record for this book is available from the British Library.

Library of Congress Cataloging-in-Publication Data
Names: Shannon, Nathan D. (Nathan Daniel), 1977– author.
Title: Absolute person and moral experience :
a study in neo-calvinism / Nathan D. Shannon.
Description: London ; New York : T&T Clark, 2022. |
Series: T&T Clark enquiries in theological ethics |
Includes bibliographical references and index. |
Identifiers: LCCN 2022004111 (print) | LCCN 2022004112 (ebook) |
ISBN 9780567707352 (hb) | ISBN 9780567707390 (paperback) |
ISBN 9780567707345 (epdf) | ISBN 9780567707383 (epub)
Subjects: LCSH: Sin, Original–History of doctrines. |
Christian ethics–Reformed authors. | Calvinism. | Reformed Church–Doctrines.
Classification: LCC BT720 .S45 2022 (print) | LCC BT720 (ebook) |
DDC 233/.14–dc23/eng/20220411
LC record available at https://lccn.loc.gov/2022004111
LC ebook record available at https://lccn.loc.gov/2022004112

ISBN: HB: 978-0-5677-0735-2
PB: 978-0-5677-0739-0
ePDF: 978-0-5677-0734-5
ePUB: 978-0-5677-0738-3

Series: T&T Clark Enquiries in Theological Ethics

Typeset by Newgen KnowledgeWorks Pvt. Ltd., Chennai, India

To find out more about our authors and books visit www.bloomsbury.com and sign up for our newsletters.

For Sabina

CONTENTS

Preface	ix
Acknowledgments	xiv
List of Abbreviations	xv

Chapter 1
DIVINE MORAL CHARACTER SELF-GIVEN	1
Edenic Theater and Cosmic Conflict	3
Prohibition and Probation: A Relational Rationale	19
Trinity, Edenic Freedom, and the Problem of Evil	30
Conclusion	35

Chapter 2
DIVINE MORAL CHARACTER TRANSGRESSED	37
Natural and Special Moral Meaning	39
The Image of God	42
Conclusion	75

Chapter 3
ABSOLUTE PERSON, REASON, AND HISTORY	77
The Structure of Reason	78
The God-Concept and Environments of Ethical Reason	83
Obedience and True Religion	88
Covenant and History	102
Conclusion	114

Chapter 4
FROM METAETHICS TO TRINITY TO ACCOMMODATION	117
Ontology and Relation	118
Trinity and Absolute Person	123
Hermeneutics and Fearless Anthropomorphism	134
Fearless Anthropomorphism and Reformed Tradition	141
Conclusion	158

Chapter 5
BAVINCK ON THE UNIQUENESS OF THE INCARNATION	161
System and the Structure of Dogmatics	162
Christology and Dogmatic System	166

Incarnation and the Trinity	168
Incarnation and Creation	173
Incarnation and Revelation	178
Uniqueness of the Incarnation	185
Conclusion	187

Chapter 6
CONCLUSION: MORAL EXPERIENCE AND THE SON FORSAKEN   191

Bibliography   197
Index   203

PREFACE

My friend Alex Tseng published a study of Karl Barth entitled *Barth's Ontology of Sin and Grace*, bearing the catchy subtitle, *Variations on a Theme of Augustine*.[1] Augustine is the inconspicuous background, the progenitor of the salient themes, to Alex's book, in which he observes Barth wrestling with the ancient African's formidable legacy. Specifically, Alex's book is a study of Barth's "actualistic reorientation of Augustine's ontology and harmatiology."[2]

In a similar vein, the present study may be viewed as an examination of neo-Calvinist theology in terms of two distinctive achievements of the bishop of Hippo. First, a theological historiography. Etienne Gilson says of *The City of God* that "in this work, perhaps for the first time, thanks to the light of revelation which reveals to it the hidden origin and end of the universe, a human mind dares to attempt a synthesis of universal history."[3] Augustine was convinced, says Johan Bavinck, that "God has a wise and holy meaning for all those goings-on," for the events of history and human experience.[4] Augustine believed that Scripture as such, as divine interpretation of history, represented this fact of the unity-in-diversity of the meaningfulness of human experience, and he believed that a theology of history was not only possible but necessary for the intelligibility of human nature and experience. So claims Johan Bavinck: "The entire course of human history remains a closed book for those who fail to recognize what in essence is the basis of it all."[5]

Bavinck in fact believed that evidence of an implicit consciousness of the intelligibility of history as such was pervasive in indigenous religions, and likely in human religious consciousness as such. He recorded, for example, this

---

1. Shao Kai Tseng, *Barth's Ontology and Sin and Grace: Variations on a Theme of Augustine* (New York: Routledge, 2020).

2. Tseng, *Barth's Ontology*, 1.

3. "Pour la première fois peut-être dans sette oeuvre, grâce à la Lumière de la révélation qui lui dévoile l'origine et la fin cachées de l'univers, une raison humaine ose tenter la synthèse de l'histoire universelle." Etienne Gilson, *Introduction à l'étude de Saint Augustin*, vol. 11, part 1, 3rd ed. (Paris: Librairie Philosophique J. Vrin, 1949), 230. It is precisely this historical revelatory approach that displeased John Hick. See his *Evil and the God of Love*, 2nd ed. (London: Macmillan, 1977). In response, see Nico Vorster, "The Augustinian Type of Theodicy: Is It Outdated?," *Journal of Reformed Theology* 5 (2011): 26–48.

4. J. H. Bavinck, *Between the Beginning and the End: A Radical Kingdom Vision*, trans. Bert Hielema (Grand Rapids, MI: Eerdmans, 2014), 7.

5. J. H. Bavinck, *Between the Beginning and the End*, 7.

observation: "One of the significant aspects concerning the thinking of some of the tribes in Asia and Africa is that they believe in an *Urzeit*, primordial time, the primeval period that preceded the time when humanity began life on earth. *Urzeit* was the time when all things were put in place."[6] Of all this evidence, Bavinck notes that many accounts around the world of such a formative prehistory are conspicuously and unashamedly imaginative. This happily fictional component of many indigenous religious traditions indicates the very nature of a formative prehistory, that it cannot be discovered or inferred; it cannot be approached or examined. It is not an object open to human scrutiny or examination. That elusiveness of a formative prehistory is due, in part, to the fact that we are always and already within it, so that what we in fact seek are the preconditions of our own inquiry. There is thus universally demonstrated in human religious consciousness "the core idea that the time in which we stand, the time in which history takes place, can never be understood in terms of itself," such that "if we want to grasp the sense of history—we must go back to primeval times, to the events that took place before the ordering of this world," when "the foundations were laid on which the structure of history rests."[7] And yet these origins are unavailable to us independently; revelation alone can disclose them to human observation.

The present study examines, in other words, a neo-Calvinist theological account of the *Urzeit* of Christian revelation, of Holy Scripture. The Bavincks, Vos, and Van Til, each in his way, contribute to what is here presented as a concerted theological retelling of human origins as found in the early chapters of Genesis. The primary terms of their account are an angelic fall; an original, covenant-creature consciousness; an irreducible theo-orientation of the human person; and the nature of an absolute and personal God self-expressed as transgressable moral norm for the creature: in a word—in a vague and vulnerable word—historical covenant relation with God. They take the events of Genesis 2 and 3 not only as historical but as *Ur*-historical, as constituting the abiding terms of human experience and self-understanding. Johan Bavinck, once again:

> The Fall into sin is a historic event: it happened in history. But it is, on the other hand, also suprahistorical because it had consequences for all subsequent centuries. All of human history can only be understood in terms of this one event. Whatever else happens with us and whatever else we do, all of it is fundamentally tied in with this awesome reality that we humans are God's creatures and that we fell into sin.[8]

Second, to Augustine we owe the idea that God and evil are contrary but not contradictory. Were there no God, there could be no evil; but evil is not the negation of God. Evil is in some way parasitic on the good. Augustine's assent to

---

6. J. H. Bavinck, *Between the Beginning and the End*, 5.
7. J. H. Bavinck, *Between the Beginning and the End*, 5–6.
8. J. H. Bavinck, *Between the Beginning and the End*, 7.

this ontology marked his break with Manichaeism and embrace of neo-Platonism on his way to conversion, and the same ontology stands to this day as a regulative framework for Christian theistic wrestling with questions of the nature, possibility, and existence of evil. And the same asymmetrical ontology, including both its victories and its vulnerabilities, serves at once as the subject matter and the boundaries of the discussion in the chapters to follow.

The classical divine ontology is faithfully maintained by the Bavincks, Vos, and Van Til, as are unqualified, decretal foreordination and sovereign, providential immanence, even with reference to the Fall—true to historic Reformed thought. It is therefore, for these neo-Calvinists, a theological tautology to say that goodness is godliness, that the good is a reflection or expression of the very character or nature of God, and that therefore, as the elder Bavinck says, evil is parasitic on the good. At this point, however, the neo-Calvinists are careful to distance themselves from the view that evil is privation. Medieval theologians, from Augustine to Anselm, struggled to explain how it is that evil could exact so much damage, and how a just God could punish sin, if evil was quite literally nothing.[9] The neo-Calvinists took note. They instead endorse a subtle ambiguity where original evil just is the primordial sin, the self-conscious self-direction of the image-bearer contrary to an express divine command of Gen. 3:6—not Augustine's misplaced or misapportioned love, but self-conscious transgression of a law of God. Chapters 1 and 2 examine the neo-Calvinists' interpretation of the relevant biblical texts, especially Gen. 2:17 and 3:6; but the primary focus of the study as a whole is their theological account of the moral conditions implicit in the Genesis account.

There is a third Augustinian feature of this study, and that is the way in which the problem of evil is approached. Modern Christian reflection upon evil has typically taken that form familiar to us from Hume's *Dialogues Concerning Natural Religion*. The task Christian thinkers set for themselves is in such cases the vindication or justification of God given the realities of evil and suffering. Phillip Cary explains that a "typical modern way of stating the problem of evil … is to ask how it can be rational to believe in the existence of a God who is both good and omnipotent when there is so much evil in the world."[10] We call this justification of God (τοῦ Θεοῦ ἡ δικαιολογία) where God is the object of our justifying efforts, "theodicy." This is not only a theological exercise but an apologetic one as well, as it is frequently claimed that evil is among the first and greatest defeaters of classical theism.[11] C. S. Lewis noted the peculiarity of this arrangement, that God is "in the dock" in a defensive mode. And so he is: this procedure takes human experience of evil and suffering at face value and demands that theism come to terms with it.

---

9. G. R. Evans, *Augustine on Evil* (Cambridge: Cambridge University Press, 1982), 98.

10. Phillip Cary, "A Classic View," in *God and the Problem of Evil: Five Views*, ed. Chad Meister and James K. Dew Jr. (Downers Grove, IL: IVP Academic, 2017), 13.

11. J. L. Mackie, *The Miracle of Theism: Arguments for and Against the Existence of God* (Oxford: Oxford University Press, 1982), 150–76; and of course, paradigmatically, Hume's *Dialogues Concerning Natural Religion*, published posthumously in 1779.

Augustine's approach was different. Since his own deliverance from sin had been facilitated by neo-Platonist ontology, there was for Augustine no possibility of returning to a creature-centered approach to the problem of evil. The question in his case was then to make sense of evil, given the eternal perfection of the divine being. Cary writes, "The classical view of evil … typically begins with questions that go in the opposite direction: for example, assuming that God is good and omnipotent, how is evil even possible?"[12] The classical, Augustinian approach "does have a great deal to say about sin and suffering, but it puts both in a larger context, which is fundamentally ontological."[13] The Augustinian question is, in Cary's words, "How can there be corruption when all things are created by one omnipotent God, who is wholly good and creates nothing bad or corrupt?"[14] If the modern approach seeks to vindicate or make sense of God, the classical view seeks to vindicate, or make ontological sense of, evil in God's world. This is the neo-Calvinist approach as well.

There are implications for apologetics. Abraham Kuyper's distrust of apologetics, as autonomously inclined, permeates neo-Calvinist thought. Herman Bavinck argues that the best apologetic is internal coherence and explanatory power, symptoms of the organic coherence of Christian thought. More or less: the best defense is a good offense. Vos responds to modern critical historicism with a robust historical account of special revelation and a theology of historical fact: doctrine is theological interpretation of historical fact.[15] Van Til puts his distrust for natural theology and speculation in no uncertain terms and argues for indirect apologetics. In this sense, the production of a substantive account, drawing from in-house resources, of the nature and possibility of evil in the world created and sustained by the God of classical theism is both and simultaneously theology and apologetics. Dan Strange says that he owes to J. H. Bavinck the idea that "non-Christian religions are 'subversively fulfilled' in the gospel of Jesus Christ."[16] Such a proposal threatens many critiques of the Christian faith, supposing they are thus outpaced by constructive theological reasoning, with irrelevance, and forces upon opponents of Christianity an embarrassment of relative explanatory poverty. One can hardly raise an objection to Christian faith based on the fact of evil if one cannot make any sense of evil on one's own terms, if the Christian account of evil convincingly overpowers one's own. This problem is aggravated if the critic is caught borrowing from the Christian lexicon in order to challenge Christianity; and without his own account of evil, this is precisely the charge he faces. In this sense, constructive exegetical and theological labor plus candid and industrious appreciation of tradition-specific theological heritage—Reformed, in this case—is

---

12. Cary, "Classic View," 13.
13. Cary, "Classic View," 15.
14. Cary, "Classic View," 15.
15. Geerhardus Vos, "Christian Faith and the Truthfulness of Bible History," in *RHBI*.
16. Daniel Strange, *Their Rock Is Not Like Our Rock: A Theology of Religions* (Grand Rapids, MI: Zondervan, 2014), 42.

itself an apologetic undertaking. And along the way, the Bavincks, Vos, and Van Til utilize terms and concepts from non-Christian discourse for constructive-critical purposes, thus forcing the question of lexical appropriation, to invent a term, or borrowed capital, as it is sometimes called.[17] But the point is that the problem of evil is, in the classical iteration, theological, quite strictly speaking. Put differently, in the Augustinian tonality, it is a theocentric inquiry. As Van Til says, one seeks greater understanding by "looking more steadfastly into the face of God."[18] Van Til declares that "God must be his own theodicy."[19] The neo-Calvinist project is not an evilology of God, in the modern mode, but a theology of evil. And all this as drawn constructively from chords first struck by the Bishop of Hippo.

To bring this full circle: the neo-Calvinist theology of evil which unfolds in the pages that follow takes its lead from revelation, takes for granted the historicity of revelation and covenant, and seeks an ontological account for evil beginning with the self-existent triune God of classical Christian thought. The fact of the Fall, the actualization of creaturely transgression, of an exercise of human will displeasing to God, receives a surprisingly robust though arguably piecemeal account in neo-Calvinist literature. And for this account undeniably the *locus* of primary importance is the doctrine of God—true, once again, to historic Calvinism and to Augustine. The neo-Calvinists claim that human moral experience presupposes and expresses a personal self-expression of the unchanging God toward that which is not God, which very self-expression is the constitution of creaturely moral volition where God remains always God. The neo-Calvinist conception of historic Trinitarianism in terms of absolute personality highlights the lively and immutable divine capacity to self-express for the sake of historical communion with a rational and moral bearer of the image of God. Thus *absolute person* signals a theological account of the possibility of evil and of human *moral experience.*

---

17. On this methodology, see, for example, Shao Kai Tseng, *G. W. F. Hegel* (Phillipsburg, NJ: P&R, 2018), 69–128.

18. Cornelius Van Til, *CGG*, 19.

19. Cornelius Van Til, "Evil and Theodicy" (unpublished paper, Westminster Theological Seminary Library Archives), Part 2, p. 83.

ACKNOWLEDGMENTS

I am glad to mention several of my students who assisted graciously if unwittingly as I worked through many of the ideas appearing in this book. Among them are Beulah Suh, Aaron Jung, Paul Kwon, Hannah Chong, and Grace Lee. A few noble souls even accepted a selfish invitation to read through and discuss drafts of the first few chapters. Their feedback was too kind but the encouragement welcome. This group included Beulah Suh, Ryan Mudge, Minsun Wei, Job Kiggundu, and Eunice Kwon. Kevin Vanhoozer and Dan Treier offered counsel and encouragement. Gray Sutanto pushed the project toward completion with his characteristic urgency. Shao Kai Tseng, whose work is an inspiration, also offered valuable counsel. Dave Garner, Scott Oliphint, Bill Edgar, Vern Poythress, Richard Gaffin, Jonathan Brack, and Jared Oliphint, mentors and friends, are always in mind as I write and formulate my thoughts, and always ready despite packed schedules to read a few pages here and there. I am immensely grateful to Mary Wells for her excellent editorial work and careful attention to the entirety of the text, and for her kindness and encouragement. I would also like to acknowledge a few dear friends, so wonderfully present during the years that I worked on this project and attempted to manage life as a foreigner in Korea: Steve and Lisa Chang and Lauren Kim. Steve and Lisa did so much to help us make our home in Korea, and Lauren made it feel like home. My wife, above all, is so very kind to put up with endless chatter about "my book" and with this so-called career whose rewards are so elusive. She and our children, Mia and Elliot, are much better company than my Samsung Notebook 9. I pray that this book does some good, and that the Lord is pleased.

ABBREVIATIONS

Herman Bavinck
ORF	*Our Reasonable Faith*
PoR	*Philosophy of Revelation*
RD	*Reformed Dogmatics (3 vols.)*
RE	*Reformed Ethics*

Johan Herman Bavinck
CBTM	*The Church Between Temple and Mosque*
ISM	*An Introduction to the Science of Missions*

Cornelius Van Til
CA	*Christian Apologetics*
CGG	*Common Grace and the Gospel*
CTE	*Christian Theistic Evidences*
DF	*Defense of the Faith*
IST	*Introduction to Systematic Theology*
SCE	*A Survey of Christian Epistemology*

Geerhardus Vos
BT	*Biblical Theology*
RD	*Reformed Dogmatics (5 vols.)*
RHBI	*Redemptive History and Biblical Interpretation*

Chapter 1

DIVINE MORAL CHARACTER SELF-GIVEN

All men seek happiness. This is the motive of every action of every man, even of those who hang themselves. ... What is it then that this desire and this inability proclaim to us, but that there was once in man a true happiness of which there now remain to him only the mark and empty trace?

—Blaise Pascal

For Herman Bavinck, Geerhardus Vos, and Cornelius Van Til, the freedom Adam enjoyed in the Garden of Eden, signaled conspicuously by the tree of the knowledge of good and evil and the prohibition of Gen. 2:17, is the primary and definitive instance of creaturely freedom, and most importantly of creaturely freedom relative to what may be called "the law" or "the will of God." Of whatever Creator–creature symmetry one may speak, and thus of moral meaning in the realm of creaturely experience, its original is found in Genesis 2. The forbidden tree represents the first great contingency of creaturely accountability and of human intercourse with God: obedience would have meant divine bestowal of an advancement of human life to imperishable righteousness consisting of the inability to sin and consummate enjoyment of communion with God, the personal source of life. Indeed, the possibility of disobedience relative to the injunction of Gen. 2:17 was presented as the singular embodiment of evil in Adam's world, and accompanying that possibility was the prospect of the initialization of divine judicial displeasure. What are sometimes characterized as "genuine" history and freedom, and the moral structure of image-bearing life, have their beginning here in the history recorded in Genesis 2 and 3, in the garden of God. As Bavinck, Vos, and Van Til see it, the nature and possibility of evil are on display here in the arrangement surrounding the two trees placed by God in the midst of the garden.

This chapter presents Bavinck's, Vos's, and Van Til's theology of the prohibition of Gen. 2:17 as a theology of the self-expression of God as moral norm for the image-bearer, even as the implicit fabric of human moral self-consciousness. This chapter seeks to demonstrate that the possibility of sin, as a prototypical instance of creaturely volitional expression, appears within an eschatological-relational structure designed and deployed by God for the purpose of cosmic glorification of himself as sovereign Lord and Creator. Human moral experience is self-conscious engagement with this structure.

Within this structure, Gen. 2:17 is the public, legal expression of God's own moral character, and as such it is a special formalization of the natural Creator–creature relationship, a relationship that is always and already exhaustively, if implicitly, moral. As such, human moral experience is experience of a moral and relational self-expression of God, and human moral self-consciousness, implicit and explicit, is therefore thoroughly theo-referential. One might say that God is man's immediate moral experience, or that human moral experience is experience of God. So says Van Til, that "God is man's ultimate environment," and that "the creature has no private chambers."[1]

This chapter comprises three sections, the first of which presents the crisis in the garden, surrounding the tree of the knowledge of good and evil, as a satellite conflict, a concentrated earthly arena hosting cosmic, kingdom confrontation. In the Garden of Eden, two superpowers, categorically unequal, clash indirectly through the historical sequence of human experience in the garden. Both kingdoms lay claim to the allegiance of the human creature and thereby to the world entrusted to him as well. The second section examines the relational rationale for the prohibition—how exactly "thou shalt not eat" figures into this confrontation, and the third examines the nature of creaturely freedom in prelapsarian Eden. It will become clear that, according to these three writers, the nature of evil itself is observable here in original form, in what they understand to be a highly structured relational environment surrounding the prohibition of Gen. 2:17. The prominence of the relational structure in which the prohibition is issued indicates that the realm of human experience must be understood in terms of divine initiative, immanence, and eschatological relation—what Bavinck, Vos, and Van Til often call "covenant."[2] The intelligibility and ethico-religious significance of human thoughts, words, and deeds are the products of a non-necessary movement of God toward that which is not himself, a movement always covenant-eschatological and revelatory of the absolute personality of the triune God.

---

1. Van Til, *DF*, 65; Van Til, *CA*, 78.
2. Throughout this study I use the word "covenant" liberally, but I do not contend for it, despite the great deal of controversy surrounding both the term and the concept in recent years. See, for example, John H. Stek, "'Covenant' Overload in Reformed Theology," *Calvin Theological Journal* 29, no. 1 (1994): 12–41; Jeffrey J. Niehaus, "An Argument against Theologically Constructed Covenants," *Journal of the Evangelical Theological Society* 50, no. 2 (2007): 259–73; Niehaus, "Covenant: An Idea in the Mind of God," *Journal of the Evangelical Theological Society* 52, no. 2 (2009): 225–46. For Bavinck's explanation and defense, see Bavinck, *RD*, 2:568–76. Overall, agreement among covenant theologians appears insufficient, so far, to restrict the use of the term too severely. My practice will be to mirror the term's use in the primary sources.

Edenic Theater and Cosmic Conflict

Angelic Uprising and Fall

Discussion of an angelic fall is unevenly distributed in the writings of Herman Bavinck, Geerhardus Vos, and Cornelius Van Til. Throughout Bavinck's *Reformed Dogmatics* one finds careful if judicious discussion of related themes. Vos makes only passing mention of the angelic fall but in biblical theological studies of messianism and the kingdom of God, and in his study of Pauline eschatology, he reflects on Satan, his kingdom, and demonology. The noetic effects of the Fall and the state of sin are addressed in nearly everything Van Til published, and often in terms of the influence or reign of sin or Satan,[3] but Van Til does not address directly the angelic fall or what bearing it may have had on the situation in the garden. But the exegetical raw material is common ground.

As described in 2 Pet. 2:4 and Jude 6, an angelic transgression precedes the Fall of the first humans. The details of this first sin receive no direct treatment beyond these two verses, with two possible exceptions: the words of Jesus in Lk. 10:18, "I saw Satan fall like lightning from heaven," and the mention of the "Day Star, Son of Dawn," "fallen from heaven," in Isa. 14:12. There are no problems of consistency between 2 Pet. 2:4 and Jude 6; in fact they are remarkably similar. Both refer to angelic transgression, which Jude specifies as attempted angelic mutiny, noting that some number of angels claimed more or greater authority than was rightly (or possibly) theirs, and both mention God's restraining the transgressors in gloomy darkness, by means of chains, until a final judgment.[4]

Vos devotes attention to the relevant material from Isa. 14, an extended censure of Babylon focusing on the sin of pride, the "highest embodiment" of which, Vos says, "was found in that king of Babel, the last representative world power that came within Isaiah's ken."[5] One called "Day Star, son of Dawn," is addressed directly in verse 12 as "you who laid the nations low." Vos understands from Isa. 14:13-14 that the sin of pride is essentially self-deification, the presence of which in this prophecy he explains as follows: "such self-deifying pride being the controlling principle of diabolical sin, it was not unnatural to find in the king of Babel here described the type of Satan."[6]

Bavinck notes at several points that Scripture teaches "distinctions of rank and status, of dignity and ministry, of office and honor, even of class and kind," among the angels.[7] "The realm of spirits is no less rich and splendid than the realm of

---

3. For example, Van Til, *CA*, 33–4.

4. Both verses mention "gloomy darkness" (ζόφος). 2 Pet. 2:4 mentions what Vos calls "the pagan term τάρταρος," in the verbal form ταρταρώσας. Most English translations render this "cast into hell." Vos says that strictly speaking it may be read "having cast into Tartarus" (Vos, *RD*, 5:302).

5. Vos, *RHBI*, 283.

6. Vos, *RHBI*, 283. Vos notes that "Satan's name *Lucifer* [was] given him from the Latin of this passage by Tertullian and Gregory the Great" (*RHBI*, 283 n.7).

7. Bavinck, *RD*, 2:452.

material beings,"[8] perhaps "more fully furnished and populated, even far surpassing the material world in diversity."[9] This fullness and complexity indicates to Bavinck that the angelic fall must have caused considerable disorder and disarray in the angelic world: "the fall of so many angels must have profoundly disturbed the organism of the angelic world," since "it lost its head, its organization."[10]

Bavinck draws attention to one significant difference, among several others, between angels and humans, that humans from their original design were intended for dominion over the earth (Gen. 1:26) and were, once created, blessed accordingly with the task of subduing its resources (Gen. 1:28) in the exercise of creaturely, image-dominion. "Dominion over the earth is integral to being human."[11] Angels by contrast are servants and ministers. But what sort of disruption is indicated in Jude 6—that they were not content in their position but coveted and sought greater dignity—Bavinck leaves unspecified. Subordination to God, to each other, or to humans, or any combination of these, may have been the original object of angelic discontent.

Clear answers to such questions are not found in the text of Scripture. The primary concern of 2 Pet. 2:4 and Jude 6 is divine response, even divine sovereignty in particular. Peter writes that "God did not spare angels when they sinned." According to Jude, God has responded by restraining the wayward angels until "the judgment of the great day," what Peter more simply calls "the judgment." These phrases signify the Lord's prerogative in the timing of a conclusive, judicial reckoning and his unqualified sway over the fallen angels until that time. In both verses the word "until," in other words, indicates that the Lord restrains the angels for a time of his choosing; he delays judgment and suspends, as it were, their destiny according to his own plan and good pleasure. Citing both verses, Bavinck says that "although it is true that after their fall the devils have been thrown into hell to be kept there till the judgment ... they have not yet been struck by that judgment."[12]

It is unclear how this provisional status squares with the timelessness of the means of restraint—Jude mentions "eternal chains" (δεσμοῖς ἀϊδίοις).[13] The implication could be that the angels' influence within the realm of human experience is severely restricted, and the form of that restriction is suspension of spatio-temporality. The transgressors are remanded and await final sentencing. Certainly divine sovereignty receives primary emphasis here. Angels have violated

---

8. Bavinck, *RD*, 2:453.

9. Bavinck, *RD*, 2:455.

10. Bavinck, *RD*, 3:473. Bavinck's use of the organic motif here is intriguing. Elsewhere he emphasizes the comparatively inorganic character of angels.

11. Bavinck, *RD*, 2:462.

12. Bavinck, *RD*, 3:186.

13. The term appears only here and in Rom. 1:20, where Paul refers to the eternal power of God (ἀΐδιος αὐτοῦ δύναμις). There appears, however, to be no significant difference in Koine Greek between ἀΐδιος and the more common term, αἰώνιος.

an authority structure of which presumably they were well enough aware, and yet there is no indication that they had transgressed an express prohibition. The point is that God responds by containing or restraining or, as these two texts have it, incarcerating the transgressors, and apart from this response, it should be noted, nowhere in the Bible are any other effects or consequences of angelic sin described explicitly as such. God restrains not only the angels but also the effects or consequences of their dissent. In that sense 2 Pet. 2:4 and Jude 6 are noteworthy on two counts. First, they describe a creaturely, volitional transgression of divine order—a free, creaturely act of which God disapproves and which contradicts his moral character. Second, both verses highlight divine sovereignty over the impact of that sin and in the administration of justice.[14]

For Bavinck, the unity of angels among themselves, and their similarity with humans, consists in their createdness, spirituality, rationality, and morality, including original integrity.[15] "In John 8:44, Jude 6, and 2 Peter 2:4," he notes, "the original state of integrity of all angels is assumed."[16] Angels and humans "were originally created in knowledge, righteousness, and holiness; both were given dominion, immortality, and blessedness. In Scripture both are called the sons of God."[17] And yet, for all that angels and humans have in common, "the difference between them is most rigorously maintained in Scripture by the fact that humans *are*, but angels are *never*, said to be created in the image of God."[18]

Bavinck also notes several differences between the angelic and the human fall, coordinate with the aforementioned differences between their respective natures. "Satanic sin," he says, "for all its similarity to human sin, is nonetheless totally different in origin, character, and consequences."[19] The primary difference in the origin of the angelic and the human falls is that the angels fell as it were on their own; they were not tempted or seduced or led astray by outside influence. Bavinck writes:

> The angels were not, like humans, led astray. Temptation did not come to them from without. They fell by their own agency. Jesus says that the devil speaks "according to his own nature" when he lies. He became discontented with his status and power on his own, that is, by his own thinking; he produced the lie

---

14. I mention here that in Jude 6 the one who subjugates the fallen angels is not "God" but "he," where the pronoun refers to "Jesus" or "the Lord" of the preceding verse. The ESV has "Jesus" but several important English translations, including KJV and NIV, read "the Lord."

15. Bavinck, *RD*, 2:454, 455, 458, 459, respectively, and 460: "In all these qualities of createdness, spirituality, rationality, and morality, angels are similar to humans."

16. Bavinck, *RD*, 2:459.

17. Bavinck, *RD*, 2:460.

18. Bavinck, *RD*, 2:460.

19. Bavinck, *RD*, 3:148.

from within himself and projected it as a realm, as system, over against the truth of God.[20]

Notice that here Bavinck records his conviction that sin is not a wrinkle in an otherwise godly situation; it signals or constitutes a realm or system opposed to God and truth. The unity of this realm or system is a negative moral unity; the unity consists in antithesis to the sovereignty of the Creator God. Since angels do not procreate as humans do, they do not constitute a racial organism. Each fell, Bavinck says, individually and independently, of himself, and so the angels derive moral unity not from one another but from opposition to God:

> As purely spiritual beings the angels are not bound to each other by ties of blood. There is among them no father-son relationship, no physical bond, no common blood, no consanguinity. However intimately they may share an ethical bond, they are disconnected beings, so that when many fell, the others could remain standing.[21]

The spontaneity and personal independence of angelic transgression indicate its particular character. Since "Satan was not led astray, but he produced sin—the lie—from within himself (John 8:44)," he "became all at once confirmed in it."[22] In other words: "The nature of his sin is such that he is no longer capable of remorse. In his case, there is no moral consciousness, no conscience; he lives off hatred."[23]

Bavinck believes that the nature of angelic sin, regarding the spontaneity of the act and the independent volition and accountability of each angelic agent, renders it and the angels irredeemable. "In the case of the angels ... the nature of sin rules out the way of salvation."[24] And yet Bavinck is careful to avoid the suggestion that this inference from the nature of angelic sin to the irredeemability of angelic sinners is beyond the control of God. He writes, on the one hand, that "the 'form' of sin is so

---

20. Bavinck, *RD*, 3:68.
21. Bavinck, *RD*, 2:462.
22. Bavinck, *RD*, 3:148.
23. Bavinck, *RD*, 3:148.
24. Bavinck, *RD*, 3:148. Bavinck includes in the work of Christ a restoration of the angelic realm that accounts only for unfallen angels:

> It is true that the fall of so many angels must have profoundly disturbed the organism of the angelic world. As an army is totally thrown into disarray and rendered incapable of fighting when many officers and men leave the ranks and join the enemy, so also the world of angels as an army of God was shattered and made useless for the service of God. It lost its head, its organization. And now it gets this back in the person of the Son, and the Son not only according to his divine nature but also according to his human nature. ... It is Christ, therefore, who as Lord of the angels and as head of the church puts both angels and humans in the right relation to God and so to each other. (Bavinck, *RD*, 3:473)

fused with the angelic nature that there is no longer any possibility of separation."[25] Nonetheless, on the other hand, "certainly it is presumptuous," Bavinck cautions, "to say that fallen angels are irredeemable even by God's omnipotence; and it is better at this point to rest in God's good pleasure. Still, it is sufficiently clear that 'good pleasure' is not identical with arbitrariness."[26] So Bavinck affirms a kind of qualitative severity of angelic sin that renders fallen angels objects of divine wrath without hope of mercy or restoration, but also divine "good pleasure" in the sense that even this situation has not somehow broken free of foreordination and providence. In other words, we may attribute the state of angels, as unavailable to the grace of forgiveness, to the nature of their transgression, but the final word on such matters is the uncompelled design and providence of God. A theological logic is evident, but deductive certainty is always checked by the incomprehensibility of God.

Bavinck also notes an enigma relative to the state of fallen angels who, although beyond the possibility of restoration, remain in existence as creatures of God. Sinful angels are judged but not annihilated. They are condemned and relegated irrecoverably to a state of rebellion, condemnation, and enmity against God, but retain the irreducible good of their creaturely nature as such: "In the essential character and concept of the devils, there is something completely incomprehensible," namely, that "they cannot be absolutely evil, for they are God's creatures and therefore good as such; yet they are only," meaning, exclusively, "an object of God's hatred and eternal wrath."[27] From Bavinck's own understanding of the nature of the captivity indicated in 2 Pet. 2:4 and Jude 6,[28] we know that he believes that fallen angels are sinful creatures to whom common grace is denied but who nonetheless do not face immediately the full wrath of God. They endure merciless delay. Bavinck offers no solution, but he appears to find in this inscrutable tension the mode of evil's operation in the world:

> The good, by a free choice, was the cause of evil and remains its substratum. Fallen angels and humans as creatures are and remain good and exist from moment to moment only by, and in, and for God. And just as sin is dependent on the good in its origin and existence, so it is in its operation and struggle. It has power to do anything only with and by means of the powers and gifts that are God-given. Satan has therefore correctly been called the ape of God. When God builds a church, Satan adds a chapel; over against the true prophet, he raises up a false prophet; over against the Christ, he poses the Antichrist.[29]

---

25. Bavinck, *RD*, 3:148.
26. Bavinck, *RD*, 3:148.
27. Bavinck, *RD*, 3:147.
28. See Bavinck, *RD*, 3:185–6.
29. Bavinck, *RD*, 3:139. Van Til suggests that when the angels fall immediately to an irreversible allegiance to evil, while the Fall of the image-bearer into sin is restrained, this difference indicates a distinction between the metaphysical and the ethical. For Van Til the

Here in his explanation of evil as parasitic upon the good, Bavinck indicates something of the ontological structure developed throughout the course of the present study. That structure does in fact provide an explanation for the conundrum of the state of fallen angels who are wholly given over to sin and yet remain, as creatures, in some sense good.

A creature cannot attain moral equality with God. A creature's moral status or character is always in reference to or derivative of God who is good, goodness itself. So even a creature who is maximally evil is nonetheless creaturely and therefore glorifies God at least twice: in reflecting, albeit inversely, the ontologico-moral uniqueness of the self-sufficient God; and historically, as set for a final and unqualified judgment vindicating and glorifying God.

Presently, it is certain for Bavinck that "sin first broke out in the realm of spirits," that "sin did not first start on earth but in heaven … and that the fall of angels took place before that of humankind."[30] And although he believes that "Scripture is silent on whether there is a connection between that fall of the angels and the creation of humankind, nor does it tell us what drove the fallen angels to seduce humans," still one detects in Bavinck that while Eden is interrupted by the prohibition of Gen. 2:17 and the entrance of sin and suffering into the world, and while the events of Genesis 2 and 3 unfold center stage, all this takes place against a grander background. More directly: for Bavinck and certainly for Vos as well, the conflict allowed but restrained by God between the Creator and a number of angelic transgressors is the broader context of the events in Eden.[31]

The relationship between the broader context and the Edenic events themselves may be observed by comparing divine responses to the angelic fall and then to the human fall. Noteworthy, in other words, are the differences between the restraint imposed by God upon angelic transgressors and the effects of angelic sin—eternal chains until judgment (Jude 6)—on the one hand, and God's response to the human fall, on the other, consisting of the imposition of protective enmity (Gen. 3:15) and consignment to disobedience (Rom. 11:32). In explaining the covenant solidarity of the human race—not only physical but also, primarily, moral[32]—Bavinck indicates by comparison that among the angels there is neither physical (genetic) nor moral unity. "Humanity is not an aggregate of individuals but an organic unity, one race, one family. Angels on the other hand, all stand side-by-side, independently of one another. They were all created at the same time and are not the products of procreation."[33] And without procreation there is no basis or context for moral unity;[34] the absence of racial unity Bavinck associates with the

point is that creatureliness as such cannot be mistaken for the purely ethical character of sin (Van Til, *CGG*, 35).
30. Bavinck, *RD*, 3:36.
31. Bavinck, *RD*, 3:36.
32. See Chapter 2.
33. Bavinck, *RD*, 3:102.
34. Or one may argue the reverse: that moral unity is the rationale for procreative succession.

absence of covenant unity. Angels stand or fall individually; the human race is a historical, perhaps basically eschatological, organism.

Notice also, then, in God's reactions to these two falls that the angels are restrained in a manner characterized as "eternal." We might take this designation to indicate perhaps "non-historical," without progress, process, or sequence—spatio-temporal suspension, in other words—while humans are held captive to disobedience in an overtly historical sense: for the sake of mercy to be revealed in the fullness of time, the sins visited on the third and fourth generations while love and forgiveness is extended to thousands (Exod. 20:5-6; 34:7). Even the reprobate are included in this history, within which the gospel is, from a historical point of view, a real option for all.[35] Fallen angels, by contrast, are excluded from the history of progressive covenant dispensations of grace. They never hear a word of redemptive hope or promise; they remain suspended in royal disfavor and condemnation. This contrast draws attention to an uneven complementarity of disobedience (wrath) and mercy (renewal by grace), since fallen angels are set for an unattenuated judgment that is relegated to unindexed delay whereas both the sin of image-bearers and divine judgment in response are mercifully restrained while the gospel is in effect: sinners may enjoy immediately the soteric, eschatological benefits of a salvation either yet to be accomplished, in the case of Old Testament saints, or yet to be consummated, in the case of both Old Testament saints and the post-apostolic church. The singular distinction here is that in the covenant context, that is, with reference to human sin, God's response takes the form of a history constituted by divine but historicized covenant compassion, while his response to angelic sin does not.[36] History is not open to angels; history is the context for God's interaction with humans.

Cosmic Backdrop to Eden

Bavinck acknowledges a sense in which the angelic fall serves as a backdrop for the drama in the garden and subsequently for human history, or a sense in which the conflict God wages against sin unfolds primarily, or fundamentally, between God and angels and only secondarily, or mediately, on earth: "humanity and the world are the spoils for which the war between God and Satan, between heaven and hell, is waged."[37] "All the power of sin on earth is connected with a kingdom of darkness in the world of spirits."[38]

This two-tier characterization of the conflict between God and evil is indicated by an emphasis upon the fundamentally spiritual nature of that which is opposed to God. It is clear from their accounts of the Fall that for Bavinck and Vos the

---

35. The question is, of course, what "real" means in this way of stating the matter. Chapter 3 is relevant though it does not address this question directly.
36. See Bavinck, *RD*, 3:100–6.
37. Bavinck, *RD*, 3:35.
38. Bavinck, *RD*, 3:35.

primary sphere of Creator–creature engagement is in fact the spiritual. The spiritual, however, is not to be identified with the immaterial but rather with the ethico-religious. In terms of the human creature, therefore, neither the sensual nor the intellectual alone, but the covenantal, implicating the human person as a composite organism and as in a primary sense a spiritual or religious or covenantal personality—the human person, considered, that is, according to the hidden principle of his behavior plain as it is before an omniscient God—is the focus of biblical religion for these three writers. So says Bavinck: "Creation culminates in humanity where the spiritual and material world[s] are joined together."[39] The material world of human experience, it should be noted, is not frustratingly or mysteriously disconnected from the spiritual realm; neither is it a material expression of the spirit nor a reduction of it. Rather, human experience itself is the culminating confluence of the spiritual and the material, of ethico-religious createdness. Somehow the self-revelation of God in what he has made culminates in the spirit-material composite that is the human creature.

One detects in this way of framing things a contact point between the angelic fall and the arrangement in the garden. In or at the point of the human creature, in other words, one observes in the text of Genesis 3 an encounter of two antithetical kingdoms. This clash of kingdoms is most conspicuous in the temptation, which is a component of the probation and should not be strictly identified with the probation. Vos distinguishes the notions of temptation and probation by noting their divergent ends: although "both work with the same material," temptation aims toward (is designed to bring about) disobedience, evil, and death, and utilizes a strategy of deception; probation has as its end (is designed to bring about) obedience, reward, life, and communion with God, and in the latter case the way forward is transparent and public.[40] Vos therefore believes that the temptation was non-essential to the situation, that Jas. 1:13 must not fall from view, and that therefore temptation should be attributed to the serpent only. Accordingly, the probation, including testing but no temptation, could have been carried out even had the serpent not entered the garden.[41] And in that case the coherence of the temptation with the probationary situation into which it was inserted is noteworthy. The temptation is built right into the probation; it is as it were customized for the situation. The serpent could have pitched worship of himself or of another creature or of creation itself; he had any number of options; but his ruse focused specifically on the object of the only negative command recorded in the Eden account.

Two observations: first, since the temptation (Gen. 3:6) suits so precisely the probation, by intensifying the same moral crisis Adam already faced in the proscription of Gen. 2:17, it is evident that the activity of the serpent—or Satan via the serpent—in the garden, is restricted to divine permission and (probationary) design. That is, Satan's activity is, one might say, in the service of the covenant

---

39. Bavinck, *RD*, 2:511.
40. Vos, *BT*, 33.
41. Vos, *BT*, 33; Vos, *RD*, 2:43.

probation as designed by God: "A probation was made use of by the evil power to inject into it the element of temptation."[42] Bavinck, similarly, endorses the view of early Reformed theologians who "could not view Satan and his angels, however powerful, as anything other than creatures who without God's will cannot so much as move."[43] And therefore a second observation: the concurrence here of divine design and supervision with Satanic connivance, constituting that controlled clash of two kingdoms, is the substance and broader context for the testing in Eden.

And the flashpoint of that encounter is marked by intractable mystery: "We do not understand," writes Geerhardus Vos, "how temptation can gain a hold on a holy man."[44] But the fact that it did—that Adam turned his goodwill toward evil— requires that the ultimate origin of sin be located elsewhere. The possibility of sin within the realm of human experience is indicated by the prohibition of Gen. 2:17, and yet, objectively speaking, transgression within a created moral order is not for the first time a possibility at that point, but already actual; transgression of the will of God—sin, one might say—did not first take shape in Eden. When God prohibits Adam from eating of the fruit of the tree, God already knew evil and defiance as an actuality, even though Adam did not. Vos writes:

> To tempt is not to produce sin; usually it [temptation] is the arousing of a sinful inclination already present in the heart so that it would express itself and result in action. That is not the case with Adam. A non-sinful inclination can be aroused—for example, the desire for more knowledge—but this desire does not explain how it became sinful. It shows that the first origin of sin is to be sought in a higher world than that of man.[45]

Vos says that sin as we are familiar with it usually requires two conditions: antecedent sinful disposition and circumstantial provocation, commonly called temptation. This structure is, however, exclusive to a fallen condition and context. In Adam's case, there was no sinful disposition that awaited external invitation or preceded his first transgression.[46] "And here the

---

42. Vos, *BT*, 33.
43. Bavinck, *RD*, 3:188.
44. Vos, *RD*, 2:50.
45. Vos, *RD*, 2:50.
46. The structure here described is not exclusive to the actualization of sin. Vos sees it operative also in the actualization of true knowledge of God in the prelapsarian situation. Here is his description of the coordination of prelapsarian natural revelation, which "consists of two sources, nature within and nature without":

> God reveals Himself to the inner sense of man through religious consciousness and the moral conscience. He also reveals Himself in the works of nature without. It is obvious that the latter must rest on the former. If there were no antecedent innate knowledge of God, no amount of nature-observation would lead to an adequate conception of God. The presupposition of all knowledge of

rule holds that originally in Adam the *actus* determined the *status*, but that subsequently for all his posterity *status* has determined *actus*."[47] Vos suggests that Adam's sin, unique in the sense that it is without precedent, is best understood—where understood at all—in light of precedent. Adam is tested, and in that testing he sees occasion to demonstrate moral integrity. Vos suggests, however, that the testing is not the whole picture, that where only testing is in view, the full moral weight of Adam's prelapsarian moment is untold. Adam is tested, but he is also tempted. In Adam's temptation he is subjected to an additional and suggestive test that is ill-intended; the serpent's overtures are designed for Adam's failure and emerge from a kingdom of darkness, the greater part of which is hidden from human view.

Vos's reasoning appears to flirt with regress or even dualism. If one takes him as attempting to prove a prior angelic fall from the narrative of Genesis 2 and 3 alone, then the same argument could be made with regard to angelic sinners who also entered existence morally upright: since their sin is without sufficient subjective precondition, a fall in another realm must have preceded theirs, and so on, until one arrives at sin or evil self-existent. More likely, however, Vos holds the Augustinian line—that a good God tempts no one and therefore cannot be blamed for the subversions of the serpent—and takes a prior angelic fall for granted (on the basis primarily of New Testament texts), and here attempts to identify, in the Genesis narrative, the fallout of the angelic fall. Noteworthy at this point, nonetheless, is this: Vos believes that the phenomena of Adam's context do not fully explain his moral experience. In this we see that an adequate explanation of the Edenic situation is a revealed, theological explanation, one that defers to the cosmic and spiritual dimensions of creation, beyond human perception and history.

Herman Bavinck writes: "All the power of sin on earth is connected with a kingdom of darkness in the world of spirits. There, too, a fall has occurred."[48] In other words, in Genesis 3 we see two kingdoms, of darkness and of light, touch for only a brief moment, and the subtle incursion signaled by the serpent's appearance and proposal in Genesis 3 indicates a broader, cosmic context, already at play, within which Bavinck and Vos are seeking to understand Eden, the Fall, and the nature of sin. They are seeking to interpret the field of human moral experience within a broader spiritual, cosmic context.

It is perhaps noteworthy that despite the reticence of Scripture regarding the fall of Satan and the angels, it is clear to Bavinck, and presumably to Vos as well, that the angelic fall temporally precedes the events of Genesis 2–3,[49] and that, certainly

> God is man's having been created in the image of God. On the other hand, the knowledge from inner nature is not complete in itself apart from the filling-out it receives through the discovery of God in nature. (Vos, *BT*, 19)

47. Vos, *RD*, 2:25.
48. Bavinck, *RD*, 3:35.
49. Bavinck believes that timing of the creation of the angels must fall between the moment indicated by Gen. 1:1 and the resting of God from the work of creation on the

in the opinion of Bavinck, this timing indicates the broader context within which the reciprocity between God and the image-bearer unfolds: "Given with the fact of religion is the very belief that its deepest causes do not lie within the circle of visible beings. Good and evil, both in a religious and an ethical sense, are rooted in a world other than that which appears to our senses."[50]

Cosmic Conflict and Progressive Organism

As indicated in 2 Pet. 2:4 and Jude 6, there is a suspension of spatio-temporality for fallen angels, but surely the point is not a simple relegation of disobedient angels to inactivity but rather the perfection of divine sovereignty over the creatures who had turned against their Creator. Divine response to angelic transgression, and then to the Fall in Eden, is not to exile Satan but to restrain him and his influence; conflict indeed ensues.

Vos's development of the progressive organism of redemption and of redemptive revelation is well known.[51] It is also clear, however, that Vos understands redemption, and the redemptive revelation that accompanies it, as the soteric aspect of the same cosmic spiritual conflict which serves as the background to Eden, and which also progresses or intensifies organically. The progressive organism of cosmic, spiritual kingdom conflict reaches minor peaks throughout redemptive history, in the Exodus in particular, but the whole of it lies in the shadow of the dual Parousia of Christ. To put it more simply: that clash of two kingdoms which unfolds in Eden unfolds progressively in much the same way that redemption does.

Note, for example, Vos's reflections on the Exodus:

> Sin is at every point more than the sum-total of purely human influences it brings to bear upon its victims. A religious, demonic background is thrown back of the human figures that move across the canvas. Not merely the Egyptians, but likewise the Egyptians' gods are involved in the conflict. The plagues come in here for notice. They are inextricably mixed up with the Egyptian idolatry. This idolatry was nature-worship, embracing the good and beneficent as well as the evil and baneful aspects of nature. Jehovah, in making these harm their own worshippers, shows His superiority to this whole realm of evil. ... The same demonic powers that were concerned in the antitypical redemption wrought by Christ, and there displayed their intensest activity, had a hand in this opposition to the redemption from Egypt.[52]

---

seventh day. See Bavinck, *RD*, 2:454–5. He believes, therefore, that the angelic fall preceded temporally the events of Genesis 3.

50. Bavinck, *RD*, 2:447.

51. See Vos, "The Idea of Biblical Theology as a Science and as a Discipline," in *RHBI*; Vos, *BT*, 3–26. See also Shao Kai Tseng, *G. W. F. Hegel* (Phillipsburg, NJ: P&R, 2019), 77–86.

52. Vos, *BT*, 111.

Vos hints here that the organic progress of redemption also implies an organic and progressive intensification of the conflict between God and the creatures who oppose his will and goodness. In this case, Vos demonstrates his biblical theological rule of thumb that "the Old Testament avails itself of earthly and eternal forms to convey heavenly and spiritual things."[53] Vos argues, conversely, that in his ministry and messianic self-disclosure, Jesus adopted the Old Testament language of kingdom and conquest in order to explain that his kingdom "is not of this world" (Jn 18:36).[54] In relating Jesus' self-understanding to the messianism of Zechariah and Isaiah in particular, Vos writes:

> It should be noticed that Jesus by no means discards the imagery and vocabulary of conquest in connection with the Messianic program. He only lifts it to a higher plane: the powers to be conquered are not political; they belong to the world of spirits. In connection with Satan and the demons the consciousness of bringing deliverance is retained without the least impairment. The exorcism of demons and the healing of miracles are liberating acts, and as such they form a part of the general Messianic deliverance. Jesus claims to have been sent for the purpose of performing them. (Lk. 4:18, 19)[55]

Jesus, in other words, is sent in order to liberate those captive to the forces of the kingdom of darkness. If Jesus' miracles bear witness to his deity, they also, says Vos, provide a glimpse of the broader conflict between two kingdoms. On his way to the cross, Jesus aggravates his angelic foes; he picks a fight. As Vos observes, "what forms the contrast of God's kingdom in Jesus' mind is never any political power, e.g., that of Rome, but always a superhuman power, viz., that of Satan."[56] And he concludes: "it is clearly implied that back of all this there lies an invisible, ethical, spiritual sphere which is the theater of the manifestation of the kingdom of power in its higher sense, and in reference to which signs and miracles are but symbols."[57]

To recapitulate: for Vos a cosmic framework for interpreting the mission of the mediator is vindicated by Jesus' own teaching and self-understanding. From Jesus' own teaching, Vos says, it is certain that the world is captive to Satan and to a kingdom of personal evil, that Jesus as Messiah has come to subdue the Satanic oppressor, and that only Jesus the Son of God can do so.

Vos argues that one of Jesus' primary objectives was to convey Hebrew messianism in precisely this light. Jesus sought to draw attention to that cosmic conflict and to encourage first-century Judaism to understand itself and its messiah

---

53. Vos, *RHBI*, 417.

54. Vos, *RHBI*, 417.

55. Vos, *The Self-Disclosure of Jesus: The Modern Debate about the Messianic Consciousness*, ed. Johannes J. Vos, 2nd ed. (Phillipsburg, NJ: P&R, 2002), 26–7.

56. Vos, *RHBI*, 308.

57. Vos, *RHBI*, 312–13.

in light of that conflict. The primary resistance he met was politicized religion and religious phenomenalism, both of which distracted from the ultimate problems of sin and evil which to be understood rightly must be understood in light of the threat of a spiritual kingdom of darkness. It was typical of the Jews with whom Jesus clashed, for example, to interpret manifestations of divine "supreme, royal power … in a national, political sense."[58] But "Jesus, in accordance with the deeper meaning of the Old Testament Scriptures, lifts the idea into a higher sphere. The foes He thought of as about to be conquered were" neither psychological nor moral nor political, nor even human, but "Satan, sin, and death."[59] Jesus sends out the twelve to proclaim the kingdom of heaven (Mt. 10:7); they ask the resurrected Christ when he will restore the kingdom to Israel (Acts 1:6). Jesus, Vos points out, does not reject the political for the religious or ethical, but for the cosmic. Writes Vos:

> It is kingdom against kingdom, but both of these opposing powers belong to a higher world than that to which Rome and her empire belong. … In the dislodgement of Satan the kingdom of God comes, exerts its inherent power of conquest. All miracles, not merely the casting out of demons, find their interpretation in this feature. The powers which will revolutionize heaven and earth are already in motion. While with reference to Satan and his kingdom this power is a destructive and subduing force, it is towards the members of the kingdom [of God] a life-giving and life-liberating activity.[60]

Curiously, Vos addressed similar misunderstandings found within modern Christology, where too often the spiritual or religious dimension of Jesus' self-understanding was, in Vos's view at least, unjustly disregarded. His concern, he writes, is the "specific" understanding of messiahship "which is present in the consciousness of Jesus," and there, in the consciousness of Jesus, Vos finds that "the indispensableness of strictly divine prerogatives in order to the adequate exercise of its functions springs into view."[61] Jesus' religious or spiritual self-understanding is the key to Chalcedonian mediatorial Christology. Vos points this out in terms of a "spiritualizing which the idea" of the messianic task "has undergone in the mind of Jesus."[62] He explains:

> So long as the Messiah's task is conceived as lying in the sphere of external, national, earthly kingship and salvation, it remains possible to regard Him as the representative of God without investing Him with divine attributes. But when His function comes to lie in the sphere of spiritual relationship to God … then

---

58. Vos, *RHBI*, 312.
59. Vos, *RHBI*, 312.
60. Vos, *RHBI*, 312.
61. Vos, *Self-Disclosure of Jesus*, 29.
62. Vos, *Self-Disclosure of Jesus*, 29.

His calling immediately places Him in the center of the field where the forces of religion play.[63]

Jesus understood that the minds of fallen image-bearers were darkened, so that they knew neither themselves nor the depths of their predicament, nor, therefore, the judgment and grace of God. Nonetheless, in Vos's understanding, Jesus' primary or foremost concern was not the subjective states of individual hearts and minds, nor the geo-political misfortunes of the keepers of the oracles, promises, and covenants of God, but an objective Satanic kingdom to which God in just response to sin had given over, to an extent strictly measured for his own ultimate purposes of grace and glory, his image-bearing creatures. Jesus understands his task as messiah and mediator primarily in terms of conflict with that objective kingdom of evil: "Jesus regarded this world of miraculous deliverance, which, wherever He went, He carried with Himself, as in the strictest sense objective. It did not consist of acts that anybody apart from Him could perform. Wherever it is delegated to others, it is delegated in virtue of Messianic authority (Mark 16:17, 18)."[64] Thus, as Vos observes, "In Matthew 12:28 and Luke 11:20, our Lord appeals to His casting out of demons by the Spirit of God as proof of the advent of the kingdom."[65]

And Vos finds the same in Paul, who, he observes, accounts in his eschatology of the resurrection for "the great demonic powers, who, with Satan at their head, rule the present age, and still in a measure retain their influence after the enthronization of Christ through the resurrection."[66] "Satan," writes Vos, "is 'the god of this aion.' As such he binds the mind of the unbelieving in order to prevent the dawning upon them of the light of the gospel."[67] "We do not wrestle against flesh and blood," wrote the apostle, "but against ... the cosmic powers over this present darkness, against the spiritual forces of evil in the heavenly places" (Eph. 6:12).

In Bavinck one discovers hints of a similar biblical theological inclination with regard to both redemption and revelation, and also with a view toward the progressive organism of cosmic spiritual conflict:

> Only gradually, in the course of the history of revelation, does the spiritual power emerge hid behind the appearance and seductive activity of the serpent. Then we learn that involved in the struggle of evil on earth there is also a contest of spirits and that humanity and the world are the spoils for which the war between God and Satan, between heaven and hell, is waged.[68]

---

63. Vos, *Self-Disclosure of Jesus*, 29.
64. Vos, *Self-Disclosure of Jesus*, 27.
65. Vos, *RHBI*, 307.
66. Vos, *The Pauline Eschatology* (Phillipsburg, NJ: P&R, 1979), 279.
67. Vos, *Pauline Eschatology*, 279.
68. Bavinck, *RD*, 3:35.

He notes the fact that "there is a big distinction between diabolical and human sin," but that "in the Old Testament we do not yet find a developed demonology."[69] And in the same section appears this intriguing but undeveloped description of Hebrew demonology: "The split between good and bad angels has not yet been effected; the evil spirit still comes from God; Satan is still among the sons of God."[70] Given the context, one wonders whether Bavinck means not that "the split ... has not yet been effected," an observation suggesting delayed eschatology, but rather the biblical theological point that it had not yet been articulated as such in sacred Scripture, the present tense signaling the historical context of messianic expectation. He may have meant either or both. He continues: "when revelation has been complete and Christ comes to destroy the works of the devil, then also the 'deep things of Satan' become manifest."[71]

As clear as it is, much of this, even in the New Testament, is left unexplained. But the eschatological substance, or progressive historical bedrock, Bavinck sees as basic:

> Scripture is silent on whether there is a connection between that fall of the angels and the creation of humankind, nor does it tell us what drove the fallen angels to seduce humans. But whatever the reason may have been, Satan is the adversary, the tempter, the slanderer of the human race, the murderer of mankind (Matt. 4:3; John 8:44; Eph. 6:11; 1 Thess. 3:5; 2 Tim. 2:26), the "great dragon," the "ancient serpent" (Rev. 12:9, 14-15; 20:2). As such he came to Christ, the second Adam, and as such he also came to the first.[72]

Bavinck also sees cosmic, spiritual confrontation as central to Jesus' interactions with the Jews of his time. According to Bavinck, in fact, the uniquely heinous character of blasphemy against the Holy Spirit is derived from the fact that in Jesus' ministry and teaching it is by the Spirit that advances are made against the kingdom of Satan. Where the very battle line between good and evil is manifest, "blaspheming of the Holy Spirit" amounts to "a defiant declaration that the Holy Spirit is the spirit from the abyss, that the truth is a lie, that Christ is Satan himself."[73] Blasphemy against the Holy Spirit is so special because there is in the simplest terms no more basic an affront than that and therefore none more insidious. The Spirit moves in the sphere of the broader, controlling field of moral battle.

Van Til, too, indicates an eye toward the progressive, historical organism of cosmic conflict when he rather memorably characterizes history as a "playground of differentiation," a playground, that is, which hosts the gradual realization of the judgment and the deliverance of God, the filling up of the number of the elect

---

69. Bavinck, *RD*, 3:145.
70. Bavinck, *RD*, 3:145.
71. Bavinck, *RD*, 3:146.
72. Bavinck, *RD*, 3:36.
73. Bavinck, *RD*, 3:156.

so that God is glorified in both judgment and salvation.[74] Van Til's unforgettable terminology—playground—is intended to capture the security of the decree and foreordination and divine restraint of the accuser of his people (see again 2 Pet. 2:4 and Jude 6) as the backdrop for the outworking of history, tumultuous as it is for the image-bearing creature unable to see past his immediate horizon apart from redemptive revelation calling his attention to the cosmic spiritual realm.

Finally, it must be noted that Bavinck, Vos, and Van Til see the angelic fall and the restraint of the fallen angels, this broader spiritual conflict, sidelined historically but still contained within the eschatological trajectory of creation as such. Bavinck, for his part, sees this in terms of ontology: "Sin *is* not: it *wants to be*; it neither has nor ever achieves true reality. ... And therefore, for all his power, Satan is finally subservient to God's glorification."[75] Van Til's unwavering interest in the noetic features and effects of the Fall may also suggest significant investment in the God-givenness of the Edenic situation. He says often that "the truth about the facts in the created universe, Adam and Eve were told in effect, could be known ultimately only if one knew their relationship to the plan of God. It is this plan of God that makes all created facts to be what they are."[76] And Van Til describes the Fall and the deceptive strategy of Satan in Genesis 3 as deliberate and conspicuous rejection of the primacy of divine design behind the facts of human experience. Satan sought the de-theologization, or the de-theo-contextualization of human experience—the same secularization of revelation and kingdom expectation that Jesus speaks against in the New Testament. As Van Til explains, Satan had God in mind when he entered the garden:

> When Satan tempted Adam and Eve in paradise, he sought to make them believe that man's self-consciousness was ultimate rather than derivative and God-dependent. He argued, as it were, that it was of the nature of self-consciousness to make itself the final reference point of all predication ... that God had no control over all that might come forth in the process of time ... that man's consciousness of time and of time's product in history is, if intelligible at all, intelligible in some measure independently of God.[77]

For Bavinck, Vos, and Van Til, it is important to note that the kingdom of sin and untruth is not invented by Adam and Eve. Rather, it is inaugurated in and by an angelic fall and then endorsed and affirmed by human transgression, and thus introduced into that world which had been placed in the image-bearer's care and protective dominion.

---

74. Van Til, "Nature and Scripture," in *The Infallible Word: A Symposium by the Members of the Faculty of Westminster Theological Seminary* (Philadelphia: Presbyterian Guardian, 1946), 267.
75. Bavinck, *RD*, 3:148.
76. Van Til, *CA*, 33.
77. Van Til, *CA*, 119.

Prohibition and Probation: A Relational Rationale

The foregoing discussion has shown that Bavinck, Vos, and Van Til understand the situation in Eden as a highly controlled imbrication of the kingdoms of God and of Satan. The following material presents their unified understanding of the purpose of this arrangement, namely, relational confirmation and consummation. Prominent in their largely harmonious accounts of Genesis 2 and 3 are intricate divine design and sacramental-symbolic arrangement and revelation, all implying a rich moral fabric for image-bearing life and advance. This "advance" in particular holds our attention presently. The Garden of Eden and the lives of the first humans are considered by these neo-Calvinist writers to be the divinely appointed precinct for Creator–creature relational reckoning and eschatology, just as the prohibition and probation are understood as serving that end.

Creation

If creation has a goal, one may assume that at the point of its origin it must have been in some sense imperfect; it must have had somewhere to go. Bavinck says precisely this, that creation was made open to completion or perfection:

> When God had completed the work of creation, he looked down with delight on the work of his hands, for it was all very good (Gen. 1:31). Granted, at that moment the world was only at the beginning of its development and hence enjoyed a perfection, not in degree but in kind. Inasmuch as it was something that was positively good, it could become something and develop in accordance with the laws God had set for it.[78]

This is not to say that in its initial moments creation was in some sense deficient, but it is to identify a possibility of advance. One might argue that there is nothing to which creation may be compared, no standard or normative expectation, and that therefore it may scarcely be found wanting. More importantly: theologically speaking, an uncompelled work of God simply as such is good. "Creation," writes Bavinck, "was very good inasmuch as it came forth from the hands of God."[79]

Creation does however come into being bearing lively capacity for development and enrichment. It is a potential that obtains in the form of native fecundity or promise, as in "seed each according to its kind" (Gen. 1:11). This capacity, of creation as such, is concentrated in the human person who has, subjectively, the potential to fruitfulness and multiplication, but also powers sufficient objectively to produce and cultivate the world around him, to raise it, intentionally and perpetually, to higher stages of doxological expression. Divine approval—"it is good"—this approach insists, must not be taken to rule out this kind of incompleteness. So long

---

78. Bavinck, *RD*, 3:28–9.
79. Bavinck, *RD*, 3:28.

as incompleteness is recognized as capacity and promise, rather than deficiency, the world as God made it lacks nothing and promises much.

The Image-Bearer and Created Moral Character

Potential not merely for sequence or continuation but for progress and development according to innate principles is indicated in the creation mandates of Gen. 1:26 and 1:28. In fact, the "cultural mandate" there announced to human beings is preceded by the world's own natural capacity for organic development. And augmented by the greater part of Genesis 2, the cultural mandate may be seen as drawing attention to the human creature as both agent and substance, both subject and object, of natural, if self-conscious, doxological advance. Van Til says that in Eden, "the flowers of the field glorified God directly and unconsciously, but also indirectly and consciously through man."[80] Adam's task, and by extension the task of the image-bearing race, "was to gather up into the prism of his self-conscious activity all the manifold manifestations of the glory of God in order to make one central self-conscious sacrifice of it all to God."[81] "Man was created a king so that he might become more of a king than he was," and in this sense "the central place given to him in this universe" indicates his moral program and moral self-understanding.[82]

Bavinck, likewise, holds a dynamic view of the image of God, which, he says, "is not a static entity but extends and unfolds itself in the forms of space and time. It is both a gift … and a mandate."[83] Bavinck believed that the image implied the unfolding of human culture, or that the flourishing of humanity was the natural extension or realization of the image. It was not good that Adam was alone; Adam and Eve together, a richer image still, were commissioned to increase (both themselves and their environment), subdue, and exercise dominion—that is, actively to image the Creator king in quantitative and qualitative amplification of the glory of God *in perpetuo*.

The controlling center of this creational potential-to-be-realized is the contingent character of the image-bearer's morally loaded relationship with the Creator. Van Til says that "the very presupposition of man's being able to sin is

---

80. Van Til, *CTE*, 44.

81. Van Til, *CTE*, 44–5. Coordinating subjective and objective dimensions of the doxological task, Van Til writes:

> If man was to perform this, his God-given task, he must himself be a fit instrument for this work. He was made a fit instrument for this work, but he must also make himself an ever better instrument for this work. He must will to develop his intellect in order to grasp more comprehensively the wealth of the manifestation of the glory of God in this world. (*CTE*, 45)

82. Van Til, *CTE*, 44.
83. Bavinck, *RD*, 2:577.

that from the outset God created him a perfect moral character," or moral agent, a subject self-consciously accountable for morally significant self-direction.[84] Van Til sees this as implied in the imperfected goodness of creation, coupled with the image-bearer's "central place" within it.

Vos for his part describes the entirety of "pre-redemptive special revelation" as "the disclosure of the principles of a process of probation by which man was to be raised to a state of religion and goodness, higher, by reason of its unchangeableness, than what he already possessed."[85] Thus, as for Van Til, the entire scene in the garden highlights Adam's mutable goodness. Unmistakably, "man had been created perfectly good in a moral sense. And yet there was a sense in which he could be raised to a still higher level of perfection."[86] Vos acknowledges that the idea of Adam's untarnished goodness possessing potential for perfection "seems to involve a contradiction," but a relational telos discloses the inner logic of this original incompletion.[87] He writes:

> Religion means personal intercourse between God and man. Hence it might be *a priori* expected that God would not be satisfied, and would not allow man to be satisfied with an acquaintance based on indirection, but would crown the process of religion with the establishment of face-to-face communion, as friend holds fellowship with friend.[88]

Herman Bavinck says that Adam "received the possibility to remain standing ... but not the will. ... He had the possibility of not erring, sinning, and dying ... but not yet the impossibility."[89] Bavinck notes that

> this possibility, this being changeably good, this still being able to sin and die, was no part or component of the image of God, but was its boundary, its limitation, its circumference. The image of God therefore had to be fully developed—thereby overcoming and nullifying this possibility of sin and death—and glitter in imperishable glory.[90]

Bavinck in fact says that moral mutability before a just and omniscient Creator God must have signaled to Adam's conscience, before the Fall, the prospect of transgression, failure, and death—and that this notion must have lingered fearsome in Adam's self-understanding. Original loving obedience "was not yet

---

84. Van Til, *CTE*, 36.
85. Vos, *BT*, 27.
86. Vos, *BT*, 22.
87. Vos, *BT*, 22.
88. Vos, *BT*, 22.
89. Bavinck, *RD*, 2:573.
90. Bavinck, *RD*, 2:573.

the invariable perfect love that casts out all fear," and so Adam "still lived in the state of one who could sin and die, and was therefore still in some fear and dread."[91]

If the human being is a "moral character," to use Van Til's words, there is a conspicuous sense in which religious advance would implicate a broad deployment of personal moral capacity. If the human is to advance from one human condition to another human condition, the means or avenue of advance may be expected to involve the human's natural capacity for self-advancement, however that may be understood. It is thus that a relational telos, in which the image-bearer self-develops as image of God, implies the mutability of the moral aspect of the image of God, of subjective or personal righteousness and holiness. In this neo-Calvinist account of Eden one discovers, in the mutability of the original state, an acute moral incompleteness of the image, making it available to a divine offer of supernatural advance that hangs on ethico-religious self-exertion.

To be sure, mutability notwithstanding, Bavinck, Vos, and Van Til affirm that obedience was already natural to Adam. Bavinck says that "the moral law," inclusive of Adam's original duties of obedience to God, "was known to man by nature," and "could be kept by man with the powers bestowed on him in the creation, without the assistance of supernatural grace."[92] Obedience came as it were instinctively to Adam, so that his natural and normal inclination—his preference and joy—was loving obedience to God. Bavinck wishes to be counted among those Reformed writers who, he explains, "defended the thesis that, aside from the probationary command, Adam was also thoroughly bound to the moral law ... even though he fulfilled it without any coercion, willingly and out of love."[93]

Prior to the entrance of sin, Adam was naturally inclined toward obedience and godliness in his every undertaking. The law of God was his moral nature. Van Til says that although the law of God "was for the most part not verbally transmitted to man but was created in his being," still "man would act in accord with his own true nature only if he would obey the law of God and ... if he would live in accord with his own nature, he would obey the law of God."[94]

So writes Vos, that Adam "knew from nature, by innate knowledge, what God could demand of him—that he stood, as bearer of the image of God, under the moral opposition between good and evil, that upon breaking this natural relationship punishment would follow."[95] More than that, Adam "was assured of the favor of God and of life, provided that he persevered in the good. All of this," notice, "Adam could know naturally."[96] The covenant of works, that legal relationship turning on Adam's keeping or not keeping the law of Gen. 2:17, Vos thinks of as "a concrete application of the natural legal relation that obtains

---

91. Bavinck, *RD*, 2:573.
92. Bavinck, *RD*, 2:567.
93. Bavinck, *RD*, 2:574.
94. Van Til, *CA*, 42.
95. Vos, *RD*, 2:44.
96. Vos, *RD*, 2:44.

between God and man."[97] Noteworthy, to risk redundancy here, is the richness of Adam's natural moral self-understanding.

There was therefore no natural reason for a command of God to take negative or prohibitive form, as in nine of the ten words of Exodus 20. In prelapsarian Eden, neither action nor hidden inclination required correction. Bavinck nonetheless wishes to recognize the imperatives of Gen. 1:28 as in an important sense law—as, in other words, enjoining morally significant, volitionally driven human activity. In their inauguration and intention, the basic tasks of human living—procreation, agriculture, domestication—are to be thought of as moral, as good before God, as acts of creaturely obedience—not strictly "meritorious" but not morally neutral either. So for Bavinck, and no less for Vos and Van Til, mutable goodness must be both affirmed and distinguished from moral ambiguity. Prelapsarian Adam does not swing unpredictable and ambivalent between morally meaningful options, nor is he positioned from his beginning as a morally capable but uncommitted personality, between divergent paths or competing options, obedient merely by coincidence or naïveté. Adam is unequivocally and self-consciously good, inclined to good, and recognized as good by his Creator; but his goodness is not fixed; it is impermanent—morally unqualified but unperfected.[98] For this reason when in the probation God would offer his image-bearer the blessing of covenant advance, for the acquisition of those blessings original goodness must confront its own mutability. Volition must stand alone, self-assert, and self-determine.

For the purpose of relational consummation, Adam's original goodness signals a situation requiring a special act of God, which distinguishes the grace of supernatural advance from the natural and normal development and imaging of God. In other words, "human beings could know the moral law without special revelation since it was written in their hearts. But the probationary command is

---

97. Vos, *RD*, 2:44. Vos notes complexity in comparing the natural and the covenantal Creator–creature relation. First, they are not identical: "to this natural relationship a *covenant* was added by God," such that "the distinction between the natural relationship and the covenant of works is logical and judicial, not temporal." Furthermore, in Vos's view for the imputation of Adam's sin natural (genetic) relation is insufficient; federalism and thus "imputation rests on the covenantal relation" (*RD*, 2:44). The fact that covenant is added to nature is most obvious in the fact that Adam "God had created mutable, and he also possessed the right to an immutable state." Therefore "the right to reward, and certainly such a glorious reward, did not proceed from the natural relationship of Adam to God and, thus, had to have another foundation. However, as soon as one must agree that there was something positive, a special condescension of God, in these matters, he also accepts the covenant of works in principle, although one may still take exception to the designation" (*RD*, 2:31, 35–6).

98. "In other words, man must needs develop the backbone of his will. Not as though man was created a volitional amoeba, which had to pass through the invertebrate stage before it finally acquired a backbone. Man was created a self" (Van Til, *CTE*, 45).

positive; it is not a given of human nature as such but could only be made known to human beings if God communicated it to them."[99]

Adam was put in the garden to work and to keep it, and gardening could be understood without special instruction from heaven. Likewise, the first humans were blessed to be fruitful and multiply, while of this duty, "concerning the mystery of the propagation of his race," writes Vos, Adam "will not have been wrongly ignorant."[100] They would have figured that out, too. All this Adam could do without facing squarely the fact of his mutability and the prospect of incurring the displeasure of God. Adam first of all obeyed God naturally and joyfully. But the prospect of supernatural advance, signaled in the mutability of Adam's character, required that volitional goodness be deprived of the aid of intuition and all the natural signals of general revelation. The image-bearer had to encounter divine authority as a problem. Bavinck explains:

> Precisely because in the prefall life of Adam the moral law was in the nature of the case entirely positive, it did not make clear to Adam's mind the possibility of sin. Hence, in addition to the *pre*scriptions there had to come a *pro*scription, and in addition to the commandments a positive law. In addition the commandments, whose naturalness and reasonableness were obvious to Adam, this command was in a sense arbitrary and incidental. In the probationary command the entire moral law came to Adam at a single throw, confronting him with the dilemma: either God or man, God's authority or one's own insight, unconditional obedience or independent research, faith or skepticism. It was an appalling test that opened the way either to eternal blessedness or eternal ruin.[101]

Thus the significance of a special word of God confronting the intuition of original righteousness and the natural availability of nature to cultivation and

---

99. Bavinck, *RD*, 2:571. Van Til helps clarify the language of positive as opposed to natural:

> In Paradise there was theologico-physics when God revealed his will with respect to the Tree of Good and Evil. Man could not know from nature itself or from himself in relation to nature that the result of eating from the Tree of Good and Evil would spell his death. Hence we may speak of this revelation as being positive instead of natural. It had to be a direct communication of thought content on the part of God to man. Then too we may speak of this revelation as supernatural in opposition to natural. (Van Til, *IST*, 125–6)

100. Vos, *RD*, 2:44.

101. Bavinck, *RD*, 2:574. Elsewhere Bavinck suggests that the proscriptive form (of Gen. 2:17) indicates the low demand placed upon Adam, since he was already a happily and actively obedient creature. See *RE*, 39–40, and the discussion in Chapter 2 below. It is not clear that the various ways in which Bavinck explains the moral function of a prelapsarian prohibitive word are always exactly harmonious, but neither is much at stake.

enjoyment, namely, the prohibition against eating from a tree that was without any natural disincentive or discouragement, the tree of the knowledge of good and evil.

For Vos as well, the mutability of Adam's original condition, the dynamicism of the image of God, and the offer of relational and personal advance imply the need for a negative command, a prohibition, a kind of sounding board for the objectification of the volitional component of image-advancement. Vos believes that the prohibited tree received its name "because by this tree the essence of evil was, as it were, objectified for Adam."[102] Vos thus develops Bavinck's understanding of the tree and the prohibition as these confronted Adam's will and mutable character. He says: "This essence of evil came most clearly to the fore when it was rid of all incidentals, harmful consequences, etc."[103] By contrast, in sin as we experience it, "in the usual transgression of law," writes Vos, "the seed of evil is always more or less covered over with other things."[104] But Adam's experience was different. Vos offers this informative counter-illustration: "If God had commanded Adam to treat the animals well and had made this the point of probation, then in the ill-treatment of the animals, which was in opposition to it, evil would have revealed itself as cruelty to the animals and not so directly as transgression against God."[105] There must be no room for the moral intuition of the creature to partner with, and thus to obscure, the authority of God. The prohibition must appear to the creature to be a challenge, or, to risk overstating, an offense, to his own moral reason.

Indicating Vos's preference for something like a covenant divine command ethic, not only but certainly in the Garden of Eden, nothing short of the nature of Christian theocentric morality is manifest in the name and function of the tree. Vos does not believe that the name of the tree indicates that such knowledge may be acquired by eating the fruit of the tree, but rather that the tree was set to reveal one's orientation to that distinction between good and evil. (Nor does he believe that the first sin is merely a lust for illicit information or understanding.) The tree certainly does not, for Vos, signal an opportunity to acquire moral knowledge, as though in their original state Adam and Eve were morally naïve. They were not, as the structure of the testing already implies: "the form of the probation command in itself already communicated a certain knowledge of evil, and, in contrast, of good."[106] Vos thus stands by his own anthropology when he rejects the notion that original righteousness was a kind of bliss of moral ignorance. Rather, Adam

---

102. Vos, *RD*, 2:48. Vos's account of the name and meaning of the tree, and thus of important aspects of the temptation, go beyond Calvin's emphasis on the first sin as expressing lust for illicit knowledge. The neo-Calvinists produced a much richer moral and covenantal account of this material than Calvin did.

103. Vos, *RD*, 2:48.
104. Vos, *RD*, 2:48.
105. Vos, *RD*, 2:48.
106. Vos, *RD*, 2:48.

already possessed knowledge of the most basic moral distinction, of the good in contrast to evil; the tree does not introduce that distinction but sacramentalizes it within the context of a formalized covenant eschatology.[107]

Here is Vos's memorable summary of the significance of the prohibition:

> That God made a morally neutral thing the point of decision appears ... to have had the purpose of ridding sin of all incidental features and to lay it bare at its core. If man sinned against this command, then it could be for no other reason than that he choose [sic] evil as evil and rejected good as good. Because God's will is for us the binding power, and love toward God should permeate all our moral relationships, a command that depended solely on God's will was extremely well suited to place man before the pointed choice: only because of God's will, or not.[108]

Therefore, as Vos understands it, the design of the probation was to invite Adam to express and enjoy a "pure delight in obedience," a delight in obedience pure and undiluted by personal instinct or intuition or moral self-evidence, and for this purpose "an arbitrary prohibition was issued."[109] Accordingly, Vos understands the prohibition itself as an instance of a covenantal divine command ethic in which

---

107. Vos notes that Satan rejects the sacramental interpretation of the tree and instead claims that the fruit imparts knowledge. He claims that the tree itself possessed a kind of magical power to bestow special knowledge that God out of pettiness, envy, insecurity, and of course dishonesty had claimed would be harmful to pursue. See *BT*, 32–3. On the other hand, Vos says that "man was to attain something he had not attained before. He was to learn the good in its clear opposition to the evil, and the evil in its clear opposition to the good" (*BT*, 31). But the point is that this increased acquaintance with moral categories would not come by a magical property of the fruit itself, but rather it hung on Adam's conduct relative to the prohibition; the question was not the power of an unusual fruit but obedience or disobedience to an express command of God. "The tree is called the tree of 'knowledge of good and evil', because it is the God-appointed instrument to lead man through probation to that state of religious and moral maturity wherewith his highest blessedness is connected" (*BT*, 31).

108. Vos, *RD*, 2:48.

109. Vos, *BT*, 32. Similarity with Calvin's understanding is worth noting: "Concerning the tree of knowledge of good and evil, we must hold that it was prohibited to man, not because God would have him to stray like a sheep, without judgment and without choice; but that he might not seek to be wiser than became him, nor by trusting to his own understanding, cast off the yoke of God, and constitute himself an arbiter and judge of good and evil. ... We now understand what is meant by abstaining from the tree of the knowledge of good and evil; namely, that Adam might not, in attempting one thing or another, rely upon his own prudence; but that, cleaving to God alone, he might become wise only by his obedience." John Calvin, *Commentary on the First Book of Moses Called Genesis*, trans. John King (Grand Rapids, MI: CCEL, n.d.), 72–3 (on Gen. 2:9).

above all value stands an "unmotivated demand of God."[110] Vos guards against arbitrariness but nonetheless defers to a classical doctrine of God: "it is possible to go back of the *mere command* of God for finding the bottom-reason for why a thing is good and evil. This bottom-reason lies in the *nature* of God regulating his command."[111] Emphasis on the unimpeachable sovereignty and self-existence of God leads Vos to develop at some length the moral superiority of obedience to God, Vos's "pure delight in obedience," over reasoned self-direction. So, while moral inquiry may have recourse to the nature of God, it may not do so in order to expose a deductive system, for example, inferring from "God is such and such" to "God must therefore legislate thus." The authority of a divine imperative must rest solely upon the personal authority of its author, not merely upon the metaphysical uniqueness of pure being, and it therefore, naturally enough, evokes the sort of eager and unquestioning obedience that issues from righteous fear and adoration. Vos writes:

> To do the good and reject evil from a reasoned insight into their respective natures is a noble thing, but it is a still nobler thing to do so out of regard for the nature of God, and the noblest thing of all is the ethical strength, which, when required, will act from personal attachment to God, without for the moment enquiring into these more abstruse reasons.[112]

In Vos's view, the design of covenant or Creator–creature relational eschatology is that God's people would know him as their God. Attempting to articulate the rationale of covenant, Vos explains that the notion of "knowledge of God" appropriate to biblical religion is not Greek representationalism, which is "to mirror the reality of a thing in one's consciousness." Rather, it is the "Shemitic and Biblical idea," which is "to have the reality of something practically interwoven with the inner experience of life."[113] "Because God desires to be *known* after this fashion," Vos writes, "He has caused His revelation to take place in the milieu of the historical life of a people."[114]

A rationale for the probationary testing, at least in retrospect (by no necessity, in other words), becomes apparent: God desires the fruit of this "knowledge," the fruit of personal communion in the form of public display or proof of obedience in love, which is little more than expressed and confirmed conviction of the

---

110. Vos, *BT*, 32. Elsewhere Vos writes that Jesus taught "not merely that the norm of righteousness is to be found in God," but also that "the aim of righteousness, the final cause of obedience, lies in God. Righteousness is to be sought in the pure desire of satisfying him, who is the supreme end of all moral existence." Vos, *The Teaching of Jesus Concerning the Kingdom of God and the Church* (Eugene, OR: Wipf & Stock, 1998), 106.
111. Vos, *BT*, 32.
112. Vos, *BT*, 32.
113. Vos, *BT*, 8.
114. Vos, *BT*, 8.

lordship of the one true God. And precisely this sort of religious undertaking is appropriate to the body-spirit composite image of God: visible deeds of obedience in demonstration and confirmation of both disposition and self-determination, of both character and volition. Vos infers from the biblical relational arrangement that God wants truly to be the object of human covenant love.

The Forbidden Tree and Moral Reason

For Bavinck, Vos, and Van Til the probation, with the prohibition at its center, is not so much focused on knowledge in the ordinary sense; the tree of the knowledge of good and evil does not stand for the limit of creaturely curiosity or the threshold of illicit knowledge, for information to which Adam and Eve or creatures in general have no rightful claim. Bavinck, Vos, and Van Til focus instead on obedience and disobedience relative to the tree and the prohibition as action indicating self-understanding and the character of human self-presentation before God. Even if the name of the tree were to signal content or information—a theory winning no favor among these authors—emphasis would still fall on the "manner in which they would obtain" that knowledge.[115] The leading interpretation among these writers is this, that the name of the tree signals the fact that in eating of it Adam and Eve would, in a practical sense, in their relation to the law, "become like God." That is, they would by exercise of will attempt to position themselves above the law or unto themselves take up the task of self-legislation and governance: in a word, autonomy. In this sense, in the structure of moral reasoning, becoming like God is self-idolization and public, incriminating affirmation of a false ontology.

Van Til describes original righteousness as self-conscious self-subjection of the creature, as creature, to God as Creator and source of all things. There is a distinct if implicit cognitive aspect to original righteousness by which the creature knows himself as derivative and dependent, and knows God as original and self-sufficient. God has no context but himself, and so is self-defined. "We do not name God; he names himself."[116] All other things derive their names—their nature, meaning, and relation to other things—from God, God's uncompelled will to create, providence, and foreordination. The creature therefore knows himself as in every epistemic moment seeking to think God's thoughts after him.

Van Til proposes, accordingly, a psychological structure consisting of a derivative, subjective "starting point" and a self-sufficient, objective point of reference. He writes: "In Paradise, man made his self-consciousness *the immediate but wholly derivative* starting point while he made the self-consciousness of God the *remote* but *wholly ultimate starting point* of all his knowledge."[117] Always the subject is the thinker of his own thoughts, but as such he is an image-thinker. Not *cogito ergo sum*, but *cogitat Dei mecum ergo sum*. The thinking subject must count himself

---

115. Bavinck, *RD*, 3:33.
116. Bavinck, *RD*, 2:98.
117. Van Til, *IST*, 129.

among the created, general revelatory facts of experience so that every thought is simultaneously an interpretation of revelation and self-interpretation. The image-bearer interprets his world, the revelatory context of his self-understanding, and in doing so is himself interpreted by that revelation. Obedience, for Van Til, begins with righteous self-understanding—the creature knowing himself as a creature—activated in the structure of knowing.

The obedience in view in Gen. 2:16-17 Van Til therefore sees as implicating the full range of human activity and self-understanding: "God did not give his prohibition so that man might be obedient merely with respect to the tree of the knowledge of good and evil, and that merely at one particular moment of time," but "so that man might learn to be self-consciously obedient in all that he did with respect to all things and throughout all time."[118] The forbidden tree strips bare the moral substance of all image-bearer activity: "Man's act with respect to the tree of the knowledge of good and evil was to be but an example to himself of what he should or should not do with respect to all other trees."[119] The prohibition, in this sense, is calculated to concentrate the will of the image-king upon the incompleteness of creation and the potential for grander realization of all things, so that by him all things, including himself, in his every conscious moment, would be declared the stuff of the glorification of God who alone is worthy.

Van Til reflects carefully and creatively upon the methodological implications of missing this opportunity. He writes: "When Satan tempted Adam and Eve in paradise, he sought to make them believe that man's self-consciousness was ultimate rather than derivative and God-dependent. He argued, as it were, that it was of the nature of the self-consciousness to make itself the final reference point of all predication."[120] In transgressing, Adam and Eve would in other words succumb to or embrace a lust for inordinate self-advancement in the form of judicial independence from God, not unlike the transgression of Jude 6: In Van Til's words, the first sin means that "man's knowledge is characterized by the same folly that marks Satan's knowledge of God," in the sense that the "first act of man's antitheistic interpretation consisted in the attempt on his part to be something that he knew he could not be."[121] Van Til continues: "It is this folly that man has carried on through the ages, and it is this that still makes sin so foolish. And it is upon this foolishness that Paul says that the wrath of God is revealed."[122] Bavinck suggests that the serpent's own heightened condition is designed to advertise the very promotion to which he invites Eve: "Undoubtedly the serpent's speaking must have seemed strange to the woman, but precisely this strangeness enhanced the seduction: even an animal, rejecting God's command, had achieved a higher level of perfection!"[123] "The knowledge of good and evil," writes Bavinck, is "the right

118. Van Til, *CA*, 69–70.
119. Van Til, *CA*, 70.
120. Van Til, *CA*, 118.
121. Van Til, *IST*, 167.
122. Van Til, *IST*, 167.
123. Bavinck, *RD*, 3:36.

and capacity to distinguish good and evil on one's own."[124] And, tragically, "when humanity fell, it got what it wanted; it made itself like God, 'knowing good and evil' by its own sight and judgment."[125] The knowledge of good and evil is judicial orientation, or forensic self-understanding: Do I judge, or am I myself judged?

Van Til says that in the first sin an "alliance" is formed "with Satan" on the basis of "a grand monistic assumption."[126] The monistic assumption is not merely a matter of the conclusion of reasoning, but "in his method and starting point" the sinner "takes for granted his own ultimacy."[127] Van Til concludes: "To the extent that he works according to this monistic assumption, he misinterprets all things, flowers no less than God."[128] He summarizes: "When man fell, he denied the naturally revelatory character of every fact, including that of his own consciousness."[129] And in doing so, the sinner "assumed that he was autonomous; he assumed that his consciousness was not revelation of God but only of himself."[130] Thus "man," in sinning, "made for himself a false ideal of knowledge," namely, "the ideal of absolute inderivative comprehension."[131] "Man" as sinner "virtually occupies the place that the ontological Trinity occupies in orthodox theology. He is self-sufficient and autonomous."[132]

The tree, the garden, and the probation have been designed by God for the purpose of testing the will and loyalty of an image-lord whose own constitution and his relationship to his surroundings indicate the gravity of the choice he would face; his future and that of the world entrusted to him depended upon his success or failure in the probationary testing. And this testing is understood not as an isolated quantification of the integrity of the human creature—not as an exam for its own sake—but as the sphere of cosmic, spiritual conflagration involving God, an enemy created and restrained by God, a world created by God, and a creature of God bearing the image of God defined in reference to God.

Trinity, Edenic Freedom, and the Problem of Evil

Two principles with regard to all that is implicated in the prohibition of Gen. 2:17 must at this point be observed. The first is that the possibility of evil is given in

---

124. Bavinck, *RD*, 3:33.
125. Bavinck, *RD*, 3:33.
126. Van Til, *IST*, 65.
127. Van Til, *IST*, 65.
128. Van Til, *IST*, 65.
129. Van Til, *CA*, 79. Though not to the same extent, Vos's attention, too, is drawn to the interpretive aspect not only of the Fall but of the temptation as well: "the central purpose of the tempter is the injection of doubt into the woman's mind" (Vos, *BT*, 35).
130. Van Til, *CA*, 79.
131. Van Til, *CA*, 42.
132. Van Til, *CA*, 42.

creation as a feature of the relational rationale for creation as such, in its original moral mutability. This is not to say that God's good intention, holy communion with a creation and a people unto his glory, required a suspension of divine influence for the sake of the integrity of freedom and historical contingency, that for his desired end God had no choice but to gamble, as is often argued, but only that there is, according to Bavinck, Vos, and Van Til, a clear rationale for human moral experience, namely, Creator–creature relational eschatology, or covenant consummation. Freedom is always freedom relative to image-ethics and the call to self-conscious glorification of the Creator-King. This rationale explains the possibility of evil in one sense—it provides an explanation of the nature of evil as we find it—but comes up empty in another sense, with regard to the possibility of evil.[133] The fact that relational eschatology and thus the possibility of transgression are given in creation as such, prior in fact to the prohibition itself, signals the difficulty of identifying cause or antecedent possibility, or even of diminishing mystery in any meaningful sense. It would seem in other words that there was never a created order free of the possibility of evil, and coordinately, perhaps consequently, conceiving of what had to precede that possibility, even if only logically, proves challenging.

For example: Bavinck insists, with reference to the supernatural advance offered in the garden and represented by the tree of life, that "there *is* no natural connection here between work and reward."[134] That is, there is nothing in nature that necessitates or signals creaturely right to an offer of greater life and righteousness on condition of obedience. On the other hand, the Edenic situation and Edenic anthropology seem both to have been designed precisely for an offer that would intensify the importance of the moral character of human self-expression. The garden and the image-bearer are open to perfection but do not expect it. More importantly, the two trees, particularly when highlighted by divine instruction, signal a new, additional situation constituted by specified eschatology, and magnify that natural moral situation which preceded the formalization of relational contingency. That is, the covenant of works is both continuous and discontinuous with the natural situation. It is continuous in the sense that it draws its moral force from the

---

133. Confusion may arise from the fact that Bavinck says on more than one occasion that, in the garden, the possibility of sin is plain (e.g., *RD*, 3:69), and that what eludes us is how it became actual. It would seem that something different is meant in each case by "possibility." In the garden, a morally self-conscious creature may transgress an express command of God. So, how is it possible for sin to enter the realm of human experience? Through violation of the prohibition of Gen. 2:17. This is indeed the possibility of sin, in one sense. But the situation in the garden is also, surely, the nature of sin in its prototypical instance. And a slightly different question—how is it that a creature can transgress the will of a self-existent, simple, and sovereign Creator God?—signals the theological mystery of creaturely moral freedom itself, a mystery to which the phenomena of the garden provide no answers.

134. Bavinck, *RD*, 2:571.

natural, created situation—the wholesome imperfection of creation and of the human creature, and in particular the natural (but exhaustively theological) moral law obtaining between the I AM and the image-bearer. The covenant of works is discontinuous, in a word, because it introduces an eschatology crowned with reward, by defining the terms of the probation (the tree of the knowledge of good and evil) and promising supervention of a state of accomplished self-realization in righteousness (the tree of life) on condition of obedience.

That is, for covenant advance offered by God a mutability created by God must be challenged in a situation designed and controlled by God in which opportunity is granted, graciously by God, for willful acknowledgment that all things are to the glory of God—and all this for the glory of God. "When man becomes truly the king of the universe the kingdom of God is realized, and when the kingdom of God is realized, God is glorified."[135] And yet, even human failure in the form of covenant transgression would tend toward the glory of God, who is himself law, legislator, and enforcer. If a person is considered a sinner or a lawbreaker, the law and the legislator are therein acknowledged as the beginning and the end of creation and finite experience. Sin may not please God, but the moral system that sin, understood as such, affirms does glorify God as God.

The narrowness of this conception, its heavy orientation toward the glory and honor of God, above all draws the focus and full scope of biblical religion around the issue of obedience, of creaturely volition relative to the requirements of God because and precisely because those requirements are from God. What is to notice here is that this orientation of all things as they are and as they should be to the glory of God simply because he is God precedes the formalization of the covenant relation, because God precedes the formalization of the covenant relation; wherever there is finite moral self-consciousness, there is the natural (but exhaustively theological) law of obedience to God. Necessarily, obligation to God as God is the "natural" situation for Adam as for all creatures. (There is no nonreligious moment for the image-bearer.) A creature is a creature to the glory of God, and a self-conscious, volitional creature is a creature to the glory of God in precisely those terms. The human creature is inconceivable apart from the basically theocentric notions of obedience and disobedience, which constitute the moral terms of human experience as such.

And here is the key to the relational rationale of the probation: Bavinck does not hesitate to associate even the possibility of sin with this understanding of the probation. He writes:

> It is God himself who, according to his special revelation, created the possibility of sin. Not only did he make humanity in such a way that it could fall, but he also planted the tree of the knowledge of good and evil in the garden, confronted Adam with a moral option by means of the probationary command, whose decision had the greatest significance for himself and all his posterity, and

---

135. Van Til, *CTE*, 45.

finally, even permitted the temptation of the woman by the serpent. It was God's decision to take humanity on the perilous path of freedom rather than elevating it by a single act of power above the possibility of sin and death.[136]

Here in this statement Bavinck presents side by side both of the explanatory issues just mentioned. First, the relational rationale is front and center; good and evil are basically and irreducibly theocentric notions that characterize the self-conscious self-direction of the human being relative to the omnipresent, immutable other. This is, it bears noting, simply to deny the impersonality of moral law, or to affirm a rich divine-personalism of moral experience.[137] Second, this statement is a sort of deferral to the mystery of the divine will, even to the divine being. "It is God himself who" and "it was God's decision" are phrases that indicate the blinding light of divine perfection and of incomprehensibility as the backdrop to intelligible revelation, a structure that here stalls creaturely inquiry in its tracks. This is noteworthy because it is typical of Bavinck, Vos, and Van Til—and historic Reformed theology, and Augustine—as they encounter theological mystery, to look "more steadfastly into the face of God."[138] The border of human understanding lies well within the light of divine self-understanding. "It follows," says Van Til, from the incommunicable attributes no less, "that in everything with which we deal we are, in the last analysis, dealing with this infinite God, this God who hidest Himself, this mysterious God."[139]

The second principle to mention as the present chapter draws to a close sharpens the first, that relational rationale for Edenic moral experience. The second principle is this: Bavinck, Vos, and Van Til articulate Edenic freedom in trinitarian terms. Adam's freedom in the garden is in the Son, by the Spirit, unto the Father, so that when he sins the Spirit is grieved, the Son assumes a mediatorial function, and the Father pronounces judicial sentence. One observes, in this sense, an immanent triune-theistic ethic in which not only are metaethical predicates accounted for theistically but the discrete moments of moral experience find their unity and coherence in terms of a trinitarian relational economy.

For example: Bavinck affirms a kind of Son-mediation or Christ-focused eschatology in the prelapsarian order, and an empowering presence of the Spirit granting and sustaining knowledge, righteousness, and holiness: "the Son was already the mediator of union before the fall," and "so also the Holy Spirit was even then already the craftsman of all knowledge, righteousness, and holiness in humanity."[140]

Interesting as well is the fact that Bavinck appears to believe that Adam's fleshly nature would have advanced beyond many of the familiar trappings of material

---

136. Bavinck, *RD*, 3:29.
137. See Van Til, *CGG*, 10–11.
138. Van Til, *CGG*, 19.
139. Van Til, *CGG*, 15.
140. Bavinck, *RD*, 2:558.

life. He says that Adam "needed food and drink, light and air, day and night, hence did not yet have a glorified spiritual body on a level transcending all those needs."[141] That is, Adam's "natural body had not yet fully become an instrument of the spirit."[142] As history would have it, what would have ensued, had obedience prevailed, is indicated for us, or takes shape, only in redemptive eschatology. But in Bavinck's view, Edenic eschatology would have included the cessation of dependence upon material sustenance—food and drink—and perhaps in some sense, sexual gratification.[143] Bavinck passes over the details too quickly, raising many questions and leaving many unanswered, but it is noted presently that he puts all of this in terms of unrealized spiritual eschatology: "It is evident from this scenario," in the garden, that is, "that the first man, however highly placed, did not yet possess the highest humanity. There is a very great difference between the natural and the pneumatic, between the state of integrity and the state of glory."[144] The point there is that, for Bavinck, Adam's covenant experience is pneumatologically conditioned; his relationship to God is, surely, an objective, forensic status, but it is also subjective and the subjective is pneumatological.

Bavinck says that "man in the state of integrity only possessed the virtues of knowledge and righteousness by and in the Holy Spirit."[145] In fact, "no truly good and perfect human being is even conceivable apart from the fellowship of the Holy Spirit."[146] Van Til describes the Spirit's influence in the prelapsarian situation as follows: "Before the fall, man also needed the witness of the Holy Spirit. Even then the third person of the Holy Trinity was operative in and through the naturally revelational consciousness of man so that it might react fittingly and properly to the words of God's creation."[147] And Vos says that one consequence of Adam's first sin for himself was "the loss of the gift of fellowship with God through the Holy Spirit."[148] More concretely: "By the fall, Adam cut himself off, in a way incomprehensible to us, from the supply of life by the Holy Spirit, so that the Spirit departed from him. Death was the natural result of this."[149]

Accordingly, Adam's reward for obedience would have included increased or perfected Son-mediation and Spirit endowment. One might speak in that case of Spirit-indwelling or even of mystical union in non-soteric terms, as in fact Bavinck does.[150] Righteous Adam would have entered into intensified communion with God primarily in the Son, by the indwelling of the Spirit, to the glory of the Father.

141. Bavinck, *RD*, 2:564.
142. Bavinck, *RD*, 2:564.
143. Bavinck, *RD*, 2:564.
144. Bavinck, *RD*, 2:564.
145. Bavinck, *RD*, 2:558.
146. Bavinck, *RD*, 2:558.
147. Van Til, *CA*, 79.
148. Vos, *RD*, 2:53.
149. Vos, *RD*, 2:42.
150. See Bavinck, *RD*, 2:558.

Adam as created—his constitution alone—signals an infralapsarian possibility of spiritual advance, a genuine Edenic eschatology without regard for sin and without a need for atonement, and this advance included a prominent covenant-eschatological role for the Son. Thus, as the remainder of this book attempts to demonstrate, human moral experience is constituted by a relational eschatology initiated by voluntary condescension of the triune God primarily in the Son.

Conclusion

The prohibition of Gen. 2:17 is not a dare or a challenge, nor is the Lord of creation fishing for extra affection. The prohibition is designed to evoke a minor crisis of self-understanding for the bearer of the divine image in the Edenic theater of divine majesty, a situation which itself serves as the flashpoint of a cosmic conflict waged between the Creator God and fallen angels. Caught in between two kingdoms contending for his loyalty, original man's every thought and deed are open and morally interesting to the omnipresent God. The image-bearer is invited to exert himself as a rational and moral creature in order to increase in godliness, and to increase godliness on the earth. In this sense Gen. 2:17 is for the glory of God and the enjoyment and creaturely advance of the image-bearer. Good and evil and moral meaning for the volitional creature are irreducibly theocentric. Prototypical human self-consciousness is permeated through and through with moral meaning that is nothing other than the self-expression of God as moral norm for the creature.

Chapter 2 examines the twofold character of this divine, moral self-giving. One observes natural and special instances or aspects, each of which bears distinguishable implications for human consciousness, experience, and history. A subtle relationship between the natural moral situation and the formalized covenant of works emerges, so that the theological importance of the covenant framework is observable. In other words, the subsequent chapter searches out and indicates the explanatory limits of the original moral situation as they are displayed in the supreme mystery of biblical origins: that a good and godly will succumbed to temptation and chose self-consciously to transgress the law of God.

Chapter 2

DIVINE MORAL CHARACTER TRANSGRESSED

The law of death, which followed from the Transgression, prevailed upon us, and from it there was no escape. The thing that was happening was in truth both monstrous and unfitting.

—Athanasius

Unthankful, dead, and dull have I been, and still am.

—Margaret Baxter

This chapter presents a theological commentary on Gen. 3:6. The goal is to demonstrate the radical covenant theocentrism of the neo-Calvinist view of the fall—the nature of sin and evil—but also the inadequacy of this account for explaining the possibility of evil. In other words, in this chapter I shall resolve the foregoing discussion of the nature of evil as relational transgression but in doing so raise the greater theological challenge of accounting for the objective possibility of evil.

It is argued in what follows that, according to Bavinck, Vos, and Van Til, a relational arrangement provided by God, in which natural design anticipates special intervention, provides the intelligibility of a fall as such and of all its consequences, including federalism and the inheritance of sin. That is, the covenant of works, for all its importance for explaining the nature of sin and evil, is not suspended supernaturally above an indifferent, so-called natural world; the roots of the covenant of works extend deep into the divine preconception of nature and of the human creature. One may therefore define primary evil as created covenant nature plus covenant formalization or enactment, followed by transgression and judicial response.

Herman Bavinck describes sin as "lawlessness" and as a violation of a command of God: "the standard of sin is God's law alone."[1] Geerhardus Vos says that "sin always has reference to a law—and not just a law in general, but specifically to a law of God."[2] Van Til defers to the Westminster Shorter Catechism: "What is

1. Bavinck, *RD*, 3:140; see also 3:133–6.
2. Vos, *RD*, 2:25.

sin? It is 'any want of conformity unto, or transgression of, the law of God.'"³ One thinks of course of the law of Gen. 2:17, but sin does not take its meaning from the transgression of Gen. 3:6 alone. As this chapter demonstrates, Bavinck, Vos, and Van Til see the original, Edenic situation as ethico-religious and basically relational—as covenantal through and through. The law of God is written on the heart of the first man, and is therefore, at the first moment of self-consciousness, vulnerable to transgression already. These three writers believe that moral meaning enters the sphere of human experience via a natural-special creational covenant organism, a dual gesture of divine, relational self-giving.

One implication of this view is that a law of God for the creature is the precondition of evil, so that, although evil is of the nature of the case none to the liking of a wholly good God, it is actualized only according to divine design and relational arrangement in which the natural and the special components are distinguishable but coordinated. As Bavinck has said, "it is God himself who … created," not "allowed," but designed, and brought into being ex nihilo, as it were, "the possibility of sin."⁴ Specifically, Bavinck, Vos, and Van Til believe that both the conversion of Adam's character from good to sinful and the effect of Adam's sin on his progeny are, first, implied in the design of creation and, second, imposed by God in response to sin. In other words, God designed things (namely, the human creature) such that sin, if actualized, would be the beginning and principle of an evil, which would hold succeeding generations captive, while at the same time, God responds to the first transgression by actively constituting Adam a sinner and imposing Adam's sin and sinful disposition upon his progeny; God both legislates (naturally) and enforces (specially). Adam does not fall passively or haphazardly into moral corruption but selects it for himself and then is inflicted with it by the just intervention of God, and consequently, those represented in him are likewise made sinners. Rather than passive bequeathal, these writers see in Scripture active imposition of Adam's condition upon others by God according to a creational structure preceding even the material constitution of the human creature. Covenant is the design of the created order. Sin takes its meaning from this order such that, when severed from the special involvement of God and from the relational context of original creation, the significance of Adam's sin, sin as such, disappears. Morality apart from Creator–creature relationality is inconceivable. Therefore, without divine design, relational initiative, and response, there is no explanation for the moral significance, the broader meaning, or the consequences of Adamic transgression. The larger portion of this chapter is devoted to demonstrating this radical theocentrism of the moral substance of Adamic experience.

At the center of all this, we find two intractable mysteries, but dogmas nonetheless: the exercise of a good creaturely will toward evil and the unqualified sovereignty of a God to whom no blame for sin may be assigned. "Sin," says

---

3. Van Til, *CA*, 18.
4. Bavinck, *RD*, 3:29.

Bavinck, "does not have an origin in the true sense of the word, only a beginning."[5] This means that neither the formal covenant arrangement nor the natural situation which precedes it can sustain—theologically speaking—the weight of a primary transgressive evil. Covenant, in other words, signals the relational formalization within which a transgression implicating the whole of the Creator–creature relation unfolds; but in doing so covenant is only descriptive of sin. As to the origin of sin, the covenant of works is phenomenological only. Thinking of covenant as a natural-special composite supplies an account of the nature of sin and thus of evil, but not of its possibility. Therefore a theology of the precondition for morally significant Creator–creature reciprocity—a theology of the possibility of the covenant relation, even of moral meaning in the sphere of creaturely experience—is still needed. In sum, therefore, this chapter presents a neo-Calvinist theology of the moral meaning of Adamic experience, and subsequent chapters take up the task of articulating a theology of the possibility of this clash of divine and human wills.

Natural and Special Moral Meaning

Bavinck, Vos, and Van Til believe that moral meaning enters the sphere of Adam's experience through both nature and special divine intervention. They believe that the natural and special principles are harmonious and that the natural anticipates but does not require the special. On the one hand, God designed the natural as preparation for the special; this means that "natural," for Bavinck, Vos, and Van Til, is not the phenomenalistic anti-supernaturalist's "nature" of modern, Western thought but creation as such.[6] And yet, despite this anticipation, special augmentation—divine enhancement and formalization of the created, covenant relational arrangement—meets no created right, warrant, or demand but issues only from the prerogative of God. This natural-special composite is therefore a purely theological, one may say theocentric, account of moral meaning in the garden.

The attribution of a volitional act bearing moral and moral-causal significance to an agent other than God is the substance of the covenant of works. That covenant makes the first sin what it is. These three writers affirm, however, that the covenant of works and the probation, concentrated as these are in the prohibition and the temptation, highlight a special case of human, morally significant, volitional self-exertion—but not the first one. Before the covenant of works is announced, Adam obeyed God and could have disobeyed, or he was at least conscious of the possibility of transgression and thus of his own mutability, so that his behavior

---

5. Bavinck, *RD*, 3:69.
6. Vos writes: "First of all, we are face to face with the fact that the immemorial conflict between naturalism and supernaturalism has, more than ever before, concentrated itself in the field of history ... historical study has become a powerful instrument in the service of the antisupernaturalistic spirit of the modern age" (*RHBI*, 461).

prior to Gen. 3:6 if uncontroversial was still personal and morally significant. Creaturely obedience prior to the prohibition was true godliness because it was righteousness volitionally actualized. Moral good does not require moral evil—not, at least, in the Augustinian tradition—but here moral good signals the moral air of primary human experience, which does include, from its first moment, at least an informal possibility of sin.

Moral value accrues to human action before the fall, and obtains, prior to the announcement of the special terms of the covenant of works, as a function of what Bavinck, Vos, and Van Til describe as the natural relationship between God and the image-bearer. Here sin is in principle already possible, and so as these writers affirm, a primal form of the covenant relation already obtains as the precondition for the moral significance of the creature's conduct before God. The covenant of works is therefore not the beginning of morally charged ethico-religious intercourse between God and the image-bearer but its eschatological formalization. The covenant of works, in other words, heightens a moral situation that preceded it. And upon transgression of the prohibition, sin and the inheritance of sin unfold according to the natural structure of creation and the human creature, as well as to the positive aspects of the covenant of works. In fact, Bavinck and Vos see even a redemptive motive behind the imputation of Adam's sin, while there certainly is no place in their thought for a natural, anthropological claim on the grace and forgiveness of God.

So, generally speaking, moral categories are actual—good and evil as for or against God are live options—for Adam and Eve from the first moment of consciousness, and therefore divine initiative in setting the relational prerequisites for the actual goodness of obedience and the possibility of the evil of transgression must not appear subsequent to but must at least coincide with the first moment of the moral self-awareness of the first humans. Creation in the image of God presupposes a natural covenant relation freely established by God of which image-bearers are naturally cognizant.

Vos distinguishes natural and positive elements of the covenant of works in terms of Adam's understanding of the covenant arrangement. Of the natural elements, says Vos, Adam "knew from nature, by innate knowledge, what God could demand of him," particularly that "he was assured of the favor of God and of life, provided that he persevered in the good. All of this," Vos says, "Adam could know naturally."[7] The special aspect, on the other hand, includes "the actual stipulations of the covenant," which "must have been communicated by God, at least in their general features, to the head of the covenant, although Scripture does not describe this explicitly."[8]

Bavinck, too, refers to a natural foundation, preceding the covenant of works, which includes creaturely understanding of the moral obligations implicit in being image of God, upon which the positive elements of the covenant in the garden rested: "the foundation on which the covenant rested, that is, the moral

---

7. Vos, *RD*, 2:43–4.
8. Vos, *RD*, 2:44.

law, was known to man by nature, and ... it was made with man in his original state and could be kept by man with the powers bestowed on him in the creation, without the assistance of supernatural grace."[9] Bavinck says that "human beings could know the moral law without special revelation since it was written in their hearts."[10] Alternatively, "the probationary command is positive" and was "not a given of human nature as such but could only be made known to human beings if God communicated it to them. Nor was it self-evident"—it was neither known nor knowable because it was not in fact natural—"that keeping that command would yield eternal life."[11]

Bavinck highlights the superfluity of merit: that "the 'covenant of works' is not a 'covenant of nature'" is conspicuous in the fact that "there *is* no natural connection here between work and reward."[12] Bavinck says that Adam knew the moral law naturally and that his actions before the Fall were righteous, never neutral, before God. Adam knows that moral goodness is the glorification of God in obedience; no separation of natural and religious would have, Bavinck thinks, occurred. But nor would Adam have had reason to presume that his own righteousness entitled him to more than he already possessed, to special favor. Bavinck insists that merit and the right to advanced life, a life characterized by immunity to sin and death, are special, additional, supernatural, gracious.

In other words, while affirming a broadly and exhaustively moral Edenic context and subjective self-understanding, Bavinck nonetheless restricts merit to the prohibition, and that because God has by verbal ratification of covenant terms, and by in a sense provoking Adam's moral intuition, distinguished this particular potential obedient act—one of self-restraint—as special, as uniquely potentially meritorious. Both Bavinck and Vos affirm this continuity in terms of the moral substance of the original situation, including Adam's good but mutable character, and discontinuity in terms of merit and reward. And Van Til puts it this way:

> As a creature of God man had to live in accordance with the law of God, that is, in accordance with the ordinances that God had placed in his creation. This law was for the most part not verbally transmitted to man but was created in his being. Man would act in accord with his own true nature only if he would obey the law of God and ... if he would love in accordance with his own nature, he would obey the law of God. True, God did communicate to man over and above what was embedded in his very nature the specific commandment not to eat of the tree of the knowledge of good and evil. But this was only to force an immediate and final test as to whether a man would really live in accordance with the law of God as everywhere revealed within and about him.[13]

---

9. Bavinck, *RD*, 2:567.
10. Bavinck, *RD*, 2:571.
11. Bavinck, *RD*, 2:571.
12. Bavinck, *RD*, 2:571.
13. Van Til, *CA*, 42.

Continuity between what Adam knew by nature and the moral weight of the positive, specific commands of God indicates significant consonance between the natural relationship between the Creator and his image-bearer and the special terms of the covenant of works. The covenant of works, in other words, was not one that required of Adam something strange or foreign to his nature, but something more or less already implied in both his context and his constitution. He was, in other words, created with this relationship in mind. His constitution and character already signaled a Creator–creature relation in which the terms of his future were determined by his personal conduct and response to divine instruction. Vos reasons: "Insofar as the covenant of works was a concrete application of the natural legal relation that obtains between God and man, man can never be released from it."[14] And he says that "the distinction between natural relationship and the covenant of works is logical and judicial, not temporal."[15] Vos would deny that Adam is even conceivable apart from the moral fabric of his person and world, apart from, that is, the Creator–creature covenant relation with its moral-religious character.

The Image of God

Anthropology provides a vantage point on all that is of concern regarding Gen. 3:6. The radical anthropological theocentrism of Bavinck, Vos, and Van Til dispels residual naturalism or impersonalism because it guarantees that the personal Creator God is always the reference point for human moral experience and self-understanding. Original righteousness and mutability are bound up in the image of God but also suggest creational anticipation of the covenant of works. That is, original righteousness indicates the dual divine self-giving of moment here because, as these neo-Calvinists understand it, the natural and the special are mutually dependent but not necessarily so. The first sin—whatever that in fact may be—indicates, no less, both the natural and special aspects of the covenant

---

14. Vos, *RD*, 2:44. Likewise Bavinck: "But though in the covenant of works, obedience to God's law had been cast in a special form and was directed to a special end (i.e., the securing of eternal life), it is, as such, grounded in the nature of humans and hence an obligation from which they can never be released" (Bavinck, *RD*, 3:226).

15. Vos, *RD*, 2:32. Van Til also makes a point to close the gap between the natural moral life of Adam and the covenant of works:

> It is necessary ... to think of this revelation of God to man as *originally internal as well as external*. Man found in his own make-up, in his own moral nature, an understanding of and a love for that which is good. His own nature was revelational of the will of God. But while thus revelational of the will of God, man's nature, even in paradise, *was never meant to function by itself*. It was *at once supplemented by the supernatural*, external and positive expression of God's will as its correlative. (Van Til, *CTE*, 22)

relation. Finally, the doctrine of original sin introduces nuanced accounts of a natural and necessary fall into sinfulness regulated and enforced by divine judicial intervention. Here again the prevailing impression is of a dual divine self-giving as the context for human moral experience.

Theocentrism

Bavinck says that if the human creature is essentially the image of God, rather than merely accidentally so, then Christian anthropology must be radically theocentric: "we cannot understand or imagine humanity without God ... all human beings always and everywhere stand in some relation to God."[16] He says that God is the "archetype, the exemplar, the original," and that we, as created reflections of the uncreated original, "are only truly human to the extent that we display God."[17] Similarly, Van Til says: "The God of Scripture is the ultimate category of interpretation for man in every aspect of his being."[18]

Van Til explains the covenant of works along these lines. He says that Adam's original moral mutability indicates the disunity of his person, of his moral character and his will. Adam was created with loose joints. In the covenant of works, he was to increase in the unity of his person so that the spontaneity of his will toward the good and godly would be perfect and his joy in obedience complete. Van Til says that in this sense Adam was presented with an opportunity to shape his own person by the exercise of his will; if he determined to obey his Creator and refrain from eating from the tree of the knowledge of good and evil, he would increase the perfection—the godlikeness—of his person. The moral perfection offered in the covenant of works featured the inability to sin, the discontinuation of mutability, and the permanence of personal obedience and holiness—in a word, moral godliness. This, says Van Til, would have signaled an increase in approximation to the unity of the divine being:

> Man was created a self. He was the creature of an absolute self and could not be otherwise created than a self. But for this very reason again man had to develop his self-determination. Man's God is absolutely self-determinate; man will be Godlike in proportion that he becomes self-determining and self-determinate *under* God.[19]

Van Til's proto-religious psychology substantiates Bavinck's theocentrism, and both suggest that the religious relation colors all of man's activity, and that in all

---

16. Bavinck, *RE*, 40.
17. Bavinck, *RE*, 40.
18. Van Til, *CTE*, 20.
19. Van Til, *CTE*, 45–6. Here "self," elsewhere "personality." For example: "Man is created *in God's image*. He is therefore like God in everything in which a creature can be like God. He is like God in that he too is a personality" (Van Til, *IST*, 34).

of his activity man is measured, one might say, theologically, according to his original, God himself. Bavinck writes: "The covenant ... involves becoming the image of God more and more through procreation, worship, and culture. From humanity's creation in the image of God it follows that humans are moral beings and have to develop as such."[20] He adds that "we cannot know proper dominion over nature apart from God and his revelation," meaning that the basic cultural functionality of the human person is religiously borne.[21]

Vos also understands the human person as oriented toward God, originally in positive fashion, from within the silent moral inclinations of his mind and heart. The image-bearer is irreducibly a religious creature, bearing, as it were beneath his consciousness, a Godward directionality of the whole person. The human creature does not express itself only in religion, but human self-expression is always in reference to God and in that sense incurably religious. So Vos's understanding of the image of God, which he attributes indiscriminately to "the Reformed," includes the notion that the human creature "is disposed for communion with God, that all the capacities of his soul can act in a way that corresponds to their destiny only if they rest in God."[22] "This is," again, not accidental, but rather "the *nature* of man," such that "there is no sphere of life that lies outside his relationship to God and in which religion would not be the ruling principle."[23] In this sense Vos may say that so far as all human expression, in word, thought, or deed, and even the secret disposition of the heart, is in this way religious, in the sense of being always in reference to God, so also every expression naturally and necessarily draws moral character from this reference to God as norm. The human person is a religious-moral creature, not merely a creature whose actions bear moral value. God is the object, directly or indirectly, of all human religious and moral self-expression, but also, or because, God himself is the substance of religious and moral reality.

Van Til develops similar themes: "God himself is naturally the end of all man's activity. Man's whole personality was to be a manifestation and revelation on a finite scale of the personality of God."[24] Van Til distinguishes religious and ethical glorification of God as direct and indirect, respectively. He adds however that since to God's glory nothing may be added, and because God is eternal and human activity falls entirely within the "temporal sphere," then "there is a sense in which all of man's activities glorify God indirectly only."[25] Nonetheless, "all of

---

20. Bavinck, *RE*, 43. See also Bavinck's discussion of the faculty of judgment; he says that hesitation and inability to see clearly the right decision is a product of the Fall and that we should grow and increase in the ease of decision-making. See parallel material in Van Til, *CTE*, 41–50.

21. Bavinck, *RE*, 43.
22. Vos, *RD*, 2:13.
23. Vos, *RD*, 2:13. Emphasis original.
24. Van Til, *CTE*, 41.
25. Van Til, *CTE*, 41.

man's activity is directed toward God" and "man's ethics is not only founded upon a religious basis but *is itself religious*."[26]

Van Til says that "God is man's ultimate environment,"[27] and that, therefore, human consciousness is creature consciousness, implicit awareness that one is a creature or creation of God; and creature consciousness is covenant consciousness; moral accountability before a self-existent personal norm is the fabric of human personality: "For man, self-consciousness presupposes God-consciousness. ... Man's creature-consciousness may therefore be more particularly signalized as covenant-consciousness."[28] "Man's mind ... is surrounded by nothing but revelation," and it "is itself inherently revelational," so that "for Adam in paradise ... God-consciousness was ... the presupposition of the significance of his reasoning on anything."[29] Therefore if man is to act at all he can do so "only in response to the revelation of God."[30] Everything man thinks and does is objectively and self-consciously characterized with reference to God. Adam would have understood himself at every moment with reference to God, and via that reference to God moral value would have filled Adam's world and characterized his life in all its parts and as a whole. And he would have known himself to be righteous and holy before God, if impermanently so.

An implication of theocentric anthropology for the first sin is that the impact of a relational breach with God cannot be relegated solely to the religious sphere, nor even subjectively to the life of the image-bearer; rather, all that lies within the realm of Adam's experience and the realm of his vice-dominion is implicated. The creation looks forward to the revelation of the sons of God because all of creation was implicated in Adam's transgression and the divine curse that followed.

This theocentrism also highlights the moral substance of the natural situation and brings into greater focus the relationship between the natural situation and the covenant of works that was added to it, and, indeed, the relationship of the first covenant to the second, covenant of grace. Vos says that "law ... can indicate a natural obligation toward God that is incumbent on us and must always be incumbent on us," or "it can indicate a specific obligation, determined by a pact, to which certain consequences are linked if it is kept or transgressed."[31] "The latter," he says, "was the case with the law in the covenant of works."[32] He also distinguishes "three kinds of relationships in which man stands to the law," first "the natural relationship of a rational being," second "the covenantal relationship," and third "the penal relationship."[33] Evidently, these "three kinds of relationships"

---

26. Van Til, *CTE*, 41. Emphasis original.
27. Van Til, *DF*, 65.
28. Van Til, *CA*, 115.
29. Van Til, *CA*, 115.
30. Van Til, *CA*, 63.
31. Vos, *RD*, 5:86.
32. Vos, *RD*, 5:86.
33. Vos, *RD*, 3:128–9.

may be viewed sequentially: the natural relationship is followed by a covenantal one; God creates Adam and then, subsequently, enters into covenant with him. The covenant relationship is then the occasion for the penal relationship, which obtains upon violation of covenantal law.

Although this sequence works, it is not the only way the three legal relationships may relate. Notice that the penal cannot replace or render obsolete the covenantal, since the penal is a subset of the covenantal. The penal relationship is a matter of covenant guilt; remove the covenant relationship and the penal loses its meaning.[34] Similarly, the "natural relationship of a rational being" might be considered temporally prior to the covenantal relationship, but Vos has said specifically that the covenantal is only logically and not temporally subsequent to the natural.[35] Once again, therefore, the covenant-legal relationship depends upon the natural in the sense that the moral weight of the covenantal may be considered, to a significant degree, an expression or formalization of the natural relationship. The prohibition of Gen. 2:17 would of course have no binding force at all were it not uttered by the self-naming Creator God to his self-conscious image-bearer; only as such may the word regarding the tree of the knowledge of good and evil bear anything like the importance attributed to it. The covenantal relationship depends upon the natural, and the natural is exhaustively ethico-religious.

Notice also that even though Vos clearly favors a divine command interpretation of the prohibition of Gen. 2:17, he will not approve of taking the special aspect of the covenantal relationship as a strange imposition on the natural. So Vos says that "the requirement of the covenant contained the natural requirement of perfect keeping of the law."[36] Vos follows Bavinck in emphasizing the fact that the obedience required of Adam in the covenant of works is on some level simply a continuation of his original righteousness; to pass the probation Adam had simply to remain what he was.[37] Vos says that the original, creaturely "supremacy of man was of the nature of a voluntary submission."[38] It was to this creature of voluntary submission to his Creator God that the prohibition was addressed. Thus there is a

---

34. Vos writes:
> The nonelect natural man is also still under the covenant of works, if one takes the covenant of works only in its broadest sense. ... He is under it insofar as his punishable culpability is at its root connected with Adam's breaking of the covenant, whether he would acknowledge it or not. By the breaking of the covenant of works, he did not revert to his natural relationship. (Vos, *RD*, 2:46)

35. Vos, *RD*, 2:32.
36. Vos, *RD*, 3:132.
37. See Bavinck, *RE*, 39. More on this below. Compare this section of *RE* with Bavinck, *RD*, 2:572, where the idea that "Adam did not have to become anything; he only had to remain what he was" represents a Lutheran rejection of Edenic eschatology which Bavinck rejects.
38. Vos, *BT*, 53.

profound anticipation of the covenantal in the natural, and therefore the natural is richly theological for Adam.

Bavinck reinforces this picture richly if indirectly. He says of course that "the very notion of sin presupposes *law*," adding that "in this regard the *moral law* must be mentioned."[39] And the moral law is, in sum, this: "love for God and one's neighbor."[40] Here again, sin is not transgression of a rule or law, which apart from such rule or law would be morally null; sin is lawlessness—Bavinck's preferred term[41]—but not a lawlessness that requires an expressed law. This means, according to the natural aspect, that sin is a violation of the rule of love for God, however that love might be enjoined in additional, specific (covenantal) stipulations. Here again, as in Vos's explanation, a subsequent legal relationship assumes a prior natural one that is no less theocentric. While Bavinck emphasizes the legislative context for sin—sin is always and everywhere a violation of law—he does not reduce sin to the material contradiction of a given law, but to a natural covenant relation as an exhaustively moral assessment of the human person and situation.

Another indication of the moral theocentrism of the natural situation is the fact that the covenant of works, when transgressed, is not repealed but rather, by the covenant of grace, patched or repaired. Vos states pointedly that the covenant of works is incorporated into the covenant of grace. The second covenant is implemented not to replace the first but in order to fulfill it. One might say that the covenant of grace is the covenant of works in which the task of obedience—the works in question—is delegated, picked up in our stead by one like us except that his sinless life has value sufficient to atone for the sins of many. First the covenant of works; then the covenant of works delegated, picked up vicariously. In this sense, for the second Adam the covenant of grace is a covenant of works, an unmediated arrangement which hangs on his own obedience, and it is a covenant of grace for the church precisely because it is a covenant of works for the mediator. Writes Vos: "The covenant of grace is the implementation of the covenant of works in the surety for us."[42] And shortly after: "By the covenant of works, the idea of covenant is introduced into humanity, and fellowship with God incapable of being lost and life flowing from that fellowship presented as the ideal. This ideal is not subsequently removed. God does not lower his demand and does not hypothetically waive his promise."[43] If the covenant of works is dependent upon a prior natural, ethico-religious covenant relation, then in order for the covenant of works to persist, the natural covenant relation must also remain. Vos writes: "Insofar as the covenant of works was a concrete application of the natural legal relation that obtains between God and man, man can never be released from it."[44]

---

39. Bavinck, *RE*, 43.
40. Bavinck, *RE*, 43.
41. Bavinck, *RE*, 101; *RD*, 3:130, 133–6.
42. Vos, *RD*, 2:36.
43. Vos, *RD*, 2:46.
44. Vos, *RD*, 2:44.

Bavinck, Vos, and Van Til believe that the human creature is, essentially, image of God, rather than merely possessing the image accidentally. They believe that this implies a radical anthropological theocentrism according to which the human creature must always be understood as a finite replica of the divine who in his every thought and deed reacts to knowledge of God. Even at the psychological level godlikeness is the rule of holiness and creaturely self-fulfillment. The fall, therefore, implicates the full personality of the image-bearer and therefore the realm of his experience and activity without remainder. Anthropological theocentrism also disallows a religiously neutral conception of the natural situation preceding the covenant of works. It is impossible, in the view of Bavinck, Vos, and Van Til, to conceive of the human creature as at any moment outside of the sphere of divine rule, law, and preeminence. The human being is a covenant creature.

Original Righteousness, Mutability, and the First Sin

Original righteousness is often inferred from the seven statements of divine approval found in Genesis 1 ("it is good," "it is very good"); from an emphasis elsewhere in Scripture on the original goodness of creation as a whole; from biblical descriptions, New Testament texts in particular, of the image of God restored; and from Pauline texts, such as Romans 5, attributing directly to Adam's sin the first entrance of sin into the world.[45] Bavinck believes that original righteousness is demonstrable from the text of Genesis:

> Creation in the image of God (Gen. 1:27; Eccles. 7:29; Eph. 4:24; Col. 3:10), the blessing of procreation and multiplication (Gen. 1:28), divine approval (Gen. 1:31), the probationary command (Gen. 2:16-17), the naming of the animals (Gen. 2:19-20), the pronouncement about Eve (Gen. 2:23-24), the manner of the temptation (Gen. 3:1ff.), and the attitude of Adam and Eve after the fall (Gen. 3:7ff.)—all attest to the truth that the first humans were created positively good, not morally indifferent.[46]

Bavinck also notes that the doctrine of original righteousness is more or less implied by the goodness of God, since without it (original righteousness) one

---

45. The Heidelberg Catechism says that "God created man good," "in true righteousness and holiness," and cites Gen. 1:31 and Eph. 4:24. So says Bavinck: "Underlying Ephesians 4:24 and Colossians 3:10, therefore, is the idea that humankind was originally created in God's image and in the re-creation is renewed on that model" (*RD*, 2:532). Similarly, for original "righteousness, and true holiness" the Westminster Confession and Larger Catechism cite Eph. 4:24, where "righteousness and true holiness" are attributed to the "new man" "after God," and Rom. 2:14-15 is cited as proof for the claim that at their creation the first humans had "the law of God written in their hearts," and Eccl. 7:29 for original ability to keep that law.

46. Bavinck, *RD*, 2:537.

"does less than justice to the justice of God, who has then allowed his creature to be tempted beyond his power to resist."[47] Accordingly, losing track of original righteousness "fails to do justice to the seriousness of the temptation … and to the character of the fall," since if the Fall is not qualitative moral conversion it "ceases to be an appalling sin and changes into a nonculpable misfortune, an almost unavoidable lot."[48]

Bavinck in fact believes that a leading implication of creation in the image of God is original righteousness; if Adam is created in the image of God, he is created good and holy.[49] For Bavinck, as for the Reformed generally, moral integrity constitutes the narrow aspect of the image of God and is therefore moral integrity received rather than accomplished; original righteousness is a gift and in no sense meritorious.

"Many theologians," Bavinck observes, "taught that humanity was created in a state, not of positive holiness, but of childlike innocence," and "it was to such pronouncements that Pelagius later appealed."[50] Against such views of original righteousness as accidental—logically or temporally subsequent to the creation of the human being—or morality itself as a process or accomplishment of personal development, Bavinck says that the "moral and the good is not an ideal hovering far off in the distance from humanity. … The good is not the end goal of life, a destination for humans, but the foundation on which we stand and the environment within which we stand."[51]

Bavinck uses the first-person plural here, even though only Adam (and Eve) actually enjoyed original righteousness. Federalism is the obvious reason he does so, but there is a bigger picture as well. Original righteousness and the original goodness of creation bear a great deal of importance for Bavinck's ethics and for neo-Calvinist ethics generally. Neo-Calvinists say, with Kuyper, that sin renders the human race "abnormal," and that what we know now as normal must not be taken as normative. Neo-Calvinists hold in this way an ethico-historical (we may say redemptive-historical) approach to ethics according to which our current situation, the state of all Adam's progeny, has the Edenic good as both its origin and its foundation. Humanity had its beginning in a situation of moral integrity, and from that golden age it fell. Bavinck says, therefore, that evil is "a parasite on the good," "it lives off the good."[52] History and sequence imply metaethics. Bavinck stands by the notion of evil as privation against Manichaeism or moral dualism, but aside from this corrective value he sees no place for privation in historic Christian thought.[53] Bavinck prefers "active privation," according to which evil is

---

47. Bavinck, *RD*, 2:538.
48. Bavinck, *RD*, 2:538–9.
49. Bavinck, *RE*, 38–9.
50. Bavinck, *RD*, 2:534.
51. Bavinck, *RE*, 39.
52. Bavinck, *RD*, 3:139, 145.
53. "When the majority of Christian theologians conceive sin as privation, they first of all have opposition to Manicheism in view. To that extent their opinion is completely

active (positive) opposition to the good and therefore, in this sense, presupposes the good.[54] In fact, it presupposes both the created good, which is a breakable good, implicated in the covenant of works; and God himself the self-existent good. God has no opposite, no comparable counter-part; but the created good, including a revealed will of God for creation, is subject to creaturely opposition. Again: "It is God himself who ... *created* the possibility of sin."[55] So a state of original integrity, against a backdrop of the goodness of God expressed as created norm, serves as a perpetual ideal for the image-bearer both morally and historically. The fallen situation is just that, fallen—having undergone a temporal and ethical transition, a moral descent, as it were, from original goodness to evil.

In addition to this deferral to historical origins, neo-Calvinists take stock of the current situation eschatologically, in terms of the redemptive principles of new creation inaugurated in the resurrection.[56] A redemptive-eschatological principle has entered the stream of history in the form of word or promise of ideal cosmic re-creation and has its center of gravity in the revivification of the flesh of Jesus the firstborn from the dead.[57] The appeal to "as it is in heaven" is, for the neo-Calvinist, eschatological.

In light of original righteousness, Bavinck explains, in the covenant of works, "Adam did not have to *become* good, he *was* good and had to ensure that he *remained* good. ... He came from the hand of God holy, righteous, and wise."[58] By thus remaining righteous Adam was to attain the prize of eternal life; he was invited to confirm his faithfulness to his Creator. So, although in his natural or original state Adam was morally upright and blameless before God, nonetheless advance was available to him as reward for confirmation of the righteousness he already possessed: "Adam had not yet reached the end; he did not yet have eternal life; he did not yet have the ability not to sin."[59] Bavinck, Vos, and Van Til feel that it is therefore appropriate to speak of a pre-redemptive grace, since God offers to man, in Adam, the possibility of an enhanced condition and increased communion with God, an opportunity to which the human creature has no

---

correct and should be accepted without reservation." On the other hand: "The case is rather that Christian theology has at all times very firmly opposed the pantheistic view of sin as pure negation ... the difference being ... that 'negation' is only a matter of 'being without' (*carere*), while 'privation' is lacking something essential to life (*egere*) ... Sin is a privation of the moral perfection a human ought to possess" (Bavinck, *RD*, 3:137).

54. Bavinck, *RD*, 3:138. Vos also approves the term *actuosa privation* (Vos, *RD*, 2:56). Bavinck believes this is the Augustinian view and he cites several reformers.

55. Bavinck, *RD*, 3:29. Emphasis added.

56. Geerhardus Vos, *The Pauline Eschatology* (Phillipsburg, NJ: P&R, 1979); Herman Ridderbos, *Paul: An Outline of His Theology*, trans. John Richard de Witt (Grand Rapids, MI: Eerdmans, 1975), on Rom. 6.

57. Vos from *BT* or inaugural address.

58. Bavinck, *RE*, 39.

59. Bavinck, *RE*, 39.

natural claim. If his nature is created, given, granted, or bestowed, he can have no claim to divine favor except on the basis of divine self-giving. Grace in the garden is not, as it is in the state of sin, demerited, but certainly unmerited; pre-redemptive divine favor is grace because it is categorically undeserved, and the meritorious character of obedience relative to the prohibition is only and exclusively a superfluous grace of the covenant Vos captures in the general sentiment: "The provision of this new, higher prospect for man was an act of condescension and high favour. God was in no wise bound on the principle of justice to extend it to man ... there was nothing in the nature of man nor of his creation, which by manner of implication could entitle man to such a favour from God."[60] Bavinck notes, accordingly, that in the original situation, Adam viewed the prospect of moral perfection from an auspicious position, as gift upon gift: "Adam did not have to strenuously exert himself to obtain it but had merely to do what his own nature recommended. ... The command not to eat was a *prohibition*."[61]

This view of the original situation and the position from which Adam faced Edenic testing heightens the significance and moral shock of the first sin. Although Adam's character was mutable and his will was not bound by his natural integrity, still he possessed no native inclination to wander from God; in order to sin, therefore, Adam had knowingly to contradict his own moral intuition, his own character. So Vos says, "as concerns its center, sin resides in the will of man. ... In its origination, however, sin comes from the will, namely from the will understood as *voluntas*, as the deeper spiritual orientation of man."[62] Sin must be charged to the account of the whole person. Sin could not have come about by causeless volitional whim (of itself an incoherent notion, in Vos's view[63]), and so the whole person must be implicated in it.

Van Til suggests that the mutability of original righteousness implies non-culpable disunity between character and will: "In the case of original man *his instincts did not hamper his freedom*."[64] More precisely, "before the fall the will of man, insofar as it was controlled by his instincts, was not therewith hindered

---

60. Vos, *BT*, 22.

61. Bavinck, *RE*, 39–40. See also his discussion of the will (*RE*, 89–90). One notes that prohibition, formally speaking, does not imply passivity, as Bavinck here suggests. It only suggests passivity in this situation, because Adam and Eve had not yet eaten from the tree in question. The prohibitive emphasis of the Decalogue, by contrast, targets well established behavioral patterns and therefore has a corrective purpose.

62. Vos, *RD*, 2:26. Vos is careful to emphasize the inseparability of these faculties, or the "organicism" (not his word in this case) of biblical anthropology: "One may never forget that the three faculties of the soul in their distinctions are abstractions of what is given to us in our experience only as a living unity" (Vos, *RD*, 2:26).

63. An incoherent notion, according to Vos. See *RD*, 2:26. Also Van Til: "A neutral will cannot develop because it cannot function" (*CTE*, 46).

64. Van Til, *CTE*, 48. Emphasis original.

in the least in the freedom of its action."[65] This disjoint signals the possibility not only of transgressing a law received from without but also of contradicting dispositional goodness within. Adam can act against his nature; he can express himself in violation of his natural goodness and contradict his inclination to obey God in love. Van Til believes that this is because his will and his good character though both components of his person as created are separate parts that are, though related, still open to greater coherence and cohesion. So Van Til says that Adam's original charter and the Edenic invitation to obedience may be thought of as an injunction to self-realization: Adam, originally good, should will to become the good character that he is by electing to move himself toward increased unity of character by means of volitional affirmation of divine lordship over the independence of his own will; he should will the submission of his own will. "Man's righteousness, which should be a reproduction of the righteousness of God, would be, first, *a proper sense of subordination* of himself to God and of coordination of himself with his fellow man."[66] And the bearer of the divine image should increase as such: "*man should realize himself as God's viceregent in history*."[67] "Thou shalt not eat" makes accessible perfected, creaturely godliness. Adam as an individual "must learn to will the will of God," and, increasing in the unity of his person, he must "grow in spontaneity" of obedience:[68] "Man's God is absolutely self-determinate; man will be Godlike in proportion that he becomes self-determining and self-determinate *under* God."[69] "Man was created to be, as nearly as that was possible for a creature, a replica of the being of God. In God there is no difference between potentiality and act."[70] Vos also emphasizes the moral superiority of obedient spontaneity:

> To do the good and reject the evil from a reasoned insight into their respective natures is a noble thing, but it is a still nobler thing to do so out of regard for the nature of God, and the noblest thing of all is the ethical strength, which, when required, will act from personal attachment to God, without for the moment enquiring into these more abstruse reasons. The pure delight in obedience adds to the ethical value of a choice.[71]

An unstable but pure delight in spontaneous obedience was Adam's starting point; an obedience of immovable spontaneity was his destination. This doctrine of the mutability of Adam's character is an anthropological, even perhaps psychological,

---

65. Van Til, *CTE*, 49.
66. Van Til, *CTE*, 47.
67. Van Til, *CTE*, 44. Emphasis original.
68. Van Til, *CTE*, 45.
69. Van Til, *CTE*, 45–6.
70. Van Til, *CTE*, 48.
71. Vos, *BT*, 32.

account of original righteousness and mutability, of Adam's ability to sin. Vos and Van Til infer this ability from the moral contingency and religious tension surrounding Gen. 2:17 and from the actualization of sin in Gen. 3:6. The prohibition is only intelligible if Adam can disobey it; therefore he must have had within himself the capacity to act against his nature, a capacity, in other words, for self-renunciation in the form of self-assertion. And Adam's moral mutability is confirmed of course in the fall. Adam's transgression, on display in the charge against him and in his fumbled confession (Gen. 3:8-13), the actualization of sin in other words, proves the precedent of potentiality. If Adam sinned, he could have sinned; if Adam sinned, he sinned first as a non-sinner.

And yet, "good but mutable" does not explain the first sin but only describes its possibility as inferred retrospectively from its appearance.[72] In fact, the sum of this account, far less than dissolving mystery, is to aggravate the conundrum of the first sin. Bavinck writes: "Sin cannot be physically or logically deduced from antecedent circumstances, reasonings, or considerations. Above all, it cannot be inferred from a holy nature created in God's image."[73] He adds: "it should be said openly and clearly: we are here at the boundaries of our knowledge. Sin *exists*, but it will never be able to justify its existence. It is unlawful and irrational."[74] So says Vos: "In Adam's disposition toward God Himself lies the mysterious ground of the origin of sin. In an inexplicable way, that inclination ceased, reversed. In it itself lay the beginning point of sin."[75] And "we are unable to explain how a cause can exist in the holy nature of Adam that turned him to sin. We must pronounce the origin of the first sin in Adam an unsolvable problem."[76]

Bavinck says: "Almost at the same moment creatures came, pure and splendid, from the hand of their Maker, they were deprived of all their luster, and stood, corrupted and impure, before his holy face. Sin ruined the entire creation."[77] As to the question of origin, "Scripture," he says, "vindicates God" and "always points us in the direction of the creature."[78] Van Til, noting the authority and the explanatory power of this account, writes: "We take our information from Scripture and then realize that what it teaches must be true."[79] Vos, too, in the end, resists resolving this tension:[80]

---

72. In the Westminster Confession and Larger Catechism the only texts cited for the claim that God made man "subject to fall" are Gen. 3:6 and Eccl. 7:29, verses descriptive of sinful acts after the fact.
73. Bavinck, *RD*, 3:69.
74. Bavinck, *RD*, 3:70.
75. Vos, *RD*, 2:49.
76. Vos, *RD*, 1:88.
77. Bavinck, *RD*, 3:28.
78. Bavinck, *RD*, 3:29.
79. Van Til, *CTE*, 21.
80. On this point see Robert F. Brown, "The First Evil Will Must Be Incomprehensible: A Critique of Augustine," *Journal of the American Academy of Religion* 46, no. 3 (1978): 315–29.

The difficulty that remains in all this is here: We can certainly understand how inciting motives from the outside can be at work in man, provided that first from within, in an immediate way, the disposition is produced to which those motives are directed. God acts in this manner in the re-creation of man. He also works from the outside through His word. That can be because He has first awakened life from within in a direct manner. But Satan could not do that. He cannot reorder the inner being of man, and if he had been able to, then man could hardly be considered responsible for it. From this follows the mysteriousness of this conjoining process. Just as it is, it seems to be nothing but an enticing to outward expression of a sinful principle that was present already from within. Yet it is more. What we can understand is the working of sin from the inside out. To that precedes the penetration of sin from outside to the inside. This precedence, this wonder, we do not understand. With us, the disposition determines the deed, both in the natural state and in regeneration; with Adam, the deed determined the disposition. One may not say that Adam fell because the grace of God left him, but through this fall, one must say, Adam fell in an incomprehensible way from the grace of God.[81]

The actualization of the first sin, remaining unexplained, occasions a conversion of character that is required by that basic anthropological religiosity. A being in this way always in reference to God, not only in matters of religion but in all matters religious, cannot undergo proportionate redistribution of moral quantities; it must convert wholesale. "The transition between evil and good," in the Fall in particular, "is qualitative, not quantitative. A being that is good becomes evil not by a decrease in his goodness but by a radical change in it, by passing over to sin."[82]

Vos does nonetheless suggest a rationale for this design. Why would God create Adam able to sin? The tree of the knowledge of good and evil, he observes, was "the God-appointed instrument to lead man through probation to that state of religious and moral maturity wherewith his highest blessedness is connected."[83] "God ... had beneficent purposes for man."[84] The stark intrusiveness of the prohibition—indeed, Van Til describes it as "arbitrary"[85]—likewise indicates the desired outcome: "pure delight in obedience."[86] These observations add to our understanding of the design of the arrangement in Eden, and of the consonance of the natural and special principles, by suggesting a rationale in terms of "what God desired": obedient character tested and confirmed.

---

81. Vos, *RD*, 2:53.
82. Vos, *RD*, 2:24.
83. Vos, *BT*, 31.
84. Vos, *BT*, 36.
85. Van Til, *CA*, 69.
86. Vos, *BT*, 32. Vos says something similar in his discussion of the *ordo salutis*:

> At the same time, this order shows us that even in what is most subjective the purpose of God may not be limited to the satisfaction of the creature's longing

But the question of means remains. Moral maturity implies moral trial; perhaps error; growth in wisdom and increased acquaintance both with one's self and with the objective norm, which classifies human thoughts and actions with a view toward all the nuances of situation and application. But if Jesus can make wine from water, omitting the naturally requisite process, God can make moral maturity, too, without the natural process of maturation. He could create personal enjoyment of maturity, the subjective impression, in one sense false, of having arrived by natural means, without bothering with such means—moral fermentation, as it were, supernaturally produced. We have therefore no explanation for the fact that God did not take this safer, more direct, non-natural route. In sum, the final cause— what he did it for—is evident. The goal of the probation was moral maturity, subjective moral perfection through testing, for the glory of God. But sufficient cause—why in this way, or why he did it at all—eludes us.

A complication thus emerges in this account of the first sin. Vos emphasizes the mysteriousness of Adam's first transgression in the sense that unlike any other sin, the outward act in Adam's case was not preceded by inward disposition; in this case and this one only (though probably in the case of Eve, as well), the outward act preceded sinfulness of character. And yet Vos also says that the "actual fall" preceded the eating of the fruit of the tree,[87] and given the development in Eve of a self-legislative posture, the "first sinful act ... could not have remained in abeyance."[88] Vos seems to be saying that the development of sinful character was the first sin. Bavinck too believes that "strictly speaking," the act of eating "was not the first sin, but the first fully matured sin."[89] "Anterior" to the act of eating, he says,

> there were sinful considerations of the mind ... and sinful tendencies of the heart ... which had been promoted by the temptation of the serpent and were fostered by the will of man. Both before, during, and after the act of eating from the forbidden tree, the relation of humans to God and his law was changed.[90]

The serpent, Vos observes, "incites Eve to regard God's prohibition as a limitation of human rights and freedoms," and Eve appears to succumb to this distortion when she, taking her lead from the serpent's opening inquiry, exaggerates the severity of the prohibition. The serpent asked whether God had forbidden

> for blessedness. If this were so, then the order that is slow and in many respects tests the patience of the children of God would be lost. But here, too, God works first of all to glorify Himself according to the principles of an eternal order and an immanent propriety. (*RD*, 4:2)

87. Vos, *RD*, 2:51-2.
88. Vos, *RD*, 2:53.
89. Bavinck, *RD*, 3:108.
90. Bavinck, *RD*, 3:108.

eating from any or all of the trees of the garden, whereas of course only one had been mentioned (or at most two, but certainly not all (Gen. 2:16)); and similarly, although the prohibition was directed at eating, Eve extended the incursion of divine legislative presumption to include merely touching. Eve "speaks about it with a note of an aggrieved sense of justice," indicating that in her mind "the two spheres of divine justice and human justice are already separated."[91] Vos observes that in Eve's response to the serpent's initial inquiry "there already shines through that the woman had begun to entertain the possibility of God's restricting her too severely," and that "by entertaining this, even for a moment, she had already begun to separate in principle between the rights of God and her own rights."[92] Thinking thus, "she had admitted the seed of the act of sinning into her heart."[93] Vos concludes: "This is *temptation*: to shift the center of our lives from God to a point outside God; and this, therefore, is already the actual fall."[94]

There appears to be no way to attenuate Vos's claim here that taking and eating expressed a sin that had already taken hold, or that in principle had already been committed: "It is, therefore, useless speculation to ask what would have happened if Adam and Eve had not proceeded to the sinful act. Humanly speaking, the act could not have remained in abeyance."[95] In the paragraph immediately following this statement, Vos at length details the location of mystery in the appearance of the first human sin, specifically this: that the first sin was not preceded by sinful disposition or character. Are there hints here of discrepancy?

One possible solution is this: that Vos's emphasis on the mysteriousness of the first sin, that it originated not from a sinful personality but from a good one, does not commit him to unintelligible spontaneity with regard to taking and eating; something perhaps psychological, short of covenant sinfulness, may have, perhaps

---

91. Vos, *BT*, 35.
92. Vos, *BT*, 35.
93. Vos, *BT*, 35.
94. Vos, *RD*, 2:52.
95. Vos, *RD*, 2:53. Elsewhere Vos indicates precisely why Eve's repositioning of herself relative to the law of God already signals ethical breakdown: "Because the ultimate root in which all the commandments are one in the nature and will of God is lost sight of, the law will become a mere aggregate of unrelated precepts, a collection of statutory ordinances, for adjusting which to the compass of the entire outward life a complicated system of the most refined casuistry will be required." Vos, *The Teaching of Jesus Concerning the Kingdom of God and the Church* (Eugene, OR: Wipf & Stock, 1998), 108; see also 106–7. Due to the legislative re-structuring that had taken place in her mind, Eve's transgression was a foregone conclusion. On this question, Bavinck makes the following observation: "Protestants, however, in considering the sin of Eve, usually have it start already with doubt and unbelief, which were later followed by pride and covetousness" (Bavinck, *RD*, 3:128). Bavinck cites M. Luther, *Lectures on Genesis 1–3*, in vol. 1 of *Luther's Works* (St. Louis: Concordia, 1958); J. Gerhard, *Loci Theol.*, IX, 2; John Calvin, *Institutes of the Christian Religion*, 2.1.4; and others.

must have, preceded the first sin. In fact, he says elsewhere, "an uncaused choice of free will is not only metaphysically and psychologically inexplicable but also ethically worthless," and later that "to tempt is not to produce sin."[96] Though it is not clear that the first sin, unique among all others, is denoted here, perhaps it is—in which case the tension is resolved, though the mysteriousness of the prior angelic sin would remain. If this statement applies to Genesis 3, even the first sin would be intelligible only as the result of a process, such as the conversation between Eve and the serpent.

Indeed, the mysteriousness of the Fall is precisely the fact of original righteous mutability. That a good character could succumb to temptation—this is the issue, not that a good character could surprise itself by committing an act that is not only morally repugnant to itself but also spontaneous, causeless, *ergo* unintelligible. By definition such an act could have no explanation and therefore no moral significance. Moral uprightness and mutability—theocentric, mutable goodness—here is the dark silence behind the transgression of Gen. 3:6.

And yet, Vos emphasizes too often and too clearly the mysteriousness of the first sin as an evil act not preceded by a sinful disposition but by a good one. Bavinck no less: "sin proves to be an incomprehensible mystery," since "we know neither whence it is nor what it is ... it exists, but no one can explain its origin. Sin itself came into the world without motivation, yet it is the motivation for all human thought and action."[97] This precise "incoherence" or surprise, or the uniqueness of it at least, carries weight in Vos's understanding of the fall, of a Reformed doctrine of sin over against Pelagianism, for Vos's emphasis on an Edenic divine command ethic, and on the innocence of God relative to Adamic violation of the prohibition. So I cannot see that this tension is resolved definitively in Vos's discussion of the fall, and yet nor can I find any reason to attenuate either the formation in Eve's mind and heart of a sinful disposition or the moral-primary significance of the act of eating. Both appear essential to the neo-Calvinist account of the fall.

That being said, for Vos accountability is the principle issue, in terms of the responsibility and the legal or judicial recognition of the first sin. That is, sin is not subtle moral discoloration but an act covenantally, even forensically, defined. The difficulty is, then, somewhat relativized, since "the first sin," not only for Vos but for Bavinck and Van Til as well, is not always a sequential designation but more often a covenantal one by which Eve's sin is not primarily in view but rather Adam's: "Adam *alone* was not the origin of the human race. Nevertheless, the sin and covenant-breaking of Adam is always spoken of, and Adam is placed in contrast with Christ, because as man he represents the woman judicially."[98] Accountability for the first covenantally significant sin falls therefore to Adam as the responsible and legally liable party. Vos says, not with reference to Eve specifically but to sinful progenitors besides her, that "through the covenant of works it is explained why the sin of our

---

96. Vos, *RD*, 2:29, 50.
97. Bavinck, *RD*, 3:145.
98. Vos, *RD*, 2:51.

natural ancestors outside of Adam is not imputed to us."[99] The sole reason that moral inheritance is specifically and uniquely Adamic is that "imputation rests on the covenantal relation, and we stand in such a covenantal relation only to Adam and not to others."[100] "Adam's first sin," not Eve's, "is representatively our sin."[101] One might suggest therefore that for Bavinck, Vos, and Van Til the term "sin" is primarily a covenantal designation. The natural aspects of the covenant relation are necessary but insufficient for sin. Not the existence of God, nor a generic reference to God, nor an intuitive moral fabric of experience, but all of this plus the formalized covenant relation established by God make sin, in its fullest sense, possible. Sin begins with Adam's covenant transgression. In that case Eve's taking and eating is sinful, certainly, but in a preliminary and judicially ambiguous sense.

On this account, "the first sin" is imprecise terminology. Eve's transgression precedes Adam's temporally and so is the first in that sense; but temporal precedent does not imply covenant significance. In the moment before Eve gives the fruit to Adam and he eats, as Vos understands the situation, the status of the covenant would have been unclear, yet undecided. If Eve eats but Adam does not, what happens? Covenantally speaking the first sin is Adam's, since, given his representative status even when only one other person is considered, the covenant arrangement hangs on his conduct relative to the prohibition. It is worth noting, in this light, that in the text of Genesis no information appears regarding Adam's state of mind before he ate. There is no evidence for or against a conversion of Adam's moral character like that of Eve. The temptation concerns Eve exclusively; as for Adam, we know only that he ate, and that when confronted by the law-giver, he blamed everyone else.

This understanding of sin strikes a delicate balance between the natural and special aspects of the covenant relation. Vos in particular demonstrates sensitivity to the integrity of each aspect and to their interdependence. What Vos calls the "formal aspect" of sin is its legal or forensic reference to God. "Sin," writes Vos, "always has reference to law ... specifically to a law of God."[102] The material aspect of sin highlights the rich personalism of the natural aspect of the covenant relation:

> Scripture teaches that the law is fulfilled in love. That law, however, is the expression of God's being insofar as it is a *norm*. Therefore, we cannot go further than to affirm that love for God is the material aspect of moral goodness and that the opposite of this is the material aspect of moral evil.[103]

If an expressed or special law is necessary and sufficient for sin, then there is no sin where this is no law. But Paul denies this, pointing out that though there is no

---

99. Vos, *RD*, 2:33.
100. Vos, *RD*, 2:33.
101. Vos, *RD*, 2:34.
102. Vos, *RD*, 2:25.
103. Vos, *RD*, 2:25.

death where there is no sin, from Adam to Moses all died. And as Vos argues, one can rule out neither the moral value of obedience nor the possibility of sin prior to Gen. 2:17. Adam's normal conduct, apart from and prior to the prohibition, Bavinck, Vos, and Van Til all think of as conscious, volitional obedience bearing positive (though non-meritorious) moral value, and that in the recesses of Adam's constitution he was always aware of the possibility of sin and consequent divine wrath. So two kinds of sin emerge relative to two kinds of divine law: sin against an express command and sin against an implicit or natural or creational law. As to whether Adam could have fallen any other way, Vos writes that "in the abstract, that possibility did not exist," but that nonetheless "we cannot show or affirm that, considered subjectively, an earlier fall for Adam would be impossible."[104] The natural situation is exhaustively moral, and even subtly eschatological (it contains hints of final reckoning); the special aspect formalizes and intensifies the covenant morality that precedes it and sacramentalizes its eschatological undercurrent.

Original Sin: Natural and Special Aspects

Another implication of the human creature's not possessing but being the image of God, according to Bavinck, is this: "the essence of human beings having been corrupted through sin."[105] Adam is the first to undergo this corruption; in him and by virtue of his sin, his progeny follow.

If in sinning Adam turns against his own inherent moral godliness, then sin is opposition to the godliness of Adam's constitution—and the human creature is nothing but concentrated godliness. Adam's moral character in particular defers; it defers to its original, to God, to whom it is ever accountable. Self-conscious hostility to that deferral signals not only opposition to external authority but also subjective discord, self-directed mutiny. Van Til writes: "Man would act in accord with his own true nature only if he would obey the law of God, and, vice versa, if he would live in accord with his own nature, he would obey the law of God."[106] So, conversely, to act against the law of God is to act against one's self, simultaneously to self-glorify and self-harm. Being essentially the image of God makes this possible. Even at the point of disobedience, the image cannot disappear, or the human would disappear; the image cannot be lost, abandoned, or destroyed, because it is not accidental but essential;[107] nonetheless, sin as such is opposition to the image as image, to the referential character of image anthropology. Bavinck puts it this way:

---

104. Vos, *RD*, 2:43.
105. Bavinck, *RE*, 43. On the other hand: "When God condemns, he speaks of sin and guilt that, though great and heavy, can be removed because they do not belong to the essence of humanity" (Bavinck, *RD*, 3:125). The distinction between broad and narrow aspects of the image affords this ambiguity.
106. Van Til, *IST*, 36.
107. Van Til quotes Kuyper to this effect. See *IST*, 50–1.

While they remained essentially and substantially the same, that is, human, and kept all their human components, capacities, and powers, the form, the character and nature, the set and direction of all these capacities and powers were so changed that now, instead of fulfilling the will of God, they fulfill the "law of the flesh." The image has changed into a caricature.[108]

Vos writes that sin is a *habitus* or disposition, in the sense that the substance of its host—the human creature—remains identifiably and essentially the same, while its disposition changes: first in Adam from good to evil, then in the regenerate from evil to good. So the human person comprises among other things a morally mutable *habitus* or disposition. Vos says that because this disposition "touches," as it were, the soul, it characterizes the whole of the human person without remainder: "Because the sinful *habitus* is inherent in the soul as a whole, it extends to every capacity of the soul, to the entire life of the soul, and leaves nothing untouched. ... Everything," the whole person without remainder, "is alienated from God and therefore the object of his displeasure."[109]

The soul and the moral disposition are distinguishable, but inseparable, and this unity leads Vos to deny separability of natural and moral ability, so that the claim that one's nature, one's capacities, are in good or at least neutral working order, while one's moral disposition leads them astray, invests in a false distinction or illegitimate separability. The whole human person, Vos says, even as it is "natural" is now "naturally" sinful. He says: "The clarity of the intellect, the power of the will, the tone of the emotions—all are damaged in sinful man. ... So, even if one would accept the distinction between natural and moral, natural inability [to do good before God] must still be maintained."[110] "It must always be pointed out," Vos says, "that inability and unwillingness are two sides of one and the same matter."[111] The implication of the unity or one might say co-termineity of disposition and spirit is that

> no love for God is present as the motivating principle of our life; that it does not dwell in us as a disposition and therefore never determines our deeds, thoughts, and words; and, conversely, that in our entire life there is an undertow

---

108. Bavinck, *RD*, 3:140. Elsewhere:

> Man lost none of his substance as a result of sin. In that sense humans are fully human even after the fall. But when man lost his original righteousness, he lost the harmony and health of his nature and became a sinner through and through. His nature in the sense of substance or essence remained, but the moral qualities naturally belonging to his nature were lost. (*RD*, 2:553)

109. Vos, *RD*, 2:57.
110. Vos, *RD*, 2:60.
111. Vos, *RD*, 2:60.

of hostility toward God that only needs an external stimulus to develop into conscious opposition to the Lord.[112]

Along similar lines, Van Til repeatedly emphasizes the fact that the Fall and sin must be understood ethically instead of metaphysically. Sin "is an attempt on the part of man to himself loose from God," but "this breaking loose from God could, in the nature of the case, not be metaphysical; if it were, man himself would be destroyed, and God's purpose with man would be frustrated."[113] Therefore, says Van Til, "sin is breaking loose from God ethically and not metaphysically. Sin is the creature's enmity and rebellion against God but is not an escape from creaturehood."[114] Elsewhere he writes:

> In the narrower sense, God's image in man is the true knowledge, the true righteousness and the true holiness that man possessed when created by God. In the wider sense, God's image in man is man's rationality and morality. Through sin man lost the image of God in the narrower sense. This means that man is spiritually blind but remains a rational nature, and as such is always confronted by the revelation of God about him and within his constitution. ... We must think of man as spiritually blind without denying his personality. His spiritual blindness presupposes his being a covenant personality.[115]

In a strange irony human sin is hostility toward just what it means to be human, toward the very glimmer of divine-paternal approbation. With this in mind, the

---

112. Vos, *RD*, 2:58.

> Inability to do good is only incompatible with responsibility if this inability has a nonmoral origin. For man this is not the case. He cannot, but that is because the direction of his will is wrong, going against God. It is not a natural capacity to will that is lacking in him, but the good moral quality of his capacity. This is what we found to be the kernel of truth in the distinction between natural and moral inability. Only we would also want to call this moral inability natural, inasmuch as it belongs to the nature of man to be moral and to be good. (Vos, *RD*, 2:62)

113. Van Til, *DF*, 69.
114. Van Til, *DF*, 69–70.
115. Van Til, *SCE*, 95. Note Van Til's apologetic investment in this distinction: "Perhaps the most fundamental difference between all forms of non-Christian ethics and Christian ethics lies in the fact that, according to the former, it is man's finitude as such that causes his ethical strife, while according to the latter it is not finitude as such but created man's disobedience of God that causes all the trouble" (Van Til, *CTE*, 31). He later adds: "The reason for reducing the tension to a metaphysical strain between time and eternity is that *men do not want the tension to be found in the exclusively ethical sphere.* If the tension can be thus reduced to something metaphysical, its seriousness is reduced or taken away, and man is no longer fully responsible for it" (*CTE*, 39).

prohibition of Gen. 2:17 may be read not as a threat but as a warning—a publication of the cause-and-effect sequence, rather than a dare. Vos in fact denies that Gen. 2:17 represents a threat of immediate physical death and separation of the spirit from the body, and that this sentence was somehow not carried out immediately following the first sin. He writes, "stressing of the phrase 'in the day' in 2:17, is not only uncalled for, but, in view of the sequel of the narrative, impossible. ... Some knowledge of Hebrew idiom is sufficient to show that the phrase in question simply means 'as surely as thou eatest thereof.'"[116] Vos believes that the death predicted, rightly understood, did follow immediately upon the first sin.[117] Bavinck captures the self-destructive nature of sin: "The human being remained a human being, not a machine, not a wooden thing or block, not a devil, but a human being. But the human became abnormal; though still human, its humanity"—its very humanity—"is cankered and rotten."[118]

The foregoing are natural explanations for Adam's moral degeneration subsequent to the first sin.[119] Bavinck, Vos, and Van Til identify causes from within the human constitution and in the nature of sin for the emergence of Adam's guilt and corruption. That is: Adam's constitution is such that if he sins, he will become a sinner; and one sees in the first sin that full scale personal conversion must follow. But these are not the only explanations for the degradation of Adam's character subsequent to his sin. In addition to this natural aspect, there is a special aspect as well.

According to Vos, in just response to sin, as a form of punishment, God himself inflicts Adam with moral corruption consistent with transgression: "Original pollution, inherent corruption, was both for Adam and for us a *punishment* for the first sin. For Adam it appeared immediately; ... It is not the only but still the principal punishment of sin, and potentially contains eternal death, since it is *separation from God* of the σάρξ, 'flesh.'"[120] Original pollution "must be viewed as a penal consequence," with this effect, that it emptied Adam's character of righteousness: "there was now nothing more in it that was in accord with the demand of God's law."[121]

---

116. Vos, *BT*, 38.

117. Vos, *RD*, 2:42.

118. Bavinck, *RE*, 43.

119. Along these lines, note this statement from Vos: "We find the essence of sin in general to be this: that man (1) divorces himself and his relationships from God; (2) places them as a separate center in opposition to God; (3) makes them act against God" (*RD*, 2:51). Observing Eve's conduct prior to taking and eating, Vos says, "one sees here how all three elements mentioned above are already potentially present" (*RD*, 2:52).

120. Vos, *RD*, 2:34-5.

121. Vos, *RD*, 2:35, 53. Bavinck explains sin as punishment for sin: "A subsequent sin may be called a punishment for a prior sin, since it distances the sinner even further away from God, makes him more wretched, and abandons him to all sorts of covetousness and passion, dread and remorse" (Bavinck, *RD*, 3:107).

Thus Vos argues that Adam underwent the corruption of his nature because his constitution once guilty of sin implies such conversion, but also that God inflicts Adam with corruption of his nature as punishment for sin. One wonders: how are these related? Are they redundant? Or are they somehow supplementary?

Vos's answer seems to be that natural and imposed (retributive) corruption are not redundant because although Adam's nature implies this or that, once the terms of the covenant are violated, God was no longer under obligation to endure Adam's existence. By sinning Adam had renounced his right to reward of course but also to natural life, and yet, graciously, inexplicably, "there was something in the pre-redemptive eschatology that was not eliminated but reincorporated in the redemptive program."[122] So the continuation of Adam's existence, its persistence despite covenant violation, signals the intervention of divine long-suffering, a willingness to tolerate the existence of sinners that can be attributed only to some kind of unwarranted favor of God. And an excessively favorable situation for the human creature can be attributed to God and God only. Delay of judgment, in fact, requires either failure of the divine justice and therefore diminution of the divine being, or mediatorial provision. Favoring the latter, of course, Vos takes this long-suffering as a side effect of the historicity and the timing of the accomplishment of redemption. He believes that in Rom. 9:22-3 Paul sees the patience of God relative to vessels of wrath as subsidiary to the outworking of his mercy relative to the elect:

> Insofar as this purpose concerning the vessels of mercy rested on, and was related to, the satisfaction of the Mediator, who could not satisfy until the fullness of time—to that extent this satisfaction became a cause of the patience of God in putting up with those who are lost. All that results from the delay of judgment, all external blessings that mankind enjoys, all that befalls them beyond curse and death, the common grace at work throughout, with all the fruits of external righteousness that it fosters—all of this is an indirect result of the satisfaction of the mediator.[123]

In other words, "there is common grace and special grace," and the one extends the patience of God as the context for the historical administration of the other.[124] Vos affirms positive aspects of common grace as well. The life of Cain, he says, includes description of "the working of common grace in the gift of invention for the advance of civilization," and that "these gifts of grace were abused by the Cainites and made subservient to the progress of evil."[125] The point here however

---

122. Vos, *Eschatology of the Old Testament*, ed. James T. Dennison Jr. (Phillipsburg, NJ: P&R, 2001), 74.

123. Vos, *RD*, 3:137-8.

124. Vos, *RD*, 5:78. Common grace as a philosophy of history is also Van Til's interest. See *CGG*, 3–19.

125. Vos, *BT*, 45. See William Edgar, "Geerhardus Vos and Culture," in *Resurrection and Eschatology: Theology in Service of the Church: Essays in Honor of Richard B. Gaffin, Jr.*, ed. Lane G. Tipton and Jeffrey C. Waddington (Phillipsburg, NJ: P&R, 2008), 383–95.

is that Vos sees the conversion of Adam's character from righteous to corrupt as a natural consequence of Adam's sin; as just punishment from God; and yet also as an indication of the mercy of God.

As Vos interprets subsequent chapters of Genesis, the diagnosis of Gen. 6:5-7 is occasioned not by accumulation of evil, by breaching a quantitative threshold, but by the amplified manifestation of a quality or principle of rebellion and wickedness operative in the heart of the image-bearer, corporately conceived, since the fall. Sin does not become or increase but self-manifests; it develops organically, one might say, within and throughout the species-organism of the image-bearing race. "Even Cain," Vos writes, "still felt the need of help from God," but "the spirit of Lamech depends upon itself alone. No trace of the sense of sin remains."[126] Genesis 6:5-7 identifies the intensity, extent, and absoluteness of evil that is anchored inwardly, and that operates habitually with and upon the human will.[127] "What was described in Gen. 6:5, was the historical culmination of a process of degeneration. ... What is here described is the natural state of evil in the human heart as such."[128]

This distinction between an aggregation of evil and a self-development is significant; by it Vos is affirming that all subsequent sin expresses the first sin. There is a basic unity to sin not only phenomenally (there are types of sin), but morally and spiritually all sin is of a kind and may trace its lineage back to the transgression of Gen. 3:6 and to a moral unity of all human beings. This is Vos's doctrine of original sin.

Bavinck, Vos, and Van Til's doctrines of original sin are not entirely unpredictable. Bavinck, for example, takes a familiar Reformed view of Rom. 5 according to which the passage teaches a two-Adam federal structure by virtue of which all human beings are implicated in the sin of the first man.[129] God in response to Adam's transgression published a judgment of guilt and a sentence of death over all humans. By virtue of and subsequent to this judgment of God, "all humans personally became sinners and all in fact die as well."[130] Bavinck thus emphasizes divine prerogative in the administration of federal representation, and Vos is rather specific about how it happens.

Guilt is "not inherited," that is, not received via natural generation, "but is imputed to us ... transmitted from Adam to us in the tribunal of God ... in an immediate way, not by heredity."[131] Imputation of guilt independent of natural means allows for the implication of preborn souls in covenant transgression: "God imputes to the soul the guilt of Adam's first sin by virtue of the covenant."[132] With regard to this imputation of Adam's sin to souls yet unborn, Vos says that first,

---

126. Vos, *BT*, 46.
127. Vos, *BT*, 51.
128. Vos, *BT*, 52.
129. Bavinck, *RD*, 3:83–5.
130. Bavinck, *RD*, 3:85.
131. Vos, *RD*, 2:66.
132. Vos, *RD*, 2:66.

by virtue of the covenant, a soul is reckoned guilty of the sin of Adam, and then appearance of the soul on earth involves dual divine involvement as Creator but also as judge, so that while God on the one hand creates a soul he withholds from it original righteousness, and, consequently, "a soul thus coming into being without original righteousness must immediately pass over into positive inherent depravity."[133] *Absentia justitiae originalis* leads immediately to *praesentia mali*, "presence of positive evil as *habitus*."[134] When Adam sinned God rendered him a sinner; likewise, when by imputation progeny figured in Adam also sin, God renders them sinners as well. Corruption is punishment for guilt imputed, and this corruption accompanies natural generation: "the corruption inherent in us as punishment for this imputed guilt ... is inherited."[135]

Vos also distinguishes original and actual sin. First is the imputation of Adam's sin, and inherent depravity as punishment. It may be most consistent with Vos's understanding to say that included in imputation are Adam's sin—effectively, the state of "having committed" that sin—the guilt for that sin, and the inherent depravity or moral decay that supervened upon Adam's character according to divine imposition and by means of a natural, anthropological cause-and-effect sequence. Out of this character, Adam's descendants produce their own sins. Vos says that a sinful act is any and "every conscious welling up of the depravity that is unconsciously present in us."[136] Since his notion of act "does not mean external action that is manifested by means of our body," but rather this welling up, "evil thoughts ... fall under this concept of actual sins as well as evil words and deeds."[137] Actual sins accrue guilt and divine displeasure on their own strength, adding yet another layer of covenant burden.

Although not all questions are answerable from Rom. 5 alone, Bavinck believes that in the end the lesson of that classic text is sufficiently clear: "judgment was pronounced over all humans because, in some fashion that Paul does not further explain here but that can be surmised from the context, they are included in Adam; all were declared guilty and condemned to death in Adam."[138]

Bavinck emphasizes the mysteriousness of the doctrine of original sin but also the fact that it can hardly be denied; the claim that in Adam's sin all humans are implicated involves an intractable element of mystery, but at the same time human nature is unintelligible without an origin or starting point for hereditary evil: "Regardless of whether we can make some sense of the fact that God—immediately, by and on account of Adam's disobedience—makes us all sinners, that fact itself is certain."[139]

---

133. Vos, *RD*, 2:67.
134. Vos, *RD*, 2:69.
135. Vos, *RD*, 2:54.
136. Vos, *RD*, 2:69.
137. Vos, *RD*, 2:69.
138. Bavinck, *RD*, 3:85.
139. Bavinck, *RD*, 3:101–2.

Bavinck believes that profound, essential, pervasive sinfulness of human beings can hardly be questioned; the depravity of the human race, corporately and universally, is so plain as to be beyond dispute. He thus lays claim to the undeniability of racial unity in sin as a post-natural anthropological condition—a condition universal and self-evident but somehow unnatural, and argues that federalism is the only viable explanation for it.

His argument opens with a concession, that original sin is a profound mystery. Consistent with Bavinck's view of dogmatics generally, he proposes to explore the doctrine against a backdrop of unsearchable mystery, which is, at the end of the day, God himself. But Bavinck does not, after conceding mystery, turn immediately to dogmatics; he turns instead to common consent. That is, he acknowledges mystery but then anticipates the charge of incoherence: "still some things can be said if not to explain this action of God, then certainly to strip from it the appearance of arbitrariness."[140] This strategy is designed to close the distance between the broader culture and the biblical teaching; all—the culture at large—already if inadvertently commend federalism.

It is evident—evidentially plain, he means—that "humanity is ... an organic unity, one race, one family."[141] Common consent and common practice, in fact, beyond the borders of the church, confirm physical unity of the human race. Bavinck notes that federalism, specifically the imputation of Adam's guilt, is said to offend modern sensibilities, even perhaps general moral intuition. So he labors to indicate the ubiquity of moral solidarity in "family, society, the nation, the state and the church, associations and federations of all kinds and for a variety of purposes."[142] He notes as well a convenient selectivity: no one begrudges the inheritance of virtue or privilege but only of guilt or burden.

> We enter into their labors, rest on their laurels, enjoy the things they have frequently acquired at great cost. We receive all this undeservedly, without having asked for it. It is waiting for us at our birth. ... The same son who ... accepts his father's inheritance refuses to pay his father's debts.[143]

Nonetheless, Bavinck acknowledges lingering tension: "And yet, to suffer for the sin of another is not the same as to be punished for the sin of another and hence to be viewed as the perpetrator of that sin oneself."[144] This widely acknowledged physical unity, says Bavinck, is alone insufficient for explaining original sin and federalism, much less the covenant headship of Christ; it is necessary for such an explanation, but does not render inherited sin intelligible. In this sense it wears its inadequacy openly.

---

140. Bavinck, *RD*, 3:102.
141. Bavinck, *RD*, 3:102.
142. Bavinck, *RD*, 3:104.
143. Bavinck, *RD*, 3:104.
144. Bavinck, *RD*, 3:105.

Bavinck at this point expands the scope of his polemic to include theological competitors to federalism. So he takes the opportunity to critique realism, the claim that physical unity is alone sufficient for the implication of all of Adam's progeny in his transgression. He offers a handful of *reductio* arguments: First, if physical unity were sufficient, imputation would be unnecessary because redundant. If comprehension in Adam were physical only, the covenant of works itself, bound up with the representational role of the first man, begins to sound overblown. Second, if physical unity were the sole and sufficient ground for implication in Adam's sin, all of Adam's sins, and those of Eve, and those of every succeeding generation, would be imposed equally on all subsequent generations.[145] In that case, again Adam is representationally unremarkable, and it would seem that not sinfulness as a quality but sin quantitatively would have been counted against those represented in Adam and Eve, and then cumulatively with each succeeding generation. The lament of Gen. 6, that all of the meditations of man's heart were only evil all the time, would signal not the organic development of sin, not the manifestation of its nature having developed organically from its singular inception, and the limit of the Lord's patience, but cumulative augmentation having reached a critical level. Bavinck also argues that realism would require that Christ assume a sinful nature and that a soteriology of grace would be impossible; physical representation in Christ entails universalism.[146]

Ironically, losing representationalism and falling back on realism "loses sight of … the independence of the human personality."[147] If sin, guilt, and corruption are primarily genetic rather than moral, racial unity has dissolved the individual. Bavinck responds:

> A human is a member of the race as a whole, certainly, but in that whole he or she occupies a unique place of his or her own. Individuals are more than ripples in the ocean, more than passing manifestations of human nature in general. Humans … are creatures with a character of their own. For that reason, physical unity in their case is not enough; an ethical, federal unity is added as well.[148]

The realist will be concerned that a notion of unity, and an account of imputation, which nature itself cannot sustain, implicates God in sin. If God imposes guilt without sufficient natural rationale, it would appear that God himself has a hand in the increase of sin. Vos for his part is unafraid of this implication; he finds it from a theological point of view incoherent:

---

145. Bavinck, *RD*, 3:103.

146. "Now if the righteousness of Christ is acquired and applied not in the way of a covenant but realistically, then in the case of Christ it consists in the fact that he assumed our nature, and in that case the satisfaction and salvation accrues to all humans, for Christ assumed the nature of them all" (Bavinck, *RD*, 3:103).

147. Bavinck, *RD*, 3:103.

148. Bavinck, *RD*, 3:103.

The ultimate legal ground for this representation in Adam cannot be specified by us. We can only say that it ... must be just simply because it is already factual. No other legal norm exists for us than the acts of God. Therefore, it is foolish to ask whether something that God does is right, as if we possessed an independent standard by which we could know that.[149]

Similarly undeterred, Bavinck refuses to reduce divine activity in federalism and the imputation of Adam's sin to providential upholding of nature; he affirms special divine judicial response in addition to predictable effects of sin once committed.

More importantly, Bavinck and Vos both take the natural itself already to be covenantal and federal. Both Bavinck and Vos in this sense distinguish the original design of the human creature from observable physical unity—a biblical or Christian-theistic "natural" as distinguished from a positivistic natural. Observable, physical unity is insufficient to account for imputation because it is an inadequate account of human nature. Both Bavinck and Vos view federal unity as necessary for imputation, but also as anthropologically original—not imposed after the fact—and irreducible.

Bavinck believes that federalism is implied, or at least suggested, in the image of God. Humanity is a "micro-divine being," which "reflects an ectypal unity-in-diversity."[150] He argues that "the image of God can only be displayed in all its dimensions and characteristic features in a humanity whose members exist both successively ... and contemporaneously side by side."[151] That is, historical succession and representationalism are equally implied in creaturely unity-in-diversity, a kind of anthropological *vestigium trinitatis* for Bavinck.[152] This signals Bavinck's notion of humanity as organism. He says: "Humanity cannot be conceived as a completed organism unless it is united and epitomized in one head. In the covenant of grace Christ has that position ... in the covenant of works that position is occupied by Adam."[153]

---

149. Vos, *RD*, 2:33.

150. Nathaniel Gray Sutanto, "Herman Bavinck on the Image of God and Original Sin," *International Journal of Systematic Theology* 18, no. 2 (2016): 178.

151. Bavinck, *RD*, 2:577. See Sutanto, "Herman Bavinck on the Image of God," 183. Elsewhere Bavinck puts the same idea in terms of prophet, priest, and king: "Only humanity in its entirety—as one complete organism, summed up under a single head, spread out over the whole earth, as prophet proclaiming the truth of God, as priest dedicating itself to God, as ruler controlling the earth and the whole of creation—only it is the fully finished image, the most telling and striking likeness of God" (Bavinck, *RD*, 2:567).

152. See Sutanto, "Herman Bavinck on the Image of God," 183–4.

153. Bavinck, *RD*, 2:577–8. Though it should be noted that the use of organic language with reference to humanity is ambiguous in both Bavinck and Vos. At times the word indicates a basically theocentric conception of the race in its spiritual, ethical unity. At other times, it seems that only physical unity is in view. Even this quotation could be taken either

Gray Sutanto observes: "For Bavinck, an organic unity-in-diversity in the triune God implies a superlative organic unity-in-diversity in the bearers of his image, in the human being and in the entire race. The archetypal unity-in-diversity obtains by perichoretic union, while the ectype finds its unity by means of ethical and natural solidarity."[154] Sutanto notes what this entails for the relationship between natural and divine explanations for original sin: "The covenant and its federal head's ethical union with the human race are conceived not merely as a voluntaristic special ordinance of God (though it includes that). It is a special ordinance of God which preserves and respects the ontologically triune features of humanity."[155]

Sutanto here points out that the will of God as it is involved in the enforcement of the moral structure of covenant is free and unsearchable—the "voluntaristic" aspect—and yet, at the same time, it tracks with the structure of the human creature as image of the triunity of God. Sutanto's aim here is to highlight Bavinck's argument for natural warrant, in this case anthropology, for corporate guilt; the imputation of Adam's sin is not arbitrary, nor therefore morally offensive, because it is to a large extent anticipated in the nature of the human creature, in the image-bearing species as such. As Sutanto reads him, Bavinck argues that unity-in-diversity in God implies an anthropological unity-in-diversity. He further argues that an organic anthropology such as this, one in which the whole is implicated in each individual, implies federalism such that the imputation of Adam's sin by God is not an arbitrary imposition but enforcement of covenant morality predictable from the point of view of the constitution of the image-bearer. In the imputation of Adam's sin, repugnant to the individualist moral instinct, God demonstrates the covenant structure of his image-bearer's nature and original, covenant conception, even the covenant unity-in-diversity of his own creativity. Imputation itself, therefore, displays both a natural covenant relation and active divine administration of the terms of the covenant.

Noteworthy in Vos's discussion is the fact that federalism and Adam's representative function is included in both the natural and the positive components of the original relational arrangement. The fact that representative function is not stated explicitly in the text of Gen. 2 or 3, in fact perhaps only with the desired specificity in Rom. 5 and 1 Cor. 15, may afford room for this distribution. Nonetheless it is certainly Vos's view that the human race was created a corporate entity and that Adam was aware of his representative function; but that federalism is a positive feature of Adam's testing and that the impact of the course of his life on his descendants must be explained in terms of a free but not arbitrary exercise of the will and authority of God. Vos writes:

---

way. Bavinck could be, in an apologetic mode, referring to an observable "organic" unity that, against the grain of naturalism, requires precisely the explanation given in Rom. 5, or "completed organism" may simply be meant dogmatically.

154. Sutanto, "Herman Bavinck on the Image of God," 184.
155. Sutanto, "Herman Bavinck on the Image of God," 184.

> The organic unity that exists between Adam and his posterity is not the ground but the means for the transmission of Adam's sin to us. ... It does not follow that Adam, because he possesses our nature, now *must* represent us. Thus unity of the nature is only a *conditio sine qua non*. ... The actual relationship is such that God, with an eye to the covenant unity for which He intended humanity, also created it as a natural unity.[156]

There may be some terminological variation here. In this instance, Vos's "organic unity" is physical unity—means only. The covenantal or federal character of Vos's anthropology appears logically prior to the conception of humanity as organism. He says here that organic unity, a genetic unity productive of difference, is necessary but insufficient for federalism, or, more simply, for the inheritance of Adamic sin and guilt. Organism in this case is observable unity, while transmission of ethico-religious status to posterity was figured into the original design of the image-bearer. Bavinck, likewise, says: "On the basis of common physical descent an ethical unity has been built that causes humanity ... to manifest itself as one organism."[157] For both Bavinck and Vos, anthropological organism is an observable phenomenon but also, more basically, a biblical, theological anthropology.

Overall, Bavinck indicates a dual purpose for his discussion of original sin and in his polemic against realism. He wishes to emphasize natural precedent for covenant unity and for the intelligibility of inclusion in the sin of a representative, but he also wishes to commend the supernatural component, a covenant anthropology. He collects these emphases as follows: "The law of solidarity does not explain the covenant (of works or grace) but is based on it and harks back to it," because, argues Bavinck, each sphere of mutual influence suggests a larger one until we arrive at the idea of a universal, uninfluenced influencer. And "only two persons have existed whose life and works extended to the boundaries of humanity itself, whose influence and dominion had effects to the ends of the earth and into eternity."[158] Adam and Christ "have the human race not behind them but before them; they do not spring from it but give rise to it; they are not sustained by it but themselves sustain it; they are not the product of humankind, but are, each in his own way, the beginning and root of it, the heads of all humanity." In sum: "They are not explained by the law of solidarity but explain this law by their own existence. They do not presuppose but constitute the organism of humanity."[159] His conclusion: "The covenant of works and the covenant of grace are the forms by which the organism of humanity is maintained also in a religious and an ethical sense."[160]

---

156. Vos, *RD*, 2:32.
157. Bavinck, *RD*, 2:579.
158. Bavinck, *RD*, 3:105.
159. Bavinck, *RD*, 3:106
160. Bavinck, *RD*, 3:106.

Still, in terms of the covenant of works, the special participation of God in response to the Fall is not the predictable covenant response. The imposition of corruption and the imputation of Adam's sin are not what the covenant of works required, and they are, in fact, kinder than death.[161] Spiritual death, represented by expulsion from the garden and the presence of God, is restrained so that it does not immediately effect physical death. Adam is expelled from the garden "lest he reach out his hand and take also of the tree of life and eat, and life forever"; expulsion from the presence of God and extension of life in sin is mercy. Bavinck for this reason sees in original sin ultimately the structure of redemption, and in the corporate inclusion in Adam's transgression the mercy of God. Original sin, Bavinck says clearly, is a function of the covenant of grace: "For when God condemns us, he at the same time offers his forgiving love in Christ. ... When God condemns, he speaks of sin and guilt that, though great and heavy, can be removed because they do not belong to the essence of humanity."[162] In the end a soteric rationale for original sin emerges: "Because God is interested, not in a handful of individuals, but in humanity as his image and likeness, it had to fall and be raised up again in one person."[163]

In this remarkable section of his discussion of sin, Bavinck offers extensive reinforcement of the natural aspect of the federal structure of the doctrine of original sin. The human race and the human condition are inexplicable, he argues, without an original, unmoved will for evil, and the moral solidarity of the race is everywhere acknowledged and everywhere enjoyed. And yet because the human is a character, a moral self, moral recoil at the notion of imputed guilt is, though hypocritical, intuitive and defensible. Moral unity and representation, indicated in but not limited to physical unity, best explains this. At the same time, Bavinck has insisted upon the theological integrity of the covenant idea. By thus claiming the inadequacy of ethics or anthropology apart from an originating sin committed by a single representative human, Bavinck has crafted a complex apologetic for federal Christianity, which includes equal parts subversion and proclamation.

---

161. A more complete picture of Bavinck's thought at this point would include common grace:

> Immediately after the fall, God delayed both eternal and temporal death. God also mitigated spiritual death in many ways. Spiritual death consists of the inability to do good and the inclination to evil, to live for sin and unto death. In many ways, God tempers this inclination to evil. From the fall onward, human life and humanity itself have come under the purview of *common grace*. It is not self-evident that humanity should exist. (*RE*, 149)

For several reasons, which will not hold our attention here, there is no offense to Bavinck's thought to indicate a close connection between the fall, original sin, and special grace, without deferring to common grace.

162. Bavinck, *RD*, 3:124–5.
163. Bavinck, *RD*, 3:106.

For our purposes, however, we note that Bavinck has rejected the idea that covenant is added to nature, or that religion is added to morality; nature/grace dualism is excluded in his account. Bavinck has not enhanced common moral inclination by recasting it in religious terminology; he has rejected realism as the best possible non-theistic account for the moral unity-in-difference of the image-bearing race and replaced it with a theocentric account in which as an anthropological category covenant precedes and explains the physical unity of humanity. Relation to God is not confined to the religious sphere of human culture; relation to God is the covenant-substance of the human creature as such, beginning from the conception and design of the human in the mind of God.

Vos leads with the idea that God on some level is responsible for the inheritance of Adamic moral corruption. It should be clear: the sin is Adam's, and the natural generation that constitutes the natural grounds for the bond between Adam and his descendants is a process largely empirically identifiable; it is a natural process. But as Vos indicates in several places, what he and the Reformed tradition are in the habiting of referring to as the "covenant bond" between Adam and his progeny is the design and actual imposition of God, but not a design "after the fact" as it were; it dates even to the pre-creation conception of the human creature. That "it is not good for man to be alone" is an indication of the corporate emphasis in Edenic or original anthropology, and as Vos points out, the relational structure that emphasizes racial unity in Adam explains two important things: "why the sin of our natural ancestors outside of Adam is not imputed to us," and "why Christ, though He assumed a human nature, was not under the curse as we are and why He could therefore assume human nature undefiled."[164] The point is that there is no natural explanation for these facts, and quite the contrary: Vos appears compelled to appeal to divine design in order to preserve these important components of his understanding of the covenant of works. So again Vos's first point: the inheritance of moral corruption, the fact that the natural is not unnatural or the normal no longer normal, is only explainable in terms of divine response to the transgression of Gen. 3:6.[165]

Vos says that the rite of circumcision "has something to do with the process of propagation," but it is "not the act but the product, *human nature*, which is unclean, and stands in need of purification and qualification."[166] "Sin, consequently, is a

---

164. Vos, *RD*, 2:33, 34.

165. It may be noted that Vos does appear to argue, with the doctrines of the image of God and original righteousness in view, not only that the first sin converted a good nature into a sinful one but that it did so necessarily. (Van Til argues similarly in *CTE*.) In that case, one might hypothesize a bit of inconsistency at this point, since here Vos argues that original pollution—the moral decay that supervened upon Adam's character subsequent and consequent to the first sin—was the stuff of divine response. On the other hand, it cannot be denied that Vos understand both of these conditions—the image of God and original, mutable righteousness—to be nothing other than the design of God.

166. Vos, *BT*, 90.

2. Divine Moral Character Transgressed

matter of the race and not of the individual only," and so "circumcision teaches that physical descent from Abraham is not sufficient to make true Israelites."[167] In fact Vos's exegesis of the threat of Gen. 2:17 does imply his claim that original corruption is imposed by God, in response to sin, as punishment. On death as "separation from God" Vos writes as follows:

> It was intimated that death carried with it separation from God, since sin issued both in death and in the exclusion from the garden. If life consisted in communion with God, then, on the principle of opposites, death may have been interpretable as separation from God. In this way preparation would be made for the working out of the idea of death in a more internal sense. ... In other words: expulsion from the garden (i.e. from God's presence) means expulsion to death. The root of death is in having been sent forth from God.[168]

In this sense the threat of Gen. 2:17 is not that on the condition of disobedience God would simply erase the existence and memory of Adam but that humanity would be expelled from communion with the source of life, goodness, and joy, from God himself. If it is remembered that the goal of the probation is volitional glorification and honor of God—not mechanical obedience to instructions, but a proper (doxological) response to the prohibition issuing from the whole person of Adam—then a rationale for the imposition of original corruption appears: the silent moral sphere must be brought into view and to the forefront of consciousness; after the Fall God leads the first humans into confrontation with himself in order that—for this purpose, in fact—they would experience a profound and personal awareness of enmity with God. Vos writes of those tense post-Fall moments: "It should be noted ... that the shame and fear operate with reference to God. The man and the woman hide themselves, not from each other, but from the presence of God. The divine interrogation," Vos points out, "reduces the sense of shame and fear to its ultimate root in sin."[169] And the intention is apparent in the fact that "God does not permit man to treat the physical," that is his nakedness, "as if it were sufficient reason for his sensation," of guilt and fear, "but compels man to recognize in it the reflex of the ethical."[170] As separation from God is symbolized geographically by ejection from the garden, so the humiliation of intimacy exposed is externalized in the shame and fear of nakedness. But the divine design evident here is to place the "ethical," a moral reckoning of the whole human person, front and center before the judgment of God. In this sense the post-fall crisis in which Adam and Eve are scrambling vainly as it were to regain their composure is the design of God with the aim of bringing about the fullest repentance and regeneration of their character and status before him.

---

167. Vos, *BT*, 90.
168. Vos, *BT*, 40.
169. Vos, *BT*, 41.
170. Vos, *BT*, 41.

Vos claims, as noted, that both the conversion of Adam's character as occasioned by his first transgression and the inheritance of Adamic moral corruption are engineered by God. This particular heredity uses natural generation as its means, but natural generation does not explain it; or if it did, it would explain too much— we would inherit the sin of every person from whom we are descended. Then the consequence is noteworthy: this corruption is the basis of guilt.

In this sense there appear to be two sources or aspects to the guilt of Adamic inheritance: guilt for Adam's transgression and guilt consequent to the inherent corruption received. So Vos explains: "God is free in the choice of the form in which He will to bring the punishment of sin," and "this fact stands on a line identical to the order that God follows in the covenant of grace, where He grants His promises to children of believing parents and generally extends the grace of the covenant."[171]

The design of God in inflicting Adam and his progeny with not only the guilt of Adam's sin but of Adamic sinfulness is evident as well in Vos's understanding of the "abiding force of the covenant of works," in particular with reference to believers.[172] In treating this matter Vos first points out that because the covenant of works comprises natural aspects of the image-bearer's relationship to his Creator, there is a sense in which to be human means to be in something like that relationship permanently and irreversibly. Because naturally and necessarily the Creator/image-bearer relationship is exhaustively moral, "even where Christ fulfills the law for us, we do not become lawless creatures ... natural law remains in force as the rule of life for the redeemed elect."[173] And even the penal consequence of the law serves a redemptive function in the lives of regenerate Christians:

> All who are led to [recognize] their guilt know themselves to be guilty because of federal sin. The covenant of works enters into the sense of guilt in an awakened soul, just as the awareness of satisfaction in the covenant head, Christ, becomes food for every soul that hungers and thirsts for personal righteousness.[174]

Vos here describes actual awareness of both guilt and the corporate origin of that guilt; and one certainly may understand Vos also to mean that this actual awareness is the desired result of federal design, of the divine imposition of corporate unity in the corruption of human character and in standing corporately under guilt and threat of death for that corruption. In this statement one sees as well the end toward which this awareness is designed: grasp of Christian grace according to the full anthropological scope of the state of sin. The purpose of the prohibition, to evoke full personal and doxological obedience, is the purpose also of imputation and becomes the accomplishment of the mediator in the fullness

---

171. Vos, *RD*, 2:35.
172. Vos, *RD*, 2:44.
173. Vos, *RD*, 2:44.
174. Vos, *RD*, 2:45.

of time. So, conclusively, regarding this divine imposition of unity with Adam in his guilt and moral corruption, Vos writes, "emphasis must be placed ... in yet another respect," according to which "fellowship with God incapable of being lost and life flowing from that fellowship" is presented as "the ideal," an ideal that is "not subsequently removed."[175]

The point here is that Vos sees a great deal of divine involvement in the reason for the sinfulness and the sinful condition of human beings. The origin of Adam's sin, in personal or subjective terms, is and will remain mysterious. But subsequent and consequent to Adam's sin, both the conversion of Adam's nature or moral character and the heredity of moral corruption are designed and imposed by God and include guilt before God distinguishable from guilt for Adam's eating from the tree. In addition to guilt for Adam's first transgression, humans descended from Adam bear guilt each for his own sinfulness, to say nothing of actual, personal sins. Although presently our interest lies in the origin and nature of sin and sinfulness, Vos it seems would encourage us to note that the imposition of Adamic sinfulness and guilt is not to no end nor an end itself, but unto the grace of God in Christ. For Vos, as Adam would have been aware of his righteousness and good standing before God, so he would have been aware of the possibility of transgression and then of the necessary just and wrathful response of God. Vos believes that before the Fall Adam would have, in the recesses of his heart, feared wrath and death and his own mutability. And all this knowledge would have been natural to him. Likewise, Vos believes that after the Fall all bearers of the divine image possess unshakable awareness of their tragic investment in the course of a primal, corporate fall and of the just and wrathful response to God. The point here is that this terror-inducing self-awareness is imposed by God as a precondition of precisely the sort of repentance He desires—perfect and personal.

Conclusion

This and the preceding chapter have demonstrated the neo-Calvinist conviction that the event of Gen. 3:6 should be understood in terms of two gestures of divine self-giving that together constitute the moral experience of Adam in the garden. The first is creational and is reflected in Adam's natural knowledge and self-understanding prior to and apart from the formalization of the covenant of works. Adam's life and person were, from the first moment of self-consciousness, naturally and necessarily contingently righteous before God. God in this sense had self-given in order to be the moral substance of Adam's contingent (mutable) moral experience, and here the mystery of the first sin, metaphysically speaking, already obtains and perplexes. The second is special and is most conspicuous in Gen. 2:17. There the moral nature of God is issued in the public ratification of covenant terms and stipulations. God gives his moral nature in transgressable,

---

175. Vos, *RD*, 2:46.

created form; establishes the required obedience as meritorious; and promises increased and perfected Creator–creature communion. The point is that this somewhat familiar covenantal interpretation of Eden derives all of its moral content from a relational immanence of God and a theocentric view of created reality and human experience.

This dual, divine relational self-giving provides us with the meaning of sin as such. What is the first sin? It is transgression, by a naturally, originally, God-honoring image-bearer, of the moral character and legislation of God, initiating a conversion of the ethico-religious condition of the transgressor and, federally, of those represented by him. But two mysteries remain: first, how a creature, devoid of evil and wholly inclined toward honoring God, could consciously, willfully sin; and second, how transgression of divine will is possible—how that possibility is even conceivable—where God is sovereign and good, or eternal and unchanging. These questions, not their answers but their persisting mysteriousness, demonstrate the explanatory limitations of this account of Gen. 3:6. Covenant is the preferred term here for the created situation in which a creature filled with divinely bestowed goodness and godliness faces the possibility of turning self-consciously against the self-subsistent personal precondition of his own self-consciousness. But as such, covenant is simply the name for the structure of this state of affairs. That deity is transgressable and in time transgressed is a mystery untouched by the narrative of Gen. 2 and 3.

What, then, of the objective possibility of sin? To answer this question, one must provide a theology of the possibility of the appearance of the relational context that gives meaning to sin, and then a theory of the divine act that actualizes it. If in the beginning there was only God, and then there was God and creation—a creation within which a divine relational initiative is the moral substance of creaturely experience—the possibility of the appearance of creation and the relation that animates it must be found in God himself. Bavinck, Vos, and Van Til deploy two concepts to this end: absolute person and incarnational condescension.[176]

Bavinck says: "The sinful act is caused by the sinful will, but who will indicate to us the cause of this sinful will? 'Trying to discover the causes of such deficiencies—causes which, as I have said, are not efficient but deficient—is like trying to see the darkness or hear the silence.'"[177] As subsequent chapters demonstrate, the neo-Calvinist instinct when facing theological mystery is, as Van Til has said, to look "more steadfastly into the face of God."[178]

---

176. The latter is my terminology.
177. Bavinck, *RD*, 3:69; quoting Augustine, *City of God*, 12.7.
178. Van Til, *CGG*, 19.

Chapter 3

ABSOLUTE PERSON, REASON, AND HISTORY

> From this proceeded that halting of holy Jacob … for although in wrestling with God he prevailed, yet he ever after bore the mark of his sinful defect.
>
> —John Calvin

Epistemology, worldview, ethics, elenctics and missiology, the structure of dogmatics, the nature of revelation, and the knowledge of God, all display the centrality and importance of the absolute personality of God in neo-Calvinist theology. And absolute personality is the key to articulating the neo-Calvinist account of human moral experience and the possibility of the first sin.

For Bavinck, Vos, and Van Til, biblical revelation grounds confession of an unconditioned God in whom ontological independence and personality are equally ultimate. This means that aseity and personality are mutually informative notions, that God is self-existent because he is internally, self-sufficiently, exhaustively personal; and his personality is everywhere characterized by the incommunicable attributes of his being.

The following material traces the significance of absolute personality through a number of the topics named above in order to provide a well-rounded view of the interdependence of absolute personalism and the covenant history that constitutes moral experience for the image-bearer. It perhaps is not an overstatement to say that neo-Calvinist thought, at least in Bavinck, Vos, and Van Til, is the exposition of triune absolute personalism. This chapter will substantiate this claim while focusing on the absolute personalism of moral experience.

Primary source material explored in what follows is drawn more or less equally from the writings of Van Til and Bavinck. Bavinck's nephew Johan Herman also figures here, and at several points connections with Vos's work merit attention. Thus the "organism" of neo-Calvinist absolute personalism will be made evident, and the relationships among the writings of Herman Bavinck the eclectic systematician; J. H. Bavinck the missiologist; Geerhardus Vos the biblical theologian; and Cornelius Van Til, the apologist, will be on display.

The Structure of Reason

In his apologetic literature, Cornelius Van Til defends a supernaturalistic worldview in which the triune God is the reference point for human interpretation of the self and the world.[1] "Christian theism is a unit," he says, and confession of the immanent Trinity is the determinative presupposition for predication and the intelligibility of human experience.[2] On this point, in fact, Van Til appears to do little more than rehearse and apply Bavinck's claim that the triune God of classical theism, in whom unity and diversity are equally ultimate, is the foundation of the Christian world and life view and the resolution of the antinomies that frustrate non-Christian systems.[3] Within this apologetic framework, Van Til distinguishes

---

1. On Van Til and worldview apologetics, see K. Scott Oliphint, "Cornelius Van Til and the Reformation of Christian Apologetics," in *Revelation and Reason: New Essays in Reformed Apologetics*, ed. K. Scott Oliphint and Lane G. Tipton (Phillipsburg, NJ: P&R, 2007), 255–93; on Van Til and cultural apologetics, see William B. Edgar, "Turn! Turn! Turn! Reformed Apologetics and the Cultural Dimension," in *Revelation and Reason*, 242–57; and on Vos, see William B. Edgar, "Geerhardus Vos and Culture," in *Resurrection and Eschatology: Theology in the Service of the Church: Essays in Honor of Richard B. Gaffin, Jr.*, ed. Lane G. Tipton and Jeffrey C. Waddington (Phillipsburg, NJ: P&R, 2008), 383–95.

2. Van Til, *CA*, 18. Elsewhere he puts it this way:

The form of the revelation of God to man must come to man in accordance with his creaturely limitations. God's thought with respect to anything is a unit. Yet it pertains to a multiplicity of objects. But man can think of that unit as involving a number of items only in the form of succession. So Scripture speaks of God as though he were thinking his thoughts step by step. All revelation is anthropomorphic. … In God's mind any bit of information that he gives to man is set in the fulness of his one supreme act of self-affirmation. (Van Til, *IST*, 270)

It deserves mention that this radical explanatory unity is characteristic of post-Kantian German idealism. As Shao Kai Tseng points out, the organic metaphor, now a prominent theme in Bavinck studies but important for Vos and Van Til as well, should be traced even to the Apostle Paul. But there is no denying that these neo-Calvinists have benefited from the organic impulse of nineteenth-century German philosophy. On this, see Shao Kai Tseng, *G. W. F. Hegel* (Phillipsburg, NJ: P&R, 2018), 69–128. Bavinck in fact argued that the organic doctrinal unity of Christian theology and theological method vindicated it as a scientific discipline in its own right. See James Eglinton and Michael Bräutigam, "Scientific Theology? Herman Bavinck and Adolf Schlatter on the Place of Theology in the University," *Journal of Reformed Theology* 7 (2013): 27–50; also Herman Bavinck, "The Pros and Cons of a Dogmatic System," trans. Nelson D. Kloosterman, *Bavinck Review* 5 (2014): 90–103.

3. For example: "Christians hold that the conception of God is the necessary presupposition of all human activity." "It is only on Christian presuppositions that the false contrast between abstract universal principle and abstract irrational particularity and his environment can be overcome" (Van Til, *CTE*, 34, 163). See James P. Eglinton, *Trinity and*

the structures of Christian and non-Christian reason in terms of two points of reference.[4]

The self, first of all, is the immediate or psychological starting point and is always operative as such. This is simply the fact that my thoughts are thought by me, but it means something more. That the creature is the subject of his own thoughts, or is a thinker in his own right, indicates that he lives and moves within what is called subjective experience, and that subjective experience is a trait of image-personality, which represents in finite form the eternal, tri-personal self-knowledge of God. Since it is anthropological, this feature of human reason is universal; to the extent that it is "religious," the human being as such is religious. So Van Til argues that with regard to this immediate or psychological starting point, between Christian and non-Christian thought there is no difference.

The important question of ultimate starting point or ultimate point of reference, on the other hand, marks divergence, and there are two options and two only: the self-existent triune God as revealed in Scripture, or the creature's self, the creature epistemically self-indexed. When all is well, the human mind knows itself to be the immediate but sub-ultimate psychological starting point and knows the triune God to be the mediate and ultimate reference point. Adam prior to the fall, for example, understood that a self-existent God was his (God's) own context; that God is self-named, self-known, and self-interpreted; and that therefore the creature's context is nothing but revelation of God—and God, if he would be known at all by the creature, must be known by self-attesting authority. "We do not name God; he names himself," says Bavinck.[5] "In the foreground here is the name as a revelation on the part of God, in an active and objective sense, as revealed name."[6] And yet, "the name of God in Scripture does not describe God as he exists within himself but God in his revelation and multiple relations to his creatures."[7] But the distinction here, between God as he is in himself and God

---

Organism: Towards a New Reading of Herman Bavinck's Organic Motif (London: T&T Clark, 2011), esp. 128–30.

4. Van Til's descriptions of Christian and non-Christian reason are dogmatic, not inductive. He provides evidence and illustration, but for the most part he is not interested in inductive religious psychology but in biblical anthropology and the transcendental structure of reason from a theological point of view. "We take our information from Scripture and then realize that what it teaches must be true" (*CTE*, 21). His interest is dogmatics for apologetics, theological principles for reforming theological reason and critiquing the thought patterns of unbelief. Here again his project is reminiscent of German philosophy, this time of the critical philosophy of Kant. Indeed, he described his apologetic as "transcendental." See Shao Kai Tseng, *Immanuel Kant* (Phillipsburg, NJ: P&R, 2020), esp. ch. 3.

5. Bavinck, *RD*, 2:98.
6. Bavinck, *RD*, 2:98.
7. Bavinck, *RD*, 2:99.

self-revealed, does not empty revelation of meaning: "This name, however, is not arbitrary: God reveals himself in the way he does because he is who he is."[8]

The revelation of God, both natural and special, always bears the authority of its personal, self-omniscient origin. So if as Van Til says, "man is surrounded by nothing but revelation," and in this sense "God is man's ultimate environment," human reason is basically and unavoidably re-productive of revelation and thus always proceeds (or should proceed) in a mode of interpretive obedience and imitation.[9] God knows himself in infinite perfection; God names himself for the creature; and God names everything else, all created things; the image-bearer learns these names of God and of things made by God so that creaturely knowledge is constituted by retracing the revelatory acts of the Creator. This derivative status of human reason, including the secondary nature of its activity and an accompanying awareness of the self-sufficiency of God, Van Til refers to as reason by analogy, or analogous reason.

> When on the created level of existence man think God's thoughts after him, that is, when man thinks in self-conscious submission to the voluntary revelation of the self-sufficient God, he has therewith the only possible ground of certainty for his knowledge. When man thinks thus, he thinks as a covenant creature would wish to think. That is to say, man normally thinks in analogical fashion. He realizes that God's thoughts are self-contained. He knows that his own interpretation of nature must therefore be a reinterpretation of what is already fully interpreted by God.[10]

Van Til's understanding of the use of human reason, accordingly, is shaped primarily by two things: ontology and covenant, or Creator–creature ontology and Creator–creature relation. The human creature, inclusive of human reason, is derivative of the divine original; it is the image of its origin and personal Creator. Again, there is no distinction here between regenerate and unregenerate. So Van Til says: "metaphysically, both parties have all things in common."[11] Van Til agrees of course with Bavinck that while "animals and plants also stand in a relation to God ... in the case of humanity, that relation is a *relationship* and

---

8. Bavinck, *RD*, 2:99. Van Til puts it this way:

> The names that God gives us of himself are not mere marks of denotation; there is none other beside himself from whom he need be distinguished. The names of God reveal to us something of the nature or essence of God. They cannot reveal his nature fully, but they nevertheless are expressive of something of that nature. If they were not, they would have no meaning at all. (Van Til, *IST*, 319)

9. Van Til, *CA*, 115; *DF*, 65.
10. Van Til, *CA*, 77.
11. Van Til, *CGG*, 9.

a *post* or *office*."[12] The human creature should indicate its derivative status in derivative self-understanding. That relationship hangs on willful acknowledgment of creatureliness as such. Human reason should understand itself as tasked with rehearsing out of a principle of obedience the data of divine self-glorification, which constitutes the creature's self and his context. "Should" in this case is alethic—truth-relevant—but also moral, given the personal nature of the environment; the image-bearer's context is God self-given.

Accordingly, the primary facet of non-Christian thought is rejection of the self's derivative status and of this two-tier structure in favor of the interpretive equality of God and man, a one-tier structure out of accord of the actual ontological state of affairs and by which the creature lays illegitimate claim to the privilege of determining the natures of things and judging good and evil. "Epistemologically," Van Til says, "they have nothing in common."[13]

In other words, unregenerate reason is reason as it operates within a state of culpable confusion regarding the status of the proximate starting point. Unregenerate reason takes itself to be non-derivative, original, and in a manner self-existent.[14] So Van Til argues that unregenerate reason as such is univocal, and says that it occurs prototypically in the garden.

Eve, in the silent shift described in Gen. 3:6, embraced a "grand monistic assumption," since by taking her own reason as equal to God's in the interpretation of the tree and her situation, she declared the self-sufficiency of her own mind and thus, at least by implication, of her own being alongside God's. She renounced her derivative, image status, and made herself like or equal to God by a single act of self-assertion and autonomous judgment. She denied that God's point of view was privileged relative to her own—she denied that he had greater access to truth, that his motives could be trusted, and that he had the right to legislate—which is to say that God is not God.

On the surface it is evident that Eve is unconvinced that God knows the future; taking the serpent's lead, she dismisses "you will surely die" as probably false; and she is unimpressed with God's presumption of authority; "thou shalt not eat" is not command but self-important suggestion. And perhaps eating of the fruit of the tree is indeed not in Eve's interest, but the point is that she will decide for herself. The unregenerate mind may very well agree, and even comply, but it cannot obey.

Thus, due to implicit monism, unregenerate reason is deaf to self-authenticating revelation, one might even say hostile to it. When functioning as ultimate, the

---

12. Bavinck, *RE*, 50. Van Til writes: "God put all things in this universe into covenant relation with one another. He made man the head of creation" (Van Til, *CTE*, 44).

13. Van Til, *CGG*, 9.

14. As John Frame argues in "Divine Aseity and Apologetics," in *Revelation and Reason*, 115–30. Daniel Strange has produced a theology of religions, in the Dutch Reformed tradition, in which false religion is constituted by treating something other than God as self-existent. See Strange, *Their Rock Is Not Like Our Rock: A Theology of Religions* (Grand Rapids, MI: Zondervan, 2015).

proximate reference point of itself cannot leverage affirmation of an absolute God; no command issuing from God can be received with the authority of God. "The revelation of a self-sufficient God can have no meaning for a mind that thinks of itself as ultimately autonomous."[15] Thus, whatever speaks to the unregenerate mind is always taken by it as affirming the interpretive ultimacy of the proximate self, even when it does not. Bavinck says that even the statement "God is absolute" is incoherent for the non-Christian.[16] Univocal description is always definition. Even more: the unbeliever "makes facts as he describes. His description is itself the manufacturing of facts."[17] The unbeliever has virtually taken the place of the self-defined God.

This methodological lockdown means that incoherence permeates unregenerate reason by the nature of the case. The (cognitive) darkness of sin involves itself in the demonstrably hopeless denial of the ontological state of affairs, that God is and that only in, by, and through the triune God does the creature exist and think rightly. Conversion, or regeneration, therefore, must involve radical methodological correction signaled by the demotion of the proximate starting point and by affirmation of God as God, as the self-originate one, of divine authority as self-attesting. Since regenerate reason (like Adam's pre-fall reason) is characterized by restored derivative self-understanding, conversion is not by process or degree but by crisis, a crisis of what Van Til calls epistemological self-consciousness. Conversion must be signaled by radical self-subjugation, or self-imposed (though Spirit-initiated) subjugation to a self-attesting, self-sufficient other—the self-named God: "to negative himself as ultimate and as correlative: *the natural man must first negate himself as normal.* This he will not and cannot do."[18]

> We accept this God upon Scriptural authority. In the Bible alone do we hear of such a God. Such a God, to be known at all, cannot be known otherwise than by virtue of His own voluntary revelation. He must therefore be known for what He is, and known to the extent that He is known, by authority alone. We do not first set out without God to find our highest philosophical concept in terms of which we think we can interpret reality and then call this highest concept divine. ... It is from this process of reasoning that we have been redeemed.[19]

He adds:

---

15. Van Til, *CA*, 113–14.
16. "Furthermore, if absoluteness precludes all limitation, and all determination is negation, it is not only not permissible to speak of God as personality, but it is equally wrong still to call him the Absolute, unity, the good, essential being, substance (etc.)" (Bavinck, *RD*, 2:49).
17. Van Til, *CGG*, 8.
18. Van Til, *IST*, 179.
19. Van Til, *CGG*, 14.

This frank acceptance of our position on authority, which at first blush, because of our inveterate tendency to think along non-Christian lines, seems to involve the immediate and total rejection of all philosophy—this frank acceptance of authority is, philosophically, our very salvation.[20]

The God-Concept and Environments of Ethical Reason

In Van Til's book on ethics, one discovers similar themes. There he outlines what he calls the epistemological presuppositions of Christian ethics, contrasting these with non-Christian ethical thought. He explains the differences in various ways, sometimes in terms of the "environment" of moral reason.[21] In another place he says that "all the differences between Christian and the non-Christian point of view, in the field of ethics, must be ultimately traced to their different God-concepts. Christians hold that the conception of God is the necessary presupposition of all human activity. Non-Christian thought holds that the Christian conception of God is the death of all ethical activity."[22] In fact these two ways of identifying the difference between Christian and non-Christian thought are, for Van Til, interdependent. "Metaphysically, both parties have all things in common" means that "both" regenerate and unregenerate "deal with the same God and with the same universe created by God. Both are made in the image of God."[23] Van Til's language of "God-concepts" surely denotes more than theology proper; it has to do with the distinct ways in which Christian and non-Christian moral reason understand the ultimate context within which good and evil are investigated and within which the creature understands himself as moral agent.

---

20. Van Til, *CGG*, 14. Much in Van Til, such as a trinitarian worldview, is drawn liberally from Bavinck and neo-Calvinism. By contrast, the foregoing section on epistemology and the present section on ethics show Van Til at his most creative.

21. For example:

> In a discussion of the metaphysical presuppositions of the ethical life, we deal with the will of man from the point of view of its ultimate environment. Is human personality independent of its environment? If it is not independent of but dependent upon its environment, how then can it be held responsible for its choices? Can there be any ethics if the will is wholly independent? Can there be any ethics if the will is wholly dependent? In theological language we call this the problem of the will in its theological relations. (Van Til, *CTE*, 33)

22. Van Til, *CTE*, 34. It should be noted that Van Til is primarily or not unequally concerned with non-Christian ethical thought as such, not as the statement suggests in actual, self-identified non-Christian or anti-Christian systems. This is one reason that Van Til will, after explaining non-Christian thought, turn immediately to examples of such from self-consciously Christian writers.

23. Van Til, *CGG*, 9.

Modulating the general epistemological structure reviewed above, according to which the self-sufficient God, if he will be known at all, must be known by self-attesting authority, Van Til says that the law of God is, morally speaking, the ultimate reference point beyond which no moral recourse is conceivable. In epistemological terms, creatureliness indicates analogical thinking, thinking God's thoughts after him. Ethically speaking, creatureliness entails analogical volition: "To act analogically implies the recognition that one is a creature of God. If man is a creature of God, he must, to think truly and to act truly, think an act analogically."[24] The epistemological role of revelation, as the primary interpretation of created facts and facts about God given among creatures, is in ethics occupied by the law of God, where the law of God whether explicit (verbal) or implicit (nonverbal, written on the heart) is the moral nature of God revealed or self-expressed as norm for the creature. So here, again, revelation is basic, or metaethically determinative and unimpeachable. It is the voice of the absolute God.

Notice that for Bavinck, Vos, and Van Til, not even the being of God can be consulted against the morality of a divine action or command. Vos says that "no other legal norm exists for us than the acts of God. Therefore, it is foolish to ask whether something that God does is right, as if we possessed an independent standard by which we could know that."[25] "A loving God would not do that" is theologically incoherent. Of the nature of the case, the creature cannot catch God in moral inconsistency. This is, first of all, because such inconsistency cannot occur. God cannot be involved in self-referential incoherence. God is his own goodness.[26] And, second, even if it were objectively possible, the creature could not catch God in moral inconsistency because as Vos says no adequate standard is available. God is knowable only in his voluntary self-revelation; therefore, the fact of voluntary revelation conditions what the creature knows. "A loving God would not do that" claims detection of inconsistency between the nature of God and the revelation of God. But the creature can make no such comparisons. The creature cannot arbitrate the self-consistency of God, because an absolute God is known only by authoritative revelation. So, specifically in the moral sense, "we do not artificially separate the will of God from the nature of God."[27] Thus the charge of the arbitrariness of divine command is silenced. "It is the nature of God as the will of God that is ultimately good."[28]

Van Til follows this with an important statement, linking the God-concept with the environment of moral reason: "Yet since this nature of God is personal there is no sense in which we can say that the good exists in its own right."[29] This means

24. Van Til, *CTE*, 37.
25. Vos, *RD*, 2:33.
26. "As God is absolute rationality so God is also absolute will. By this we mean primarily that God did not have to become good, but has from everlasting to everlasting been good. In God there is no problem of activity and passivity" (Van Til, *CTE*, 34).
27. Van Til, *CTE*, 20–1.
28. Van Til, *CTE*, 21.
29. Van Til, *CTE*, 20.

that the ultimate good—good itself, in the realm of creaturely experience—is what God desires. The good is not arbitrary, since it is not artificially detached from the being of God; but since God for the creature is unsearchable, the good hangs on unsearchable divine desire expressed, or self-given, or revealed, for the creature. Human reason must be oriented analogically relative to authoritative revelation; human volition, likewise, and moral reason must be oriented analogically—obediently—relative to the moral nature of God expressed as norm for the creature. "When God says, 'Come let us reason together,' he does not therewith put the sinner on an equality with himself. He asks man himself to see that obedience to God is the best for him, but whether or not man sees this he must be obedient still, or suffer the consequences."[30]

The distinction between "the good" as the desire of a personal God and "the good" as self-existent marks a basic difference between Christian and non-Christian conceptions of the moral environment. Even Plato's absolute God, "to the extent that he was personal, was metaphorical and, in any case, dependent upon an environment more ultimate than himself."[31] The question is whether the moral character of God self-expressed as law for the creature is ultimate, or whether a moral environment to which even God is subject is the ultimate point of reference in moral reason. Here, in a word, is the difference: "If man acts self-consciously before the background of an absolutely personal God he acts *analogically*. On the other hand, if man acts self-consciously before the background of an ultimately impersonal principle, he acts *univocally*."[32] Elsewhere Van Til puts it this way:

> Suppose we begin with man as a moral being, taking for granted that we know to a large extent, if not fully, what purpose means in his case, in order then to conclude that there must be a God to conserve the purposes or values of man. That would be univocal instead of analogical reason. It would be to make God the derivative of man instead of man the derivative of God. We would be thinking of a god who is but an extension of man.[33]

Van Til says that for non-Christian thought it is "impossible to speak intelligently of man's thought as being analogical of God's thought."[34] It is impossible, that is, short of conversion. This "impossibility" signals Van Til's doctrine of total inability to will or to do good: "He cannot be obedient unless he reverses his entire position, and this he cannot do of himself. It takes the regenerating power of the Spirit to do that."[35]

---

30. Van Til, *CTE*, 26.
31. Van Til, *CTE*, 35.
32. Van Til, *CTE*, 36.
33. Van Til, *IST*, 185.
34. Van Til, *CTE*, 18.
35. Van Til, *CA*, 195.

All sin, whether self-conscious and premeditated or habitual, is disobedience signaling rejection of the divine ontology. One can rationally disobey a finite god; strictly speaking this is merely disagreement. But disobeying God indicates metaethical incoherence. Van Til therefore characterizes non-Christian ethics as moral predication, which to any degree qualifies or disregards the authority of the revealed commands of God. In fact there are no degrees of such disregard. Either the judging self defers to an external, authoritative word or it does not.

Van Til says, for example, that if one finds objectionable the Lord's commanding Abraham to sacrifice Isaac, one's indignation can only be explained in terms of implicit resistance to the authority of God, and thus to God as God. Distaste for the content of even this startling command represents discontent with self-sufficient deity and the office of the image-bearer. One might argue that God did not actually intend for Abraham to kill Isaac, or even that God, being good and loving, could not actually have meant this command sincerely. Van Til argues that it is "unwillingness to show this same obedience" that Abraham showed that "makes us give such an interpretation."[36] To take ethical issue with God's sending Abraham to sacrifice Isaac his son, a command no less unimpeachable and sincere than shocking, or to qualify God's moral right to make such a command, or to assume that such a command taken at face value would necessarily tarnish the moral integrity of God, is to have "reduced the command of an absolute God to the advice of a finite God," and "this can be done only on the assumption ... that there is an ultimately impersonal atmosphere surrounding both God and man."[37]

Accordingly, Van Til utilizes the same notions of points of reference and self-understanding to identify and differentiate Christian and non-Christian moral reason. In terms of the two points of reference, proximate (or immediate) and ultimate (and mediate), Christian moral reason is characterized by implicit affirmation of a Christian ontology comprising Creator and creation, the self-sufficient God and his created image-bearer. Christian thought takes the proximate starting point as derivative and sub-ultimate, and the Christian moral thinker understands himself as ever duty-bound to defer to the self-authenticating self-disclosure of the self-existent God as the ultimate and unimpeachable authority and point of reference for all moral predication. The creature as such knows itself to be a servant of God, finding his freedom, fulfillment, and delight in personal obedience and service. It is a matter of createdness that the human defers self-consciously to divine moral rule.

In terms of the ethical environment, it is a matter of createdness that the human defers consciously and subconsciously to divine self-expression as the morally charged context for the creature's every thought and deed. Says Van Til, "the moral consciousness is no more than the *immediate* or *proximate* source of information on ethical problems," whereas "the revelation of the self-contained God, the

---

36. Van Til, *CTE*, 28.
37. Van Til, *CTE*, 26. This is said in reference to Newman Smyth, *Christian Ethics* (New York: C. Scribner's, 1892).

ontological Trinity, as found in Scripture, is the ultimate reference point in all ethical ... questions."[38] "God is the infinite moral personality who reveals to man the true nature of morality," so that, "in Christian thought, man's moral activity is thought of as being *receptively reconstructive*."[39] This means that in terms of both explicit obedience to express commands and implicit obedience or glorification of God in response to an environment and conscience exhaustively revelatory of God, the creature is always and everywhere in a mode of obedient response to relational, morally rich expression of the divine being. In the previous chapter natural and special moral environments were distinguished, and discontinuity between the special and the natural—between the original state of nature and the graciousness of the covenant of works, in other words—was found to assume considerable continuity. Van Til here argues that this is because the self-sufficiency of God already requires that the image-bearer as such does nothing but respond to an exhaustively moral divine self-disclosure that meets him wherever he goes. A neutral or indifferent creaturely will is a contradiction. "Creatures have no private chambers."[40] "A neutral will," he says, "cannot function."[41]

Non-Christian thought differs in that the proximate starting point is also the ultimate starting point. "For non-Christian ethics the autonomous moral consciousness of man is the ultimate reference point," and "man's moral activity is thought of as at once *creatively constructive*."[42] Underappreciation of the authority of divine command or of divine revelation may constitute a non-Christian moment in the mind or life of a Christian. But non-Christian method is an implicit self-understanding characterized by diminution of the moral authority of Scripture or of the self-revelation of God in and about the human. Van Til is arguing that recoil at the thought of God commanding the sacrifice of Isaac signals implicit deference to self-legislation, to a moral autonomy incompatible with Christian ontology.

Non-Christian method, in this sense, imagines the moral agent in an impersonal environment, in a moral context anticipating in silence the judgment of man. An impersonal moral environment, as impersonal, cannot desire, command, or speak; it cannot self-reveal. The elephant cannot speak and there is no one who can know that it is an elephant. It thus can wield no authority as objective truth or moral command. An impersonal context for moral deliberation and judgment cannot self-name, so it cannot but be named by the creature. Impersonality, on Van Til's analysis, is tantamount to the subjugation of metaethics to creaturely self-rule. "The point is that if the most ultimate environment that surrounds man is impersonal it is in the last analysis the task of the consciousness of man to determine the nature of that impersonal environment."[43]

---

38. Van Til, *CTE*, 20.
39. Van Til, *CTE*, 22.
40. Van Til, *CA*, 78.
41. Van Til, *CTE*, 46.
42. Van Til, *CTE*, 20, 22.
43. Van Til, *CTE*, 19.

The basic posture of right ethical understanding is reception rather than discovery—moral truth is given before it is found—and awareness of the derivative status first of creaturely being and then of creaturely thought, and thus of the need for and appropriateness of revealed moral instruction. Van Til makes the point that receptivity does not indicate passivity; rather, it is properly the impetus of creaturely activity. Being a derivative, analogous creature, the image-bearer finds his actuality in obedience. Divine commandments are not the end but the beginning of human freedom.

> We should observe … that when we speak of obedience we are not thinking of a passive virtue. Obedience does, to be sure, emphasize man's receptivity. But it does not emphasize his passivity. Obedience is the foundation of a great activity. It is the foundation of a great constructive program of action. But it is the foundation of a constructive program which is reconstructive. By this we do not mean that a program which has once been constructed has broken down so that it needs reconstruction. We mean rather that back of the constructive activity of man lies the constructive activity of God. God has a program for man to realize on earth. When man willingly and spontaneously accepts this program with all his power, then he is truly obedient.[44]

Obedience and True Religion

From the foregoing discussion it is clear that, as far as Van Til is concerned, obedience is the primary, original, and proper disposition of the image-bearer's volition and self-understanding—obedience is righteousness—and that the absolute personality of God is implied in that very notion of creaturely obedience. But this needs emphasis.

Personality indicates capacity for the free derivation of expressable moral norms from the eternal self-knowledge and self-sufficient goodness of the absolute God, and for the issuing forth from absoluteness of those moral norms for the creature; personality means that morality is forthcoming from an absolute God into the sphere of human experience, or that the sphere of human experience is constituted by that divine self-expression. The absoluteness of the divine personality renders those expressed norms authoritative for the creature because they are in themselves authoritatively self-sufficient, and it renders creaturely compliance a matter of baseline moral uprightness. In this sense, the confluence of absoluteness and personality in the Godhead is the bedrock of human morality. To put it another way, for Van Til, obedience as such, in its pure, original form, assumes two things: Creator–creature ontology and a Creator–creature relation that is also a relationship.[45]

---

44. Van Til, *CTE*, 43.

45. It is worth noting that the obedience enjoined upon children, as obedience of one creature to another, is qualified by the supervening authority of God. In Exod. 20, the fifth

Missiologist Johan Herman Bavinck, son of pastor theologian Coenraad Bernardus and nephew of Herman,[46] develops this connection between absolute personality and obedience as demonstration of the distinct coherence of Christian theism. J. H. Bavinck believes that the defining question, the question to ask of all religions, is, "what have you done with God?"[47] He asks specifically, in any human religion, whether the deity is conceived of as personal or impersonal: "Who or what is the background of this amazing world? Must we speak of a 'he,' a 'she,' or an 'it'? Do we have to do with a personal God (male or female), or do we meet with an eternal, impersonal being, a primeval ocean from which all originates?"[48] The history of religions, he says, leans heavily toward the impersonal. Even when one does encounter the "I-thou relation" of personal religion, that relation invariably turns out to be "merely an aspect of a much greater and vaguer relation."[49]

For its own theistic personalism, Christian theism must first of all qualify the notion of personality. J. H. Bavinck notes that "the word *person* as applied to God renders only very imperfectly what God says concerning Himself."[50] "We must realize that," when speaking of the personality of God or of God as personal—even as person or persons—"we thereby say something that applies to Him in an

---

commandment is predicated upon divine deliverance (20:2), which J. H. Bavinck calls a "word of covenantal faithfulness, of deep and holy love" (*ISM*, 263) specifically, but also on the first four commandments taken together and accompanied by a promise of blessing (the latter part of v. 12). The rationale for honoring parents is conspicuously theological. The Apostle Paul says that children are to obey their parents "in the Lord" (Eph. 6:1), and Jesus makes the point with alarming clarity: "Whoever loves father or mother more than me is not worthy of me, and whoever loves son or daughter more than me is not worthy of me" (Mt. 10:37). Human relationships social and familial have a certain integrity (Mt. 18:15), but the fact that one must pray for one's persecutors (Mt. 5:44) indicates the subordination of human relationships to the religious one.

46. For a brief biography, see Paul J. Visser, "Introduction: The Life and Thought of Johan Herman Bavinck (1895–1964)," in *The J. H. Bavinck Reader*, ed. John Bolt, James D. Bratt, and Paul J. Visser, trans. James A. De Jong (Grand Rapids, MI: Eerdmans, 2013), 1–92.

47. J. H. Bavinck, *ISM*, 223. This is, J. H. Bavinck says, the "all-important question" of elenctics, which he defines as follows:

> Elenctics is the science which is concerned with the conviction of sin. In a special sense then it is the science which unmasks to heathendom all false religions as sin against God, and it calls heathendom to a knowledge of the only true God. To be able to do this well and truthfully it is necessary to have a responsible knowledge of false religions, but one must also be able to lay bare the deepest motifs which are therein expressed. This can actually occur only if one recognizes and unmasks these same undercurrents within himself. (*ISM*, 222)

48. J. H. Bavinck, *CBTM*, 185.
49. J. H. Bavinck, *CBTM*, 186.
50. J. H. Bavinck, *CBTM*, 186.

infinitely higher sense than we can even suppose."[51] One conspicuous difficulty is this, that the idea of personhood implies a kind of independence that only obtains between human persons, not between Creator and creature. Even young children may speak in the first-person singular, and truly have existence independent of their parents and others. But "the relation between God and man is always different from that between two 'persons,'" in the sense that "we are at each moment wholly dependent upon God, and without Him we cannot exist for one second."[52] In other words, theological deployment of the concept of "person" must be sensitive to Creator–creature ontology, to the Creator–creature distinction. A term used of a creature cannot be used univocally of the infinite and self-sufficient Creator. And given the ontological "distance" between the Creator and the creature, "we must be aware," he warns, "of the depth of the mystery that confronts us."[53] J. H. Bavinck even points out that although God is for good reason portrayed in Scripture as Father and thus as male, divine personalism as such transcends gender. He points out that the Bible includes female or motherly characterization of God.[54]

It should be noted that J. H. Bavinck thus situates divine personalism against a backdrop of the absoluteness of God. The history of religions, as noted, shows everywhere a similar pattern: approachable personality mediating between helpless creatures and the terrible darkness of the absolute. But in the case of Christian theism, there is no tension between absoluteness and personality but

---

51. J. H. Bavinck, *CBTM*, 187.

52. J. H. Bavinck, *CBTM*, 187. Vos argues, against the more popular view that consciousness of the other precedes and first evokes self-consciousness, that self-consciousness precedes consciousness of the other. Subjective experience, in other words, is a necessary precondition of knowledge of the other as such. See Vos, *RD*, 1:15. Vos surely has human relationships in mind. Alternatively, as J. H. Bavinck indicates, the Reformed instinct is with Calvin to understand "being thought by God" to be the precursor to "being" at all, and to acknowledge that the interdependence of the image-bearer's knowledge of self and of the supreme other, the Creator God, is therefore unsearchable. Van Til's term "covenant consciousness" means that human consciousness is, irreducibly, consciousness of creaturely status, and thus at least implicitly consciousness of the absoluteness and personality of God against which all human activity is measured.

53. J. H. Bavinck, *CBTM*, 187. So says Herman Bavinck:

> Still we have to grant the truth of what the older Fichte said, namely, that personality is a concept borrowed from the human realm and hence, when applied to God, always to some extent falls short. The concept of personality, when applied to God, is not fully adequate and in principle no better than all other anthropomorphisms we use with reference to God. (Bavinck, *RD*, 2:50)

54. See J. H. Bavinck, *CBTM*, 190–3. He argues that if the image of God is female no less than male, it may be supposed that God is the prototype of biblical femininity (p. 191). He also points out that Isa. 66:13 and the parable of the lost coin (Lk. 15:8-10) characterize God as mother and as "motherly and tender and caring," respectively (p. 192).

rather resolution of this tension in the co-equal personal absoluteness within the triune life of the God who self-reveals. So, even while there are conceptual deterrents to theological use of the concept of personality, special revelation sets authoritative precedent, and thus warrants confession of absolute personality. J. H. Bavinck says that when "we apply the word *person* to God, this concept receives an infinitely greater meaning than it generally has," but "meanwhile we must remember that it is not we who took the liberty to call God a person, but that He Himself in His revelation always describes His relation to us as that of one person to another."[55] Van Til, too, defends biblical precedent in this regard: "The Bible uses anthropomorphic names of God constantly, but nowhere presents a limited deity."[56]

J. H. Bavinck emphasizes the fact that biblical revelation contains not occasional or even frequent divine personalism or anthropomorphism, but as a whole presents a religious-personal encounter unintelligible unless God is characterized as absolute and personal. Biblical revelation is redemptive divine self-expression, a self-conscious and gracious self-revelatory overture of the absolute, personal God.

> He is the divine I, the Creator, the Originator, the King, the Father, and we are the created ones, those who are being addressed. He speaks of Himself as I or Me. He calls us *thou*. The whole Bible depicts the relation between Him and us in this fashion. Right to the last page, He is presented as the calling, saving God and we as the saved ones, the children.[57]

J. H. Bavinck waxes polemical, arguing that when "the relation of God to man is no longer in the personal sphere and is thought to be a relation between the small, human *I* and the great, ineffable *It*, the primeval ocean from which we originated,"

---

55. J. H. Bavinck, *CBTM*, 188. J. H. Bavinck's reference here to "a person" and then to "one person" is noteworthy. Both Herman Bavinck and Van Til speak of the unipersonality of God, while Vos only mentions it to express his disapproval. He writes: "God's being also exists as personal. However, we should consider that God's being may not be called personal in the abstract but only in His threefold existence as Father, Son, and Holy Spirit. In God personality is not one but three. There are not four but only three persons in the Godhead" (Vos, *RD*, 1:15). Van Til says: "We do assert that God, that is, the whole Godhead, is one person" (*IST*, 363). Bavinck says, on the one hand, that "thanks to revelation, it is certain, first of all, that God is a person" (*RD*, 2:30), but on the other, that the "Christian church and Christian theology, it must be remembered, never used the word 'personality' to describe God's being; and in respect of the three modes of subsistence in that being, they only spoke of persons reluctantly and for lack of a better term" (*RD*, 2:50). If "person" applied to the threefold personality of God is an approximation, then "person" applied to the personal unity of God may also be an approximation, perhaps with different revelatory data or dogmatic clarification in view.

56. Van Til, *IST*, 320.

57. J. H. Bavinck, *CBTM*, 188.

in cases of impersonal religion, in other words, "religious life as a whole is completely changed."[58] Specifically, "serving God" is traded for being "drowned in the divine ocean and suffused with His greatness."[59] If the divine personality is obscured, so too the human personality is reduced to delusion,[60] and "happiness and complete religious surrender are then sought in a Dionysian ecstasy."[61]

One may also encounter subtler depersonalization within religious practice, even Christian religious practice, when the law drifts from its personal source and relational context and, lacking the unifying effect of personalism (Jas. 2:10-11), dissolves into an endless series of discrete tasks and obligations. The surest sign that this has occurred is that "the little word 'I' becomes much more important than the word 'God.'"[62] "Jesus disclosed the alarming poverty of this religion," of Pharisaic legalism; but Islam is paradigmatic, and "anyone who has experienced this piety in practice knows how easily Allah is reduced to a distant, unapproachable concept, to something really unimportant. ... Here again, the word 'I' threatens to engulf the full intensity of religion, and Allah remains only as the lawgiver and the final rewarder."[63]

It is striking that the law of God could serve to divert attention from God himself, but J. H. Bavinck is convinced that the suppressive impulse expresses itself in precisely this way, within the sphere of religious practice, under the guise of

---

58. J. H. Bavinck, *CBTM*, 188.
59. J. H. Bavinck, *CBTM*, 188.

> Not only is it impossible to serve God, but the very possibility of praying to him is ruled out. One cannot speak to God; at the most one can simply listen to him in the serene stillness of the night, listen to the mystery that sounds in all things. There is no meaning in voicing our needs to him, or in confessing our guilt. And there is no guilt for the man who has once felt in his deepest being the vanity of all existence. There is only illusion, ignorance, and terrible deceit. (J. H. Bavinck, *ISM*, 269)

60. Van Til emphasizes the interdependence of created and uncreated personality: "Not as though man was created a volitional amoeba, which had to pass through the invertebrate stage before it finally acquired a backbone. Man was created a self. He was the creature of an absolute self and could not be otherwise created than as a self" (Van Til, *CTE*, 45). Similarly, exchanging "character" for "self," he writes: "To act analogically implies the recognition that one is a creature of God. If man is a creature of God, he must, to think truly and to act truly, think and act analogically. Man is created as an analogue of God. Hence man has been created as a character. God could not create an intellectual and moral blank" (Van Til, *CTE*, 36).

61. J. H. Bavinck, *CBTM*, 189. For the foregoing discussion, see also J. H. Bavinck, *ISM*, 247–72.

62. J. H. Bavinck, *ISM*, 264.

63. J. H. Bavinck, *ISM*, 264.

piety.[64] He believes that it can hardly be denied—"it cannot escape us"—that "man here again grasps at the norm given by God in order to escape from God."[65] Eluding God requires depersonalizing, or "secularizing," as J. H. Bavinck says, the law. On one end, the personal unity of the lawgiver is abandoned, and this affects on the other end not only a dissolution of the principle of holiness but also covenant or relational anthropology; the image of God loses meaning. Van Til says that if we have an absolute God then we must have an absolute Christ;[66] for this very reason, J. H. Bavinck says, this secularization of the law and the fetishization of personal conduct undermine the idea of renewal according to the image of Christ. "It is thus a fatal error when a person hypostatizes the norm, and pushes God into the distance. Such an act results solely in breaking the norm into an endless number of commands and prohibitions, but its deepest meaning, its relationship to God, is hereby lost."[67] Van Til says this of the ministry of Zephaniah: "When God was no longer recognized either in his promises or his threats, the climax had been reached of all that the devil could possibly desire. To ignore God is to go to perdition without so much as a bump."[68]

J. H. Bavinck and Van Til, in other words, agree that the inseparability of absoluteness and personality are implicated in the biblical notion of obedience, and in this notion of obedience as covenantal, as basically religious-relational. They agree, in other words, that the absolute and personal God is the singular principle of the Christian conception of righteousness and therefore constitutive of human personality and ethico-religious self-understanding.

Herman Bavinck also highlights in a polemical mode the uniqueness of Christian theism in its juxtaposition of absoluteness and personality. He argues that true religion requires fellowship and personal communion with the deity; that no religions have achieved this—all have broken on the mutual repulsion of absoluteness and personality—and that Christian special revelation alone has presented absoluteness and personality as equally ultimate. "True and genuine

---

64. See J. H. Bavinck, "Human Religion in God's Eyes: A Study of Romans 1:18–32," *Scottish Bulletin of Evangelical Theology* 12 (1994): 44–52; first published in *Themelios* 2, no. 2 (1964): 16–23. Similar is "Human Religion in God's Sight," in *CBTM*, 117–27. Van Til says, along similar lines: "Satan is not opposed to personalistic philosophies. He can sometimes use them when he wants to make non-Christians believe that they really are Christians." Cornelius Van Til and Louis Berkhof, *Foundations of Christian Education: Addresses to Christian Teachers*, ed. Dennis E. Johnson (Phillipsburg, NJ: P&R, 1989), 10.

65. J. H. Bavinck, *ISM*, 264.

66. "The Christian-theistic conception of an absolute God and an absolute Christ and an absolute Scripture go hand in hand. We cannot accept one without accepting the others" (Van Til, *CTE*, 28).

67. J. H. Bavinck, *ISM*, 265. Here J. H. Bavinck identifies a hypostatization of the law. While the person or personality of God, the author of the law, is obscured, a phantasm of personal relationship with the law replaces it.

68. Van Til and Berkhof, *Foundations of Christian Education*, 10.

religion … no religion has ever understood; all peoples either pantheistically pull God down into what is creaturely, or deistically elevate him endlessly above it. In neither case does one arrive at true fellowship."[69]

Bavinck puts it this way. He wishes first to contend for the covenant of works, for thinking of the religious relation in the garden as a covenant. He revisits Genesis 2, Hos. 6:7, Romans 5, and 1 Corinthians 15, offering exegetical arguments. He reviews church history, claiming the support of Augustine and various church fathers, and, noting inconstant appreciation of the doctrine in recent Protestant history, he proclaims: "the doctrine of the covenant of works is based on Scripture and is eminently valuable."[70]

But Bavinck adopts a second strategy as well. He argues that human familial, social, and professional life may be viewed as a complex of overlapping covenant relationships, relationships in which there is "an agreement between persons who voluntarily obligate and bind themselves to each other for the purpose of fending off an evil or obtaining a good."[71] "Love, friendship, marriage, as well as all social cooperation in business, industry, science, art, and so forth," are all covenantal in that sense, and finally, summarily, religion, "the most richly textured life of human beings," also "bears this character."[72] If religion is the essence of human life and culture, then, naturally, "covenant is the essence of true religion."[73]

Bavinck appears to argue from common consent. One easily gets the impression that he has come to a conclusion regarding the essence of true religion inductively; after gathering data, he concludes that religions have largely agreed that a reciprocal relationship such as a covenantal one is what matters most, and so it would behoove Christian theologians also to invest in this idea.[74] Clearly, however, this is not Bavinck's meaning: "no religion has ever understood." His nephew was if possibly even less conciliatory: "There is no direct uninterrupted path from the darkness of paganism to the light of the gospel."[75]

Rather, his claim is that in Scripture and the history of the church, "'covenant' is the fixed form in which the relation of God to his people is depicted and presented," and that the full scope of the cultural industry of the image-bearer witnesses to the

---

69. Bavinck, *RD*, 2:569–70.
70. Bavinck, *RD*, 2:568.
71. Bavinck, *RD*, 2:568.
72. Bavinck, *RD*, 2:568–9.
73. Bavinck, *RD*, 2:569.
74. For an argument along these lines, see John Bolt, "An Opportunity Lost and Regained: Herman Bavinck on Revelation and Religion," *Mid-America Journal of Theology* 24 (2013): 81–96. Alternatively, see Marinus de Jong, "The Heart of the Academy: Herman Bavinck in Debate with Modernity on the Academy, Theology, and the Church," in *The Kuyper Center Review, Volume Five: Church and Academy*, ed. Gordon Graham (Grand Rapids, MI: Eerdmans, 2015), 66–8; Nathan D. Shannon, "Ontology and Revelation in Bavinck's Stone Lectures," *Scottish Journal of Theology* 73, no. 2 (2020): 112–25.
75. J. H. Bavinck, *ISM*, 136.

basically covenantal makeup of the image-bearing body, mind, and soul. Humans are covenant beings. This claim puts a great deal of pressure on the failures of other religions to account for creaturely communion with God, while it commends by contrast the absolute personalism of the Christian religion. Herman and J. H. Bavinck in this sense make the same argument.

Bavinck says that between God and the creature "there is only difference, distance, endless distinctness," and that "if God remains elevated above humanity in his sovereign exaltedness and majesty, then no religion is possible, at least no religion in the sense of fellowship."[76] Religion without fellowship, as Bavinck has indicated, is a strange imposition on the human creature whose life is variously and multiply covenantal. No satisfaction of the yearning of the soul is on offer in a religion without fellowship. If religion is the gravitational center of human culture and self-understanding, it should satisfy and animate both; religion without fellowship, religious cult tossed into ineffable darkness, undermines rather than satisfies this structure. Furthermore, as J. H. Bavinck has argued, religion without fellowship has sharp recoil. In such cases, says the elder Bavinck, "the image of the potter and the clay is still much too weak to describe that relation because clay has existence—and hence rights—independently of, and over against, the potter, but human beings have nothing and are nothing apart from God."[77] Such a religion fails utterly to engage the human person as such. This fact alone, that a religion without fellowship signals the dehumanization of religion, marks conspicuous discrepancy between religion and "men and women" as "rational and moral beings,"[78] argues Bavinck. Rational and moral "is how God created them, and that therefore is how he treats them."[79] Religion therefore must somehow be a covenant of mutual and personal "I–thou" reciprocity between God and the creature.[80] The God of true religion must be the absolute personal God who initiates a covenant relationship with the creature.

In Bavinck's discussion of this question, toward the close of *Reformed Dogmatics*, in volume 2, *God and Creation*, the notions of covenant and of the

---

76. Bavinck, *RD*, 2:569.

77. Bavinck, *RD*, 2:569.

78. Bavinck, *RD*, 2:570. "If not just one relation but all relations and all sorts of relations of dependence, submission, obedience, friendship, love, and so forth among humans find their model and achieve their fulfillment in religion, then religion must be the character of covenant" (*RD*, 2:569).

79. Bavinck, *RD*, 2. 570. "For the individual man the ethical ideal is that of self-realization ... he must will to will the will of God for the whole world; he must become an ever better king than he already is ... just because man was created with this will, God wants men to develop this will" (Van Til, *CTE*, 45).

80. "For that reason it [religion] must by its very nature take the shape of a covenant in which God acts, not coercively, but with counsel, admonition, warning, invitation, petition, and in which humans serve God, not under duress or violence, but willingly, by their own free consent, moved by love to love in return" (Bavinck, *RD*, 2:570–1).

personal condescension of God are interchangeable; Bavinck's point there is to emphasize this identification. Where, for J. H. Bavinck, religion is impossible without the equal ultimacy of absoluteness and personality, in the same way, for Herman Bavinck, religion is impossible apart from the personal relationship that constitutes the religious center of human culture and self-understanding—namely, covenant. In this sense, for both Bavincks, for neo-Calvinism in fact, the absolute personality of the Christian God is theism come into its own; covenant is religion come into its own; and the revealed Christian religion the subversive fulfillment of false religions as such.[81]

> For then God has to come down from his lofty position, condescend to his creatures, impart, reveal, and give himself away to human beings; then he who inhabits eternity and dwells in a high and holy place must also dwell with those who are of a humble spirit (Isa. 57:15). But this set of conditions is nothing other than the description of a covenant. ... Scripture insists on both: God is infinitely great and condescendingly good; he is Sovereign but also Father; he is Creator but also Prototype. In a word, he is the God of the covenant.[82]

Some five hundred pages prior, at the opening of *God and Creation*, a closely related discussion unfolds. There Bavinck addresses the difficulty of religious fellowship, putting it in terms of the incomprehensibility of God: "the moment we dare to speak about God the question arises: How can we?"[83] He rehearses the challenge of the "ontological distance" between God and the creature, the infinite

---

81. "Subversive fulfillment" is Daniel Strange's term, for which he credits missiologists Hendrik Kraemer and J. H. Bavinck. See Daniel Strange, *Their Rock Is Not Like Our Rock: A Theology of Religions* (Grand Rapids, MI: Zondervan, 2014).

82. Bavinck, *RD*, 2:569, 570. And Vos: "He is the God of the covenant, and it is intrinsic to His being that He wants to be" (Vos, *RD*, 2:32).

83. Bavinck, *RD*, 2:30. The coordination of knowledge and relationship is found through the relevant primary sources. Well known is this statement from Vos:

> A second ground for the historic character of revelation may be found in its eminently practical aspect. The knowledge of God communicated by it is nowhere for a purely intellectual purpose. From beginning to end it is a knowledge intended to enter into the actual life of man, to be worked out by him in all its practical bearings. The Shemitic, and in particular the Biblical, conception of knowledge is distinguished from the Greek, more intellectualistic idea, by the prominence of this practical element. To know, in the Shemitic sense, is to have the consciousness of the reality and the properties of something interwoven with one's life through the closest intercourse and communion attainable. (Vos, *RHBI*, 10)

Although the connections are complex, evident here is the interdependence of Reformed absolute personalism, covenant theology, the historicity of revelation, and biblical theology as Vos undertook it.

and the finite, "between the All and the nothing," noting that despite mystery and conceptual clash, "in Scripture ... the knowability of God is never in doubt even for a moment."[84]

"Outside the domain of this special revelation," in both "religious and philosophical systems the unity of the personality and absoluteness of God is broken."[85] Bavinck appears to find greater candor in the latter, in philosophical reflection, than in the former. "Knowledge of the absolute," say the philosophers, "is a contradiction in terms."[86] Outside of Scripture, the "insoluble antinomy" between absoluteness and personality, between the ineffable and the knowable, presents nothing but "the choice between gross realism and vacuous idealism, between a God who is nothing but an enlarged version of a human person and a cold abstraction that freezes and destroys the religion of the heart."[87] The philosophers have come to frank realization that absoluteness and personality are mutually repellent, and that one may have either deity or religion but not both, whereas religions appear less interested in conceding defeat before that dim dilemma. Vos notices the same self-awareness in modern thought specifically: "Almost the whole of modern philosophy claims," he says, that "infinity and personal existence exclude each other."[88] And yet, says Bavinck, "thanks to that revelation" which we have in Scripture "it is certain, first of all, that God is a person."[89] Christian theology, Bavinck explains, trades contradiction for mystery.[90]

---

84. Bavinck, *RD*, 2:30.

85. Bavinck, *RD*, 2:34.

86. Bavinck, *RD*, 2:47. "Man cannot think an absolute self-contained being; that is, he cannot have a concept of it in the ordinary sense of the term. God is infinitely higher than the highest being of which man can form a concept" (Van Til, *IST*, 328).

87. Bavinck, *RD*, 2:47.

88. Vos, *RD*, 1:15. Also: "It is an indisputable fact that all modern views of revelation which are deficient in recognizing its objective character, fit far better into a pantheistic than into a theistic theory of the universe" (Vos, *RHBI*, 19). Van Til says:

> In the literature that deals with the problem of creation at all, such phrases as 'the nature of thought' and 'the nature of reality' recur again and again. The assumption of such statements is that *all* thought and *all* reality, whether divine or human, is subject to the same laws and limitations. Whether or not God can be personal is determined, for example, by asking whether thought, that is thought *per se*, can allow for the conception of absolute personality. That God cannot be absolute is sometimes deduced from the 'fact' that all thought is relative. The only thing really known is that human thought is relative, but the assumption is made that divine thought must be also. (Van Til and Berkhof, *Foundations of Christian Education*, 47)

89. Bavinck, *RD*, 2:30.

90. Bavinck distances himself first, immediately upon the opening of the volume, from Rome: "Mystery is the lifeblood of dogmatics. To be sure, the term 'mystery' (*mysterion*) in Scripture does not mean an abstract supernatural truth in the Roman Catholic sense" (*RD*, 2:29). And then from philosophical contradiction: "But mystery and self-contradiction

The theme here is captured in Bavinck's well-known opening statement: "Mystery is the lifeblood of dogmatics."[91] The reason for this is simple: "It is all mystery with which the science of dogmatics is concerned, for it does not deal with finite creatures, but from beginning to end looks past all creatures and focuses on the eternal and infinite One himself."[92] So the problem of the knowability of God is predicated on the absolute nature of deity.

Bavinck will make essentially two points about this here in this section. The first is that dogmatics is always worked out against a background of the infinity of the divine being. Dogmatics defines nothing; it only describes that of the infinite that has been rendered knowable for the creature.[93] Bavinck, furthermore, has either a reductionistic view of theology or an expansive view of the reach of the doctrine of God. The backdrop of the infinite being of God is not limited to the doctrines of God and Trinity but characterizes all of dogmatic theology as likewise unfolding at the threshold of ineffability. In this sense, dogmatics may be said to be nothing other than the science of God. He makes this point forcefully:

> The knowledge of God is the only dogma, the exclusive content, of the entire field of dogmatics. All the doctrines treat in dogmatics—whether they concern the universe, humanity, Christ, and so forth—are but the explication of the one central dogma of the knowledge of God. All things are considered in light of God, subsumed under him, traced back to him as the starting point. Dogmatics is always called upon to ponder and describe God and God alone. ... It is the knowledge of him alone that dogmatics must put on display.[94]

Notable especially for present purposes is the fact that Bavinck's theocentricism is not the latest methodological theory nor a philosophical habit Bavinck picked up at university; rather, he positions the dogmatic calling covenantally. Bavinck insists that dogmatic knowledge of God is covenant historical, even eschatological: "The knowledge of God-in-Christ, after all, is life itself."[95] This is the closest possible

---

are not synonymous" (*RD*, 2:49). On Bavinck's view of mystery, see Eglinton, *Trinity and Organism*, 95–100. On contradiction versus mystery, apparent contradiction, and limiting concepts, see Van Til, *CGG*, 15–19.

91. Bavinck, *RD*, 2:29.

92. Bavinck, *RD*, 2:29.

93. "We cannot give a definition of God but only a *description*" (Vos, *RD*, 1:2). Emphasis original.

94. Bavinck, *RD*, 2:29.

95. Bavinck, *RD*, 2:29. "Christ," being a mediatorial designation, indicates that Bavinck understands the task and nature of dogmatics historically. Dogmatics would have been undertaken differently had there been no fall; it is here and now the business of the post-apostolate regenerate Christian, who knows the name of Christ and whose citizenship lies in the eschatological country; and it will be different in the new heavens and the earth. "Life itself" refers to the covenant of life not only as it was presented in the Garden of Eden but also as the covenant structure remains in place until consummation.

association of dogmatics with practical religion, and of religious fellowship with the covenant structure of human history. The similarity with Vos on the personalist rationale for the structure of revelation is striking, and the similarity with Van Til on the matter of epistemological theocentrism is equally noteworthy.

The second point is this: the absolute personalism of the Bible is the subversive fulfillment of this "antinomy." "Agnosticism ... sees here an irresolvable contradiction in what Christian theology regards as an adorable mystery."[96] It is a mystery that "cannot be comprehended; it can only be gratefully acknowledged."[97]

After having introduced the role of mystery in dogmatics, Bavinck turns to the question of the knowability of the absolute, as noted above. He turns immediately to Scripture, where "the knowability of God is never in doubt even for a moment," and in which the "personality of God is so prominent everywhere that the question may arise whether by it oneness, spirituality, and infinity are not being shortchanged."[98]

But it is not the coincidental, haphazard, or boldfaced juxtaposition of two irreconcilable themes which distinguishes the Christian Bible. Countless religions and philosophies are reviewed in these opening pages of *God and Creation*, which also present the concurrence of absoluteness and personality without resolution of the natural tension between them. And as Bavinck has said, comprehension is not on offer. What distinguishes Scripture is that its very nature as authoritative revelation expresses the irreducible union of absoluteness and personality in the being of its primary author. Scripture is not another human attempt at forcing the cooperation of the round peg and the square hole; it is the self-giving of the absolute God and as such properly designated "revelation" and the actualization of the knowability of God.

Bavinck says that "the question concerning God's knowability has been reduced to another question, namely, whether God has willed and found a way to reveal himself in the domain of creatures."[99] The knowability of God is deferred to native capacity for self-revelation in the being of God—to personality comingling with absoluteness. He continues: "Then, however, it is also self-evident that the denial of the knowability of God coincides completely with the denial that God has revealed himself in the works of his hands."[100]

An interesting comparison may be made with an essay by Edmond La Beaume Cherbonnier, "The Logic of Biblical Anthropomorphism."[101] Like J. H. Bavinck a scholar of religion, Cherbonnier, who founded the religion department at Trinity College in Hartford, Connecticut, pits the anthropomorphic god of Scripture

---

96. Bavinck, *RD*, 2:49.
97. Bavinck, *RD*, 2:49.
98. Bavinck, *RD*, 2:30.
99. Bavinck, *RD*, 2:50.
100. Bavinck, *RD*, 2:50.
101. E. LaB. Cherbonnier, "The Logic of Biblical Anthropomorphism," *Harvard Theological Review* 55, no. 3 (1962): 187–206.

against the ineffable god of mystical religion. The "God of the Bible," he points out, "is quite as anthropomorphic as any in the Greek and Roman pantheon."[102] The prophets never faulted the false gods for anthropomorphism but for ineffectiveness, for their inability to act: "The gods of Canaan and Babylon were at least good imitations. The prophets do not charge them with being anthropomorphic, but with being frauds."[103] "You are a God of seeing," announced Hagar.[104] Of Isaiah 46, Cherbonnier writes:

> The intent of such passages is to distinguish Yahweh from idols by precisely these anthropomorphic activities: "They have mouths, but do not speak; eyes, but do not see; they have ears, but do not hear; noses, but do not smell" (Ps. 115:5, 6). Pagan gods are contemptible because of their impotence. They cannot even do the things a man can do, whereas Yahweh does these things *par excellence*.[105]

Theism requires divine capacity to act: "For the Bible, to say that God is unlimited is simply to say that with God, all things are possible—even creation. This is the difference between monism and monotheism."[106] Cherbonnier argues, therefore, that "only an anthropomorphic God can be omnipotent"[107] and that it is the concrete identity of a personal God which makes true religion possible and defines theological truth over against culpable religious creativity. The false piety of the mystics, which affirms endlessly the ineffability of god, has no defense against an abundant polymorphism such as that found in Hinduism.

Evidently, Cherbonnier observed much the same religious phenomenon as J. H. Bavinck had observed, and as Herman Bavinck had observed in modern philosophy: an irresolvable tension between absoluteness and personality. "Since each concept of God," the mystical and the anthropomorphic, "presupposes a corresponding philosophy, each with an inner logic of its own, such confusion may be expected to issue in logical inconsistencies."[108] Cherbonnier, however, devoted all his resources to defending personalism as such. It is not clear from his argumentation to what extent he wished to personalize our understanding of the absolute God. He systematically casts suspicion on the incommunicable attributes and the language of transcendence; he denies a distinction between God revealed and God as he is in himself; and makes no mention of the Trinity.[109] In other

---

102. Cherbonnier, "Logic of Biblical Anthropomorphism," 187.

103. Cherbonnier, "Logic of Biblical Anthropomorphism," 192.

104. The Hebrew is: וַתִּקְרָא שֵׁם־יְהֹוָה הַדֹּבֵר אֵלֶיהָ אַתָּה אֵל רֳאִי. The King James Version reads: "And she called the name of the LORD that spake unto her, 'Thou God seest me.'"

105. Cherbonnier, "Logic of Biblical Anthropomorphism," 192.

106. Cherbonnier, "Logic of Biblical Anthropomorphism," 195.

107. Cherbonnier, "Logic of Biblical Anthropomorphism," 193.

108. Cherbonnier, "Logic of Biblical Anthropomorphism," 203.

109. There is no mention of the Trinity in this article or in his chapter "In Defense of Anthropomorphism," in which he argues that "neither Jews, nor Mormons, nor other Christians need be embarrassed by the idea that God is a Person." Edmond LaB.

words, Cherbonnier sees the tension between absoluteness and personalism and simply sides with personalism. The divine personality is not to be thought of in terms of the absoluteness of classical articulation.

For the neo-Calvinist, on the other hand, the solution to the knowability of the absolute God is absolute personality, the absoluteness of God's personality and the personality of his self-originate nature. So that, he says, to deny the knowability of God is to deny the fact of revelation. The point to notice is that for Bavinck revelation is necessarily a personal act. Only a person is able to self-reveal; an impersonal absolute is mute and still and so can only be known univocally, which is not at all. Unless God is absolute person, there is no divine revelation and the word "God" is only the residue of a cognitive miswiring by name of religion.

"Rightly considered," absolute personality is simple: "all it means is that God's self-consciousness is equally deep and rich, equally infinite, as his being."[110] Absoluteness and personality, if they are equally ultimate or coterminous in this sense, must be treated as mutually explicatory. It is the personal fullness that God enjoys within his own being that constitutes his absoluteness. All humans, by contrast, are persons derivatively and correlatively; the personality of God is wholly self-referential and self-sufficient. His ontological independence is his personal independence. "In the case of God personality is and can therefore be the eternal synthesis of himself with himself, infinite self-knowledge and self-determination, and therefore not dependent on a nonself."[111] Van Til puts it this way: "God is self-determinatively internally active. God is the self-predicator. God is life in himself. And because he is thus life and internal activity, the God of Christianity ... could become the self-contained source of the created universe."[112]

Opportunity to revisit this material returns in Chapter 4. For present purposes, note should be taken of the confluence of a number of themes in Bavinck's treatment of these questions—specifically, two pairs which serve as bookends to *Reformed Dogmatics*, volume 2. The first is absolute personality and the knowledge of God, the former serving as the necessary precondition of the latter. The absolute is knowable because the absolute is personal.[113] It should be noted that Bavinck's absolute personalism is self-consciously unfriendly to Hegelian process ontology

---

Cherbonnier, "In Defense of Anthropomorphism," in *Reflections on Mormonism: Judaeo-Christian Parallels*, ed. Truman G. Madsen (Provo, UT: Religious Studies Center, Brigham Young University, 1978), 174.

110. Bavinck, *RD*, 2:49.
111. Bavinck, *RD*, 2:49–50.
112. Van Til, *IST*, 336.
113. Vos makes precisely this point with reference to the objectivity of revelation. Precisely because God is "conscious and personal," revelation is objective and does not "in a mysterious manner loom up from the inexplorable regions that underlie human consciousness." Implications for biblical hermeneutics begin to emerge: "The revelation of God being not subjective and individual in its nature, but objective and addressed to the human race as a whole, it is but natural that this revelation should be embedded in the

and monism.[114] The primary distinguishing notion is the Creator–creature distinction of which Bavinck often speaks under the doctrine or the idea of creation. This pairing of absolute personality and the knowledge of God, as resolution of the antinomy of the personalism of religious communion and the absoluteness of deity, dominates the first twenty pages of Bavinck's *God and Creation*. The second pair is Bavinck's defense of the doctrine of the covenant of works, reviewed above only briefly, which appears in the final pages of the penultimate topic of the same volume. Bavinck insists on the importance of the doctrine and on the cost for biblical religion of understating its importance. "This richly valuable idea of Scripture has not always come into its own in Christian theology," but now "we must completely set aside the fragmentary development of this doctrine."[115] When Bavinck describes the God of the Bible as "the God of the covenant," he indicates just how profound he takes the notion of covenant to penetrate and permeate the Christian religion and worldview.

This pairing of absolute personality and covenant as the fabric, the relational bedrock, of true religion, brings to the foreground a major component of the neo-Calvinist doctrine of God: that in a sense and to an extent unmatched elsewhere, in this tradition the absolute God is not merely the cause or the source or the foundation but is himself the environment of human self-understanding. In everything that we do we have always to do with the *ad extra* self-expression of the self-predicating triune God of the Bible.

Covenant and History

The editors of the English translation of Bavinck's *Reformed Dogmatics* insert a subtitle, "Reformed and Other Views of Human Destiny," when in his discussion of the covenant of works, Bavinck turns to engage Roman Catholic and Lutheran views of prelapsarian Adam. This insertion gives the impression that constructive reflection on the doctrine of the covenant of works is settled, and that Bavinck at that point turns to compare, contrast, and defend, but no longer develop, his view of the first covenant.

Rome indeed enters for critical treatment here, and Lutheranism, too; but Bavinck's aim remains basically constructive, and in fact it is on the heels of this brief clash with Rome, which opens this section that he draws out the broader implications of the covenant of works. It is in fact possible, as shall be demonstrated presently, that the subtext of this particular section signals a noteworthy advance of the notion of covenant and an expansion of the dimensions of its theological import. Bavinck's attention in these pages is indeed given to a

---

channels of the great objective history of redemption and extend no further than this." Vos, "The Idea of Biblical Theology as a Science and as a Discipline," in *RHBI*, 19, 8.

114. See Tseng, *G. W. F. Hegel*, 69–128.

115. Bavinck, *RD*, 2:565, 571.

comparative exercise, but the driving, if inconspicuous, theme is the teleological fabric of human experience—not only "human destiny" itself, and what various traditions have made of that destiny as it is presented primordially in Genesis 2, but the theological implications of there being a destiny at all. Bavinck draws attention to a covenant eschatological backdrop, to a theology of history, which human experience always expresses. Put more directly: here Bavinck at the very least suggests a strong relationship between the absolute personality of the God of covenant religion and the historicity of creaturely experience.

A view of the context is in order. Preceding this discussion of Roman Catholic and Lutheran views, Bavinck's exposition and defense of the covenant of works includes a three-part defense of the claim that "covenant is the essence of true religion."[116] Naturally, each of these three parts serves the same purpose, that of introducing true religion and covenant as mutually explanatory notions. Several ideas coalesce, therefore, including absolute deity and absolute personalism, and a divine condescension that results in a reciprocal relationship between the absolute God and the creature, a relationship known as "religion."

Bavinck notes first that since "God is the Creator" and "man a creature," there is "an infinite distance between the two," and of the nature of the case "no fellowship" and thus "no religion between the two seems possible."[117] Bavinck basically argues here that if God is God, and man a creature, this ontology in itself renders fellowship, religion, and any meaningful relationship with or creaturely knowledge of God impossible. This is a familiar argument at this point, but here Bavinck is not thinking exclusively about the distinctiveness of Christianity among the religions—of the church between the temple and the mosque, as J. H. Bavinck has said. What holds his attention is a problem with impressive historical pedigree (it dates at least to the Greeks) that now constitutes the singular modern problem for dogmatic theology—namely, the knowability of the absolute.

Bruce McCormack puts the modern problem this way:

> The question of whether and how God is known stood at the heart of theological reflection in the modern period. The problem had been created by the coincidence of two developments: the rise of biblical criticism with its concomitant distinction of revelation from the Bible and the much celebrated "turn to the subject" which occurred in philosophy from Descartes through Kant. It was, above all, Kant's limitation of theoretical knowing to the intuitable which made knowledge of God so deeply problematic to modern theologians. For if God is a transcendent, wholly spiritual being as the Christian tradition maintained, then God is unintuitable and—if Kant's restriction holds—cannot be known. Moreover, Kant had also shown that the attempt made by traditional metaphysics to overcome this limitation resulted invariably in antinomies. The

---

116. Bavinck, *RD*, 2:569.
117. Bavinck, *RD*, 2:569.

result was that Kant reduced God to a regulative idea wholly lacking in content; a postulated Guarantor of the meaningfulness of moral behavior.[118]

It is important to keep the modern problem in view because it constitutes not a distant historical curiosity, nor a pet issue for academics, but an enduring problem for Christian self-understanding, for the very possibility and definition of theological knowledge, which had reached crisis level in the late modern era.[119] Neither Bavinck's articulation of this modern problem, nor—much less—his ways of responding to it should be taken lightly. Arguably, to allow this particularly modern issue to recede into the background would constitute a promising prelude to misreading Bavinck and to overlooking his creative side. To date, Bavinck scholarship appears to suffer somewhat from an oversight of precisely this kind.[120]

And Bavinck responds as follows. In order for there to be any relation of any kind between the Creator and the creature, "God has to come down from his lofty position, condescend to his creatures, impart, reveal, and give himself away to human beings."[121] It cannot be that Bavinck responds off the cuff, with pious, theoretically naïve platitudes, to the singular theological problem of the age. He must mean what he says; and it would appear that what he says is this: the transcendental condition for human experience as we know it and for the satisfaction of the religious yearning of the human soul is a voluntary condescension of the absolute God, beyond or without regard for the traditional logic of the absoluteness of his being, to establish a relation, that is also a relationship, which may on account of the immanence of the divine personality issue into meaningful religious knowledge

---

118. Bruce L. McCormack, "Revelation and History in Transfoundationalist Perspective: Karl Barth's Theological Epistemology in Conversation with a Schleiermacherian Tradition," *Journal of Religion* 78 (1998): 20–1. In this article, McCormack's goal is "to interpret Barth as a nineteenth-century theologian," by which he means that he will "contend that the wealth of problems to which Barth addressed himself were, in many cases, given their characteristic shape as a result of nineteenth-century developments and that even his solutions to those problems often took up elements of nineteenth-century solutions and transformed them by placing them in a different framework of thought" (pp. 19, 20). Much the same would appear to be true of Herman Bavinck, Geerhardus Vos, and Cornelius Van Til.

119. George Harinck's observations are helpful: "The modernism Abraham Kuyper and Herman Bavinck are said to have rejected does not concern the practice but the program of some of the modernists: the emancipation from the pre-modern worldview and the implementation of the worldview of the French revolution, with at its core the rejection not just of the church, but of God and religion." George Harinck, "The Religious Character of Modernism and the Modern Character of Religion: A Case Study of Herman Bavinck's Engagement with Modern Culture," *Scottish Bulletin of Evangelical Theology* 29 (2011): 62.

120. See Bruce R. Pass, *The Heart of Dogmatics: Christology and Christocentrism in Herman Bavinck* (Göttingen: Vandenhoeck & Ruprecht, 2020), on the modern question.

121. Bavinck, *RD*, 2:569.

and experience, so that from this original religious self-understanding creaturely relations of all kinds—creature to creature relationships—may take shape. That is: *God moves*, and then human experience. Thus for Bavinck, the uncompelled movement of the absolute God to establish a religious relationship with his image-bearer is the initiation of creaturely experience as such—religious, cultural, and moral; it is the unifying center, source, and beginning of human culture and subjective self-consciousness.

One notes also that the problem as Bavinck presents it here—the impossibility of fellowship between an absolute God and the finite creature—is hypothetical or illustrative. Bavinck does not in fact believe that such a state of affairs, one in which there is an absolute God and a finite creature and as of yet no relationship between them, does or could obtain. The question of a relationship between the infinite and the finite is not "how might it come about?" or "what must God do to reach out to his creature?" Rather, the relational question is a transcendental one that inquires as to the precondition of asking the question in the first place. "Creation awaits the relational condescension of God" is incoherent because creation is constituted by divine relational initiative. In this sense, theological reflection on the nature and possibility of a Creator–creature relationship is reflection upon the precondition and possibility of such reflection.[122] The relation already obtains, or the question is impossible. As was demonstrated previously, in terms of the moral law, there is no pre-theistic context for creaturely self-understanding. The image-bearer's thoughts and his world are exhaustively theological, or theologico-personal.

The second component of his argument focuses on this religious relationship and the rights enjoyed by the creature within it. A creature, by the nature of the case, has no rights before God—no merit, no access, no recourse. "When we have done everything we have been instructed to do, we are still unworthy servants (*douloi achreioi*, Luke 17:10)."[123] He emphasizes the fact that the possibility of a higher level of blessedness is granted, though uncompelled and unexpected, by God, who "in his condescending goodness gives rights to his creatures."[124] "Every creaturely right is a given benefit, a gift of grace, undeserved and nonobligatory."[125] Bavinck here speaks, evidently, of the covenant of works.

It may be noted that this bestowal of rights presupposes the self-consciousness of the creature. It is as though the creature exists and, though self-conscious, is unaware of the God of his origin until God "in his condescending goodness" installs a morally charged relationship between himself and the creature. But

---

122. Van Til says: "By this rejection of God, agnosticism has embraced complete relativism. Yet this relativism must furnish a basis for the rejection of the absolute. Accordingly, the standard of self-contradiction taken for granted by antitheistic thought presupposes the absolute for its operation. Antitheism presupposes theism. One must stand upon the solid ground of theism to be an effective antitheist" (Van Til, *SCE*, xi).

123. Bavinck, *RD*, 2:570.

124. Bavinck, *RD*, 2:570.

125. Bavinck, *RD*, 2:570.

Bavinck affirms no such thing, that a non-theistic self-consciousness preceded the covenant of works. This second point regarding "rights enjoyed by the creature," it should be noted, follows upon the first in which, prior to the moral question, the ontological question is addressed, where Bavinck says that there is no God to think or speak of, until God comes down. But with such words Bavinck is not recounting a course of events, as though there were men able to speak and think of many things but unable to think or speak of God, and who were capable of thriving while in the place of religion there was only silence. Bavinck's account of the covenant of works is not a sequential history, but an account of the present and of the creature's ability, as it is now observed, and the creature's desire, as it is now experienced, to inquire as to his origins and the reason for his being the way that he is. Bavinck's point is, first, that in him—in God condescended—human creatures live and move, and that, second, God has formalized the covenant relationship by covenanting (committing) to count as righteous Adam's obedience and to identify Adam's destiny in terms of relational consummation. The enduing potential obedience relative to the tree of the knowledge of good and evil with life-earning merit is the primary and definitive instance of graciously bestowed legal and moral importance in the face of the absolute God condescended. And the establishment of a destiny consisting of an increase of life by perfected communion with God is the primary and definitive instance of graciously bestowed eschatology—a historical covenant relationship with the absolute God. Here, then, is the natural moral situation fulfilled not necessarily in the special or positive covenant stipulations, a fulfillment—as Vos has said—which follows not temporally but logically upon the first establishment of creaturely self-consciousness. Bavinck summarizes:

> The covenant is rooted in a free, special, and gracious dispensation of God. It proceeds from God and he decrees all the parts of it: condition and fulfillment, compliance and reward, transgression and punishment. It is monopleuric (unilateral) in origin, and it is added to the creation in God's image. The covenant of works, accordingly, does justice to both the sovereignty of God—which implies the dependency of creatures and the nonmeritoriousness of all their works—and to the grace and generosity of God, who nevertheless wants to give the creature a higher-than-earthly blessedness.[126]

The covenant relationship "maintains both the dependence" of the image-bearer upon the absolute God, "as well as the freedom of mankind," because God has expressed himself as moral norm for the creature and has thus constituted the image-bearer a creature morally self-directed and morally accountable to the self-sufficient all-determining personal God.[127]

In Bavinck's brief explanation of the rights enjoyed by the creature, two themes appear, intertwined but distinguishable. The first is relationship. On account of

---

126. Bavinck, *RD*, 2:572.
127. Bavinck, *RD*, 2:572.

God's "condescending goodness," human beings "have the freedom to come to him with prayer and thanksgiving, to address him as 'Father,' to take refuge in him in all circumstances of distress and death, to desire all good things from him."[128] The image-bearer looks toward God in self-conscious dependence upon him, such that a graciously established relationship with God signals a natural right to have one's case heard before the judicial seat of the Creator. The image-bearer enjoys a right of appeal or of covenant recourse to the uncompelled self-giving of God as the supreme object of human devotion and concern. Concerning the course of events in the world, the creature bears within his very self-consciousness, by a creative grace of God, an instinct to appeal to the world's maker and supreme governor, and the derivative self-importance to go with it. This is the religious relationship at the seat and center of human culture and self-understanding, established by the covenant condescension of God, and it is what the image-bearer will take to be his nature and natural environment. As noted previously, this entire situation trembles with the subtle angst of moral mutability. So the natural situation harkens toward the published covenant. Bavinck says that "there *is* no natural connection here between work and reward."[129] And a few pages later, he writes:

> The probationary command relates to the moral law as the covenant of works relates to man's creation in God's image. The moral law stands or falls in its entirety with the probationary command, and the image of God in mankind in its entirety stands or falls with the covenant of works. The covenant of works is the road to heavenly blessedness for the [first] human beings, who were created in God's image and had not yet fallen.[130]

Accordingly, the second theme appearing in Bavinck's discussion of the rights enjoyed by the creature in covenant with God is eschatological reward, or relational consummation as historical end. In this sense, in addition to divine covenant condescension as the foundation of creaturely self-consciousness as such, a primary or summative right is graciously granted in Gen. 2:17 as the first public covenant recognition of the lowly image-bearer. Here, against the backdrop of covenant self-consciousness a right of moral importance before God is bestowed upon the creature and now illuminated and amplified with, indeed promoted to, eschatological influence.

The moral law of itself, as the religious fabric of creature consciousness, independent of the covenant prohibition of Gen. 2:17, indicates no relationship beyond an unqualified obligation to obedience. Apart from the special command and the placing of the two trees in the midst of the garden, perfect obedience earns nothing before God; it is nothing more than the ethico-religious state of nature—but this situation knows its own provisionality. It yearns for completion

---

128. Bavinck, *RD*, 2:570.
129. Bavinck, *RD*, 2:571.
130. Bavinck, *RD*, 2:572.

and is subsequently but not necessarily guided toward the settled eschatology offered in the tree of life. By establishment or publication of the covenant of works God answers to no creaturely right or objective obligation but freely draws the creature and his moral environment into a relational eschatology constituted by a contingency focused entirely on the creature's response to a peculiar and conspicuous intrusion of divine rule. A contingency suspended between meritorious obedience and the mutability of original righteousness is conveyed to Adam not by one tree alone, but by two. Destiny here, that indicated by the tree of life, moves quietly toward the foreground of Adam's experience. Not the singularity or sameness of eschatology, in a universalistic or deterministic sense, but the unity of the fact of eschatology—that a destiny of all image-bearers is determined in the same covenant eschatological framework—emerges here as Bavinck's deepest conception of covenant religion. Covenant is history with a definite terminus. The unchanging God has condescended to make himself the singular moral absolute that will, in the course of history, divide fathers and sons. Bavinck says:

> For religion, like the moral law and the destiny of man, is one. The covenant of works and the covenant of grace do not differ in their final goal but only in the way that leads to it. In both there is one mediator: then, a mediator of union; now, a mediator of reconciliation. In both there is one faith: then, faith in God; now, faith in God through Christ; and in both covenant there is one hope, one love, and forth. Religion is always the same in essence.[131]

The point here is that covenant condescension is for Bavinck the theological explanation for creaturely experience as such. The unity of the Creator–creature relation affirmed in this quotation, and here described as permeating redemptive history, already indicates that. If this statement gives the impression that Bavinck has in mind not creaturely experience undifferentiated but only the positive religious experience of grace as it relates to original righteousness, it needs to be stated only that since Bavinck is no universalist; the covenant of grace is for him intelligible only as implemented and unfolding against the backdrop of sin and condemnation. Grace is a principle of division. Looking at it another way, when Bavinck says that the covenant of works and the covenant of grace have the same goal, he makes a soteriological statement, namely, that the same destiny that was offered in the covenant of works—and subsequently lost—is offered still, and secured for the church, in the covenant of grace. His focus is soteriology; but what he actually says is that the human race is corporately and singularly figured under the same covenant arrangement that was introduced in the garden, and will be divided according to that arrangement when history reaches its goal.[132]

---

131. Bavinck, *RD*, 2:570.

132. Then Bavinck emphasizes, this time not against Rome but against Lutheranism, the fulfillment of Edenic eschatology by Christ the second Adam. Bavinck draws attention to the "beautiful thought" that Christ does not return himself or others to the contingency of Adam's original state but instead he recovers the eschatological opportunity squandered in

So the covenant of works, in which obedience is meritorious, is a non-necessary completion and realization, a fulfillment without remainder, of human life as rational and moral. That is, all human rationality and morality are by a pre-redemptive grace of God directed toward obediential, covenant assessment before the face of God. Adam in this sense, standing before the tree of the knowledge of good and evil, and looking beyond it to the tree of life, in the full rational and moral character of his constitution, bears the whole of historical contingency before the adjudication of God. He is at that moment the eschatological man, who lives and moves in the mutual implication of historicity and covenant religion: the covenant relationship is historical, and human history as such is this covenant relationship with the absolute God.

For this reason, throughout this discussion of differing views of human destiny, Bavinck repeatedly draws attention to suspended teleology, to the fact that "Adam did not yet enjoy the highest level of blessedness."[133] The idea of destiny or of a historical point of arrival retroactively characterizes Adam's conduct with reference to that goal. Adam's words and deeds will be understood and evaluated in terms of progress toward the goal to which he is called. Adam's religion and his status before God—the state not of a relation but of a relation that is also a relationship—is figured historically.

The third component of Bavinck's argument for the covenant of works explores the manner of God's interaction with the human creature as this manner is implied in the design of the creature. Moral mutability and the kindly endowment of the meritoriousness of obedience do not modify but engage the human creature. There is, in other words, a profound consonance between the demands of the covenant and the manner of Creator–creature "reciprocal fidelity," on the one hand, and the constitution of the human creature, on the other. The covenant relationship is designed for human beings, and human beings for the covenant relationship:

> Religion is freedom … it must by its very nature take the shape of a covenant in which God acts, not coercively, but with counsel, admonition, warning, invitation, petition, and in which humans serve God, not under duress or violence, but willingly, by their own free consent, moved by love to love in return.[134]

---

the garden in order to acquire—to earn, passively and actively—the offer of eternal life first announced in the garden. Negatively stated, in Bavinck's view, the scope and magnificence of neither the objective work of Christ nor its subjective enjoyment are appreciated without taking account of the continuity between the first and second Adam.

133. Bavinck, *RD*, 2:576. "Still, everyone acknowledges that Adam did not yet possess the highest humanity, a truth implicit in the probationary command, the freedom of choice, the possibility of sin and death" (*RD*, 2:566).

134. Bavinck, *RD*, 2:570–1.

Again, when Bavinck explains religious fellowship in terms of covenant, he is not retracing sequential history. Religious fellowship is not supplementary to human self-consciousness but precedes it. Human self-consciousness as such is constituted by an awareness of divine relational immanence, by the personal fabric of experience. Van Til calls this covenant-consciousness.[135] Historically speaking, Adam's moral mutability hearkens as it were toward resolution, looks to God for permanence, and meets in the covenant of works the eschatological relational promise that by nature he longs for. The contingency of original righteousness, "this being changeably good, this being able to sin and die," did not belong essentially to the image of God. Bavinck characterizes original moral mutability as the "boundary," "limitation," and "circumference" of the image of God; it was in that sense a restraint that God imposed upon Adam in order to engage his full rational and moral capacity for a relational consummation that would entail the personal self-realization of the image-bearer as such.[136] The covenant relation, in other words, is not designed for the human creature, as though the relationship were devised after humans walked the earth, but the human creature is designed for the covenant relationship in which personal obedience would be the summative virtue. Nathaniel Gray Sutanto summarizes:

> For Bavinck, the covenant is central in defining the Creator-creature relationship. A covenant preserves this relationship in such a way that God's transcendence is uncompromised even while human beings have genuine moral freedom. A relationship between Creator and creature presupposes the condescension of the former to grant obligations and rights to the latter. Only in the establishment and fulfillment of a covenant can religion begin and flourish.[137]

This shines a rather different light on Vos's statement that the "Shemitic and Biblical idea" of knowledge is "to have the reality of something practically interwoven with the inner experience of life," and that "because God desires to be *known* after this fashion, he has caused His revelation to take place in the milieu of the historical life of a people."[138] Vos's idea of biblical theology is to study the personal self-objectification of God in redemptive-revelatory acts in history, those historical acts of God that are subsequently recorded in Scripture. For Vos, personality and the objectivity of revelation are mutually implicatory notions: "If … God be conscious and personal, the inference is that in His self-disclosure He will assert and maintain His personality, so as to place His divine thoughts before us with the stamp of divinity upon them, in a truly objective manner."[139]

---

135. See also J. H. Bavinck's work on religious consciousness in *J. H. Bavinck Reader*, 114–299; J. H. Bavinck, *CBTM*, 25–113.
136. On this idea of self-realization, see Van Til, *CTE*, 45–6.
137. Sutanto, "Herman Bavinck on the Image of God," 184.
138. Vos, *BT*, 8.
139. Vos, *RHBI*, 19.

Vos believes that special revelation is simply relational, eschatological self-objectification of God for man, of the God whom man always already knows in his inner experience. God does not become personal for the sake of covenant. "He is the God of the covenant," Vos says, "and it is intrinsic to His being that He wants to be."[140] And although covenant is somehow "intrinsic to His being," Vos attributes the covenant of works to "something positive, a special condescension of God."[141]

Vos sees his approach to biblical theology as a higher development of Reformed covenant theology, as closing the circle, one might say, between covenant, history, and revelation.[142] In this sense, yet again, absolute personalism drives a neo-Calvinist modern orthodoxy. Richard Lints summarizes Vos's intentions as follows: "Biblical theology," as Vos undertook it,

> was the study of the actual self-disclosures of God in time and space prior to the first committal to writing of the biblical documents, and which for a long time continued to run alongside of the inscripturation of the revealed material. In this sense, biblical theology attempts to understand the redemptive and revelatory activity of God in its historical unfolding.[143]

For Vos, biblical theology "is not concerned with the text per se," as many contemporary evangelical biblical theologies are, "but with what the text reveals to us about the redemptive activity of God in history."[144] This reflects Vos's concern for the field of history as the primary battle ground of his day,[145] and his contention that doctrines are "theological interpretations of facts," and thus

---

140. Vos, *RD*, 2:32.

141. Vos, *RD*, 2:36. Similarly, of the covenant of grace, he says: "Although man had no right to this promise of eternal life, still there is something in the nature of God that disposes Him to this justice-inflicting kindness and takes man up into a fixed and unbreakable covenant where he cannot again fall away" (Vos, *RD*, 2:41).

142. See Vos, "The Doctrine of the Covenant in Reformed Theology," in *RHBI*, 234–67. Van Til likely learned from his Princeton professor that "covenant theology is Reformed theology. As such it implies the exhaustively personal relationship of man to God" (Van Til, *IST*, 271).

143. Richard Lints, "Two Theologies or One? Warfield and Vos on the Nature of Theology," *Westminster Theological Journal* 54 (1992): 241. As to the late development of the discipline, Lints writes: "The irony here is that the discipline which was to provide the basis for systematic theology was nonexistent for most of the historical life of systematic theology. The child was apparently much older than the parent (though roughly the same age as the grandparent)" (p. 238). At Vos's installation, "Warfield ... notes the changes necessary to the curriculum as a result of this appointment" (p. 237 n.11).

144. Lints, "Two Theologies or One?," 241.

145. "First of all, we are face to face with the fact that the immemorial conflict between naturalism and supernaturalism has, more than ever before, concentrated itself in the field of history" (Vos, *RHBI*, 461).

basically historical.¹⁴⁶ The exegete is first of all a historian.¹⁴⁷ In other words: "For Vos, the discipline of biblical theology dealt with revelation in the active sense, as an act of God."¹⁴⁸

Van Til was sensitive to the connections Vos had in mind. Drawing together absolute personalism, covenant, and redemptive history, while hinting also at biblical hermeneutics, he says that "the New Testament believer sees more clearly than the Old Testament believer did that there must be *one unified controlling principle back of all his ethical striving.*"¹⁴⁹ Elsewhere he makes the connections explicit:

> Covenant theology is Reformed theology. As such it implies the exhaustively personal relationship of man to God. Man never deals with the essence of God as such. He always deals with God. God has self-consciously placed himself before man. It is only in the Reformed faith that one can speak of the divine-human confrontation as over against impersonal views of reality.¹⁵⁰

In Van Til, one discovers the coalescence of Bavinck's and Vos's absolute personalist accounts of covenant and history. He says of Adam in the garden, of the righteous race that could have been, and of the regenerate now eschatologically reclaimed, that "in proportion that man develops his self-determination does he develop God's determination or plan for his kingdom on earth. God accomplishes his plans through self-determined characters."¹⁵¹ Van Til celebrates the equal ultimacy of absoluteness and personality in this and other apparent contradictions. He repeats often the startling claim not that unqualified foreordination and freedom are compatible, but rather that creaturely volition is unintelligible apart from the sovereign and all-encompassing decree of God:

> It is on this ground, then, that, from the point of view of the necessity of the ethical life, we hold to the absolute will of God as the presupposition of the will of man. Looked at in this way, that which to many seems to be the greatest hindrance to human responsibility, namely, the conception of an absolutely sovereign God, becomes the very foundation of its possibility.¹⁵²

---

146. Vos, *RHBI*, 468.
147. Richard B. Gaffin, explaining Vos, writes: "Biblical interpretation is necessarily historical work. The exegete, among other things, is a historian. ... The biblical documents have a historical origin and background to be investigated, but also ... their subject matter is historical" (Gaffin, introduction to *RHBI*, xx).
148. Lints, "Two Theologies or One?," 246.
149. Van Til, *CTE*, 107.
150. Van Til, *IST*, 271.
151. Van Til, *CTE*, 46.
152. Van Til, *CTE*, 35. In the polemical mode: "It is well to observe in this connection that a natural concomitant of the failure to distinguish between a Christian and a non-Christian foundation for true logic is the denial of the genuine significance of the historical.

Van Til says such things because he holds to the incommunicable attributes—the absoluteness and metaphysical simplicity of deity—but also to the absoluteness of the divine personality. "Man never deals with the essence of God as such" means that there is no impersonal essence; man deals always with divine personality. "The Scriptures speak anthropomorphically of God and could not do otherwise, but for all that, God in himself is immutable."[153] In this sense Van Til makes clear the stark distinction between actualism—a Hegelian, panentheistic historical becoming—and absolute personalism. God does not become personal, and his personality is never less than immutably absolute. In this sense it is Van Til's classical orthodoxy that both grounds and motivates his constructive appreciation of absolute personalism:

> As God is absolute rationality so God is also absolute will. By this we mean primarily that God did not have to become good, but has from everlasting to everlasting been good. In God there is no problem of activity and passivity. In God there is *eternal accomplishment*. God is finally and *ultimately self-determinative*. God is finally and absolutely necessary and *therefore* absolutely free.[154]

Bavinck did not miss the polemical tone of his own theological culture, but he distinguished himself by indulging his eclectic side.[155] Vos's work is self-consciously polemical, though this fact is often missed by his readers.[156] Van Til, on the other hand, unmistakably, made of polemics something of a way of life. And it may be that for this undertaking as well, absolute personalism is the deeper conception. A programmatic statement from his study of ethics may be seen as bearing this out:

> In order to avoid misunderstanding, however, we should distinguish the concept of the absolutely personalist environment in which the Christian believes, from philosophical determinism. It is all too common for men hastily to identify consistent Christianity with philosophical necessitarianism. Yet they

Given the belief in a self-sufficient God, the idea of temporal creation and genuine historical development is absurd. So says the non-believer" (Van Til, *CGG*, 38).

153. Van Til, *IST*, 334.

154. Van Til, *CTE*, 34.

155. It troubled his family, friends, and church community that he left Kampen to study at Leiden University. See Ron Gleason, *Herman Bavinck: Pastor, Churchman, Statesman, and Theologian* (Phillipsburg, NJ: P&R, 2010), 43–4. On his eclecticism, see Cory Brock and Nathaniel Gray Sutanto, "Herman Bavinck's Reformed Eclecticism: On Catholicity, Consciousness and Theological Epistemology," *Scottish Journal of Theology* 70, no. 3 (2017): 310–32.

156. See Vos's "The Idea of Biblical Theology as a Science and as a Theological Discipline" and his "Christian Faith and the Truthfulness of Bible History," in *RHBI*, 3–24, 458–71.

are as the poles apart. Philosophical necessitarianism stands for an ultimate impersonalism: consistent Christianity stands for an ultimate personalism.[157]

The themes at work in this statement no longer require elucidation. Suffice it to say, in sum, that for Bavinck, Vos, and Van Til, the creature's moral environment and the historicity that renders volition meaningful is the self-expressed personality of an absolute God.

Conclusion

This chapter has demonstrated that Vos and Van Til have worked as biblical theologian and apologist, respectively, drawing out the implications of a fresh rearticulation of divine personality, and that this rearticulation of divine personality was something of a modern polemical tactic marketed well by Bavinck.

It could be argued that Van Til has recast apologetics as a subset of Christian theistic religious psychology, such that awareness of and acquaintance with God are taken as identical with human self-consciousness; God is the fabric of subjective experience. Human reason is taxonomized according to one of two attitudes toward this bedrock theistic acquaintance: either suppression in Adam or doxology in Christ. For Van Til, God is not a hypothesis proposed for consideration but the attentive, personal context for human self-understanding and self-expression, and the necessary precondition of human subjective experience. Additionally, Van Til makes clear the significance of absolute personalism for ethics. In this sense, he articulates the doctrine of God as it is operative, implicitly, in Vos's theology of the covenant of works, as discussed in Chapter 2.

Vos's distinctive program for biblical theology views Scripture as the by-product of, or better, divinely appointed accompaniment to, the redemptive work of God in history. Scripture is not a retrospective, religious revisionist history, but the authoritative treatise on a supernatural view of history, a Christ-centered account of the omnipresent God self-presenting for the sake of covenant eschatology and relational consummation in the Son. As a historical study of the progressive and organic work of redemption and self-revelation, biblical theology is for Vos a union of biblical and dogmatic concerns officiated by absolute personalism.

J. H. Bavinck, as well, has capitalized on absolute personalism as he undertook missiological articulation of Christian theism and the natural hopelessness of counterfeits. Absolute personalism vindicates the relational fullness of religious longing and the transcendence of the object of religious concern. Absolute personalism also signals the knowability of God and, therefore, it guards Christian theism against mysticism and pluralistic agnosticism. Only an absolute and personal God can demand obedience and present himself as the object of loving submission and glorification. Only the absolute and personal God of the Bible can

---

157. Van Til, *CTE*, 35.

satisfy the religious longing of the image-bearer—because that longing expresses hostility to him and him alone (Ps. 51:1).

All this has enriched the neo-Calvinist theology of the moral situation of the image-bearer. Sin and evil are meaningless notions if they are not descriptive of a willful transgression of a law issuing from the self-objectification of the God who is there, who is the very personal fabric of human self-understanding in the first place. Thus, absolute personality is the neo-Calvinist language for the sort of theism that validates human moral experience.

In what follows, the clarity and resolution of theological vision, as it were, shall be once again increased, so that for further elucidation of the mystery of moral experience one continues to look "more steadfastly into the face of God."[158] Exploration of two themes, that of ontology and relation, and that of Trinity and absolute personality, open the way to a trinitarian account perspective on created response to non-necessary self-objectification. In other words, in the following chapter, absolute person will be brought to bear on the question of theological consciousness and human speech about God.

---

158. Van Til, *CGG*, 19.

Chapter 4

FROM METAETHICS TO TRINITY TO ACCOMMODATION

It was a groundless fear to be afraid of making Christ subject to so great sorrow, lest they should diminish his glory.

—John Calvin

The notion of absolute person is the key to this neo-Calvinist Christian theistic account of the Creator–creature relation. Absolute person affords a robust personalization of the law of God that is always known to the image-bearer implicitly, as the moral fabric of experience and history, and is made known explicitly in the covenant of works and in redemptive special revelation. It shall be demonstrated, furthermore, that Bavinck, Vos, and Van Til view absolute person as classical Trinitarianism come into its own, and that, accordingly, absolute person expresses Trinity itself and in particular the capacity of Trinity to account for moral experience. Van Til's discussion is highlighted in what follows, along with his claim that absolute person in this way retrieves the theistic moral absoluteness of Augustine.

Absolute person has hermeneutical implications as well. Van Til makes the arresting claim that absolute person suggests a theology of accommodation that vindicates what he calls "fearless anthropomorphism," an interpretive rule Van Til takes to be maximally faithful to classical theism and to Scripture as the self-attesting self-expression of God. Van Til's discussion of these matters is historically unsubstantiated—he makes no effort to demonstrate precedent—but evidence appears to show that Van Til is more faithful to Calvin's theology of accommodation than Calvin himself, and that Van Til finds refuge from many challenges to accommodation in Chalcedonian Christology, as Vos had already at least hinted. This chapter demonstrates the role of absolute person in Bavinck, Vos, and Van Til's metaethics and the further value of absolute person in closing the distance between Trinity and religious experience.

Ontology and Relation

This notion of absolute person provokes several questions. But a specific challenge has emerged already from the foregoing discussion of God's relationship to both the possibility and actualization of sin, the question of ontology and relation. Absolute person settles the matter of there being a relation, of a relation obtaining, a relation that is also a relationship, between the absolute God and the creature. Human religion, as Herman and Johan Bavinck have argued, is predicated on the actuality of fellowship with the personal absolute. But this settles only the matter of the actuality of religious relationship, not the initial actualization of that relationship in terms of its theological relations: what exactly is that relationship, and how did it come about? Absolute person gives a name to the foundation and context of the religious fellowship the image-bearer seeks and Christian Scripture conveys; but thus far little has been said regarding the first introduction of that religious fellowship, or regarding the origination of that religious fellowship in God and in God alone. In fact, in terms of both religious and philosophical polemics, absolute personality in the vague form of the foregoing discussion is already taught in the failures of alternative systems. Thus far in the present study, however, no account for fellowship between creature and the personal absolute has appeared.

Bavinck's summons to the further development of the notion of covenant highlights this limitation. He warns that while Reformed scholars bicker over the covenant of works,[1] covenant theology still holds considerable yet untapped potential in a different direction: "This richly valuable idea of Scripture," the notion of covenant, that is, "has not always come into its own in Christian theology."[2] In order to capitalize on this potential, "we must completely set aside the fragmentary development of this doctrine."[3] Precisely, as the debates over the covenant of works demonstrate, standard treatments of the covenant doctrine are theologically

---

1. As covenant theologians still do today: Niehaus, Bolt, et al. Bavinck has a noteworthy explanation for the fact that the word "covenant" does not appear in the early chapters of Genesis:

> The word was admittedly first employed in the profane world of everyday for contractual provisions and agreements between people. Long before God established his covenant with Noah and Abraham, covenants had been made between humans. And this *had to be* the case for Noah, Abraham, and Israel to understand and appreciate religion as a covenant. This is also why the word does not yet occur in Genesis 3:15. Only when covenants were needed in a sinful and deceptive human society for the defense of acquisition of any good could the value of a covenant be appreciated and religion be regarded from this point of view. (Bavinck, *RD*, 3:203)

2. Bavinck, *RD*, 2:565.
3. Bavinck, *RD*, 2:571.

shallow. In such discussions, the operative understanding of covenant is, evidently, literary, even phenomenalistic, at best an exegetico-inductive notion descriptive of the events of Hebrew religion as they unfold within the pages of Scripture and ancient history, but also in the broader religious culture of the ancient Near East. This common—and, again, according to Bavinck, stunted—understanding of covenant merely reports the actuality of Creator–creature reciprocity in its Judeo-Christian form; it does not consider the religion of Scripture in its theological relations; it is, in other words, religious phenomenological and thus only sheepishly supernatural. The fact that so much confusion surrounds the hermeneutical relevance of ancient Near Eastern religious covenant documents and political arrangements, and that hermeneutics has proven vulnerable to pluralistic theories of comparative religions and ancient literature, broadcasts that very theological anemia. In this unsubstantial form, covenant theology only vaguely suggests, and appears of itself incapable of producing, a theology of the possibility of religious fellowship between God and the human creature. Covenant theology, in this literary, phenomenalistic form, offers only a description of practical religion, and Bavinck sees the need for a theological account of historico-religious relation, an account that begins with absolute personality and moves on to relieve the tension between ontology and actual relationality even from within the doctrine of God. This chapter engages the efforts of Bavinck, Vos, and Van Til to provide such an account.

Relative but Not Correlative

The question at hand may be put in terms of the moral law and moral experience by making an important distinction. It may be noted, first, that it is one thing to outline a theology of moral value based upon the self-sufficiency of God, and then to understand sin as transgression of that moral value, or failure to conform to the moral character of the unchanging God. This way of framing the question of moral value and of attempting a definition of sin is, in broad strokes, Augustinian. Thus it is important to note the relationship between the metaethics of absolute personalism and that of the Augustinian tradition. Gillian Evans describes Augustine's personal crisis in striking terms:

> It was his preoccupation with the problem of evil above all which held him in thrall to the Manichees for nine years. The Manichees did not attempt to avoid the problem of evil; indeed, by finding a place for evil in the universe they made it a fundamental principle in their system. More, they appealed to a deep sense of something at war within himself in Augustine; they recognized what he has himself felt about his soul and his body, 'that they have been enemies since the creation of the worlds' (*Manichean Psalm-Book*, ccxlviii). ... They took from Augustine the private responsibility for his own soul's health ... and allowed him to cast his burden into the cosmic maelstrom. When he was young, he notes wryly, he was readier to believe that the universe was out of joint than that there was something wrong within himself (*Conf.* VII.iii.4). He came close to

believing that God could be affected by evil, rather than admit that he himself was the agent of evil.[4]

Dualism had, she notes, strong personal appeal for Augustine as a man still unrepentant. Augustine would acknowledge, in retrospect, that the Manichees' cosmology was rather too convenient for one unwilling to face God. "The Manichean explanation took away the need to search his heart and to avert his eyes from the troubled state of his own conscience, and allowed him to turn his attention to the world, to argue grand issues concerning the structure of the universe."[5] In the end, the futility of moral dualism sparked the crisis that resulted in Augustine's conversion. When Augustine renounced dualism, he embraced an ontology of the divine being which would bequeath to historic Christianity the enigma of the origin of that which contradicts God, namely, sin and evil.[6]

In Augustine's new paradigm, ontological security is front and center, and the moral picture as a whole hangs on the self-sufficient goodness of God. But this approach lacks relationality. The good is well defined but it does not—because as impersonal it cannot—enter the sphere of human experience in objective form. It behaves like a Platonism insufficiently Christianized, a theo-ontological account of moral value without the personal context sufficient to render obedience religiously meaningful.[7] Justice is secure but it remains aloof, impersonal, and ahistorical; God legislates—if at all—deductively from his own moral nature, and sin may be metaphysically construed.

---

4. G. R. Evans, *Augustine on Evil* (Cambridge: Cambridge University Press, 1982), 13.

5. Evans, *Augustine on Evil*, 15.

6. Some believe that Augustine was not always able to let that mystery alone. See "The First Evil Will Must Remain a Mystery." Augustine converted from Manichean dualism to Christianity with the help of neo-Platonist philosophy. So strong was the influence of neo-Platonism at that juncture in Augustine's life, that some have argued that Augustine in fact converted to neo-Platonism rather than to Christianity. This does not matter at the moment. The relevant point presently is that Augustine's conversion featured ontological correction, namely, his embrace of the self-sufficient goodness of the God of Scripture, an ontological view taken presently as Platonist.

7. Van Til clearly believed that Augustine's religion was better than Platonist ontology. He refuses to grant the objectivism of Platonic thought, repeatedly accusing it of relativism, and qualifies strongly its association with Augustine, whose

> thought is at bottom the polar opposite of Plato's. For Plato the Ideas or laws are next to or higher than God; for Augustine the ideas or laws are expressive of God's nature. No more radical difference is conceivable. For Plato God wants the good because it is good in itself; for Augustine the good is good because God wants it and God wants it because it is expressive of his nature.

Cornelius Van Til and Louis Berkhof, *Foundations of Christian Education: Addresses to Christian Teachers*, ed. Dennis E. Johnson (Phillipsburg, NJ: P&R, 1989), 58.

4. From Metaethics to Trinity to Accommodation

At this point, in a corrective mode, Van Til defers to absolute personalism:

> There is not and cannot be any evil in God. This is involved in the very idea of God as an absolute person. If there were evil in his being there would be a mutual cancellation instead of a mutual complementation of the attributes of God. Absolute negation and absolute affirmation would cancel one another. Plato says that somehow the Good had to be supreme if there was to be intelligible predication, but he could not get rid of the "mud and hair and filth" in the ideal world. Satan is not as old as God, but was a creature of God and sinned as a creature of God.[8]

This statement is somewhat out of order, but worth the trouble. Van Til attempts here to replace a Platonist theo-ontology, or metaethics, with a Christian alternative. He does so first by affirming the discovery that delivered Augustine from Manichean dualism, the absolute goodness of the absolute God, or rather, the absolute goodness that is the absolute God. So Van Til rehearses a Platonist dismissal of dualism on the basis of the moral incoherence dualism implies; the good must be self-sufficient, for if evil is its ontological complement, the distinction is arbitrary and meaning is lost. If neither team will win, or the game will never end, it hardly matters who you support. He then introduces Plato as the name associated with the discovery of the supremacy of the Good but also as the one who could not outlive the problem of the ontology of that which contradicts the Good. Ironically, Plato's high, abstract good still needed evil for meaning. Plato ended up with problems on both ends. So Van Til argues that from this impersonal system, no relational arrangement affording relativity without correlativity, opposition but not opposites, is forthcoming. Plato's Good lacked relational capacity, but relation there must be if not-Good is to have being at all and if Good can really oppose not-Good within the realm of experience. Van Til's mention of "God as an absolute person" comes into its own in the asymmetry that closes the quotation, "Satan is not as old as God." Divine personality allows for relativity without correlativity and thus for that relation apart from which the absoluteness of the Good has turned out to be a mixed blessing. One must discover a relation that can sustain contradiction of the moral nature of God or one must deny evil altogether; Good is being itself and therefore ontological descent and moral descent are one. "Satan is not as old as God" is a rejection of dualism; that "he was a creature of God" and "sinned as a creature of God" means that evil is creaturely. In other words, ontologically evil is created, meaning that it has an ontology but is not equal to God. Evil is moral but not ontological complementation, and it is afforded ontology by the free and personal movement of the unchanging God toward that which changes, where that which changes is the realized object of his own creative act. God created the possibility of opposition to God; and opposition to God is moral only, not ontological, as it is a creature of God. The cosmic origin of volitional transgression

---

8. Van Til, *CTE*, 21.

is that wicked angelic person who in Scripture is called Satan, and there at the very threshold of the appearance of sin and evil Van Til highlights the "very idea of God as an absolute person."[9]

Absolute person, or, more fully, "the complete self-consciousness of God which we have found to be the epistemological and metaphysical foundation of Christian ethics," indicates that "it is possible to have something that is relative without being correlative."[10] That is, where absoluteness alone mutes moral meaning, absolute personalism vindicates that which is contrary to goodness but not its contradiction. "The temporal universe is relative without making God correlative to itself. Evil is relative without making God correlative to it."[11]

Law and Personal Relationship

On the other hand, to define sin as transgression of or lack of conformity to a law of God is not obviously adequate, as it is vulnerable to the depersonalization described above by J. H. Bavinck. Although this definition maintains greater proximity to the biblical text and to practical religion, it is vulnerable to the worry that divine (absolute) authority is inadequately represented, that God's commands are or could conceivably be arbitrary because no one can specify the relationship between divine will and divine nature. And, indeed, there is a sense in which divine commands are arbitrary, the prohibition being an obvious example. The same could be said of the command to sacrifice Isaac, which, without confidence in the divine origin of the command, would stand morally repugnant in the extreme. It is the divine origin alone that saves these imperatives from meaninglessness and moral absurdity. And this is basically an ontological concern, in terms of the need for confidence that divine commands have not issued forth from darkness, from the infinite unsearchability of an unknowable being of God—from infinite unsearchability as such—and that Christian ethics is not thus abandoned to metaethical actualism.

Adam knew, indeed, he was aware in the fabric of his self-understanding, that his state of mutable righteousness before the unchanging Creator God was at the mercy of his own volition. That there were not simply laws as such, nor even laws suggestive of the legislative privilege of a greater being, but laws from God of a provisional, historical-covenant character signals, somehow, a harmonious juxtaposition of the ontological and the relational. In other words: How could it be that a prohibition against eating from a particular, created tree bore unimpeachable authority and eschatological significance? How could human destiny hang on wholehearted obedience to an arbitrary rule? The resolution signaled in the notion of absolute person is this: the expressed moral law is only an explicit form of the implicit moral law, that law which is written on the heart. And the law written on

9. Van Til, *CTE*, 21.
10. Van Til, *CTE*, 123–4.
11. Van Til, *CTE*, 123–4.

the heart is not a law unarticulated; it is not published legislation minus linguistic iteration, amounting to a vague sense of obligation open to clarification by trial and error; the law written on the heart is a personal relationship. In personal relationship with the absolute person, moral order is preserved; recourse to a higher, ineffable good is eliminated; and the unimpeachability of divine prerogative and lordship is embraced.

Notice that on this neo-Calvinistic account, natural law is defined as consciousness of the attentive omnipresence of the personal God. Adam's natural law was a knowledge of personal and religious acquaintance. Subsequent (logically, not temporally) to the natural law, the expressed law serves to publicize and objectify that personal relationship. The notion of absolute person thus denotes two facts: that God can establish a relation that is a relationship that places the image-bearer into a moral-relational environment constituted by a self-expression of the moral nature of the absolute God, first of all, and second, that God has done so. Here, again, for these neo-Calvinists, the notion of "covenant" signals this arrangement, including both its natural and positive aspects.

And yet, absolute person—thus far—has clarified little about how this came about, or rather, how it could have come about. Absolute person is the theism of the moral situation, a theological descriptor that relieves a great deal of tension in the theological account of moral experience. But how, theologically speaking, may the establishment of that moral-relational environment be understood?

Trinity and Absolute Person

As to the development of neo-Calvinist absolute personalism, Van Til excels. He develops, applies, and defends absolute personalism in dogmatic literature and in his work on apologetics and ethics, and, with surprising force, in his essays on Christian education. As shall be made evident in what follows, Bavinck set important precedents for Van Til's work. Indeed, the entire first chapter of Bavinck's *God and Creation* is dominated by discussion of absolute personalism. The relative silence of the secondary literature on this material and on absolute personalism[12] is perhaps due to the inconspicuous nature of the development in Bavinck's work not only of absolute personalism but of its importance for other dogmatic *loci*. It is there but not emphasized. It may even be the case that Bavinck himself had not made such connections in his own mind, although it is certainly the case that they

---

12. But for the famous opening statement—"Mystery is the lifeblood of dogmatics"—chapter 1 receives no sustained secondary attention, and absolute personalism is all but completely ignored. Exceptions are Ximian Xu, "Appreciative and Faithful? Karl Barth's Use of Herman Bavinck's View of God's Incomprehensibility," *Journal of Reformed Theology* 13 (2019): 26–46; Nathaniel Gray Sutanto, *God and Knowledge: Herman Bavinck's Theological Epistemology* (London: Bloomsbury, 2020); Cory Brock, *Orthodox yet Modern: Herman Bavinck's Use of Friedrich Schleiermacher* (Bellingham, WA: Lexham, 2020).

were beginning to manifest themselves in his writing. Hindsight aids interpretation in this case, and Van Til's constructive work, which capitalizes on the dogmatic and apologetic promise of absolute personalism, renders the influence of absolute personalism elsewhere in Bavinck's thinking more easily detectable.[13] Among the three, Vos spends by far the least amount of time on the topic. In fact, it is not clear that he uses the words "absolute person" in publication. On the other hand, since Vos understands his approach to biblical theology as implied in and continuous with Reformed covenant theology, it stands to reason that via the notion of covenant, absolute personalism would have exercised influence, even if implicit, in his approach to the progressive and organic nature of redemptive revelation. Perhaps this should be stated the other way around: given the particularities of Vos's polemical interest—namely, an anti-supernatural historicism—it stands to reason that his reconfiguring the notion of history as the realm of the historical working out of religious relation, Vos, too, would betray an interest in absolute person.

With regard to the interpretation of Vos, it is worth noting Richard Gaffin's suggestion that between the two, Bavinck, although he was "virtually silent" on biblical theology, was ahead of Vos in the development of a progressive and organic conception of historic redemption and redemptive revelation.[14] And yet

---

13. A leading instance of implicit absolute personalism is Bavinck's 1908 Stone Lectures at Princeton Seminary, published as *Philosophy of Revelation*, trans. and ed. Cory Brock, Nathaniel Gray Sutanto, and James P. Eglinton (Peabody, MA: Hendrickson, 2018). See Nathan D. Shannon, "Ontology and Revelation in Bavinck's Stone Lectures," *Scottish Journal of Theology* 73, no. 2 (2020): 112–25. It is worth noting that Vos helped to organize this event, hosted Bavinck at his home in Princeton, and facilitated the translation of the lectures into English, as Bavinck wrote them initially in Dutch. See Ron Gleason, *Herman Bavinck: Pastor, Churchman, Statesman, and Theologian* (Phillipsburg, NJ: P&R, 2010), 225–6, 361; Brock and Sutanto, "Introduction to the Annotated Edition," in *Philosophy of Revelation*, xxx. In these lectures as much as anywhere else, one finds language strongly reminiscent of Vos's approach to biblical theology. Thus the Stone Lectures capture in many ways the "organic" interdependence of neo-Calvinist thought on several important *loci*, including the doctrines of God, incomprehensibility, and revelation, as well as redemptive history, biblical theology, hermeneutics and anthropomorphism, and apologetic method.

14. Gaffin writes:

> Bavinck is virtually silent on biblical theology. Relevant, however, is what he has to say in a section of his Dogmatiek dealing with special revelation. So far as its content is concerned, he identifies three basic characteristics of special revelation. It is (1) historical and progressive, (2) made up of deeds as well as words and teaching, and (3) soteriological. He also observes that the first two characteristics, that is, the historically progressive and the deed character of special revelation, have been better recognized in more recent theology than in the older theologians. In other words, according to Bavinck the basic material qualification of biblical revelation is that it is redemptive-historical and it is just

on the other hand, Richard Lints claims that it is difficult to identify a precedent to Vos's distinctive approach to biblical theology, which indeed focuses on historical divine activity—where absolute personalism would prove especially relevant—as the subject matter of biblical revelation.[15] Bavinck says "absolute person" and lays the foundation for what would become Vos's "biblical theology." Absolute person, in other words, is the unifying notion at work where the thoughts of Bavinck and Vos overlap.

Vos

Vos appears at one point to express concern that absolute personalism flirts with heterodoxy. In his *Reformed Dogmatics*, one statement in particular comes across as designed to restrain the unipersonal tendency implicit in talk of God as absolute person. Vos says that "God's spirituality" means "that God's being also exists as personal," and then he says:

> However, we should consider that God's being may not be called personal in the abstract but only in His threefold existence as Father, Son, and Holy Spirit. In

---

this factor that needs further, more concerted attention. Again, perhaps even more so than in Kuyper, the work of Vos is on the horizon.

Richard B. Gaffin Jr., "Systematic Theology and Biblical Theology," *Westminster Theological Journal* 38, no. 3 (1976): 287. It is also worth noting that from his student days Bavinck had a strong background in Old Testament studies. At Leiden, he studied Semitic languages with his friend Christiaan Snouck Hurgronje, who would become a recognized expert in Hebrew and Eastern languages. Bavinck's studies included special attention to exegesis of the Old Testament, Israelite literature, and the history of Israelite worship. On the occasion of Bavinck's first encounter with Abraham Kuyper, Kuyper encouraged him to select an Old Testament subject for his dissertation, and there is evidence that Kuyper had hoped to recruit Bavinck to teach Eastern languages at the Free University. See Gleason, *Herman Bavinck*, 56, 57, 63, 64.

15. Lints describes Vos as "the first evangelical proponent of that theological method which has come to be called biblical theology." Richard Lints, *The Fabric of Theology: A Prolegomenon to Evangelical Theology* (Grand Rapids, MI: Eerdmans, 1993), 182. While "Vos surely shows some indebtedness to Bavinck and Kuyper in his appreciation for the historical character of revelation and redemption," evidently he was aware of the fact that "the hermeneutical distinctions did not have any (or many) historical precedents in the evangelical tradition and that evangelical theology was embarking on a relatively new venture." Richard Lints, "Two Theologies or One? Warfield and Vos on the Nature of Theology," *Westminster Theological Journal* 54 (1992): 236, 242, 243. "Unprecedented" must be of course taken with a grain of salt. Bavinck, it may be noted, attributes to Augustine the idea that "the New is concealed in the Old Testament, and the Old is revealed in the New Testament" (see Bavinck, *RD*, 3:207).

God personality is not one but three. There are not four but only three persons in the Godhead.[16]

Again, one easily gets the impression that Vos wished to qualify his participation in the developing interest in absolute personalism and to suggest that when Bavinck says that "God is a person," he goes too far, and that Van Til, stating on several occasions that "God is one person," disregards his teacher's wise counsel and flirts with heterodoxy.[17]

There is first of all chronological challenge to this interpretation. Given the early date—Vos's *Reformed Dogmatics* was first published in 1896—it is next to impossible that Vos was concerned about unipersonality in the developing thought of Bavinck, whose *Gereformeerde Dogmatiek*, volume 2, would not be published until the following year.[18] More likely, Vos was concerned about unipersonality in German idealism ("personal in the abstract sense"). That is, given the chronology, this can hardly be called a disagreement between Vos and Bavinck, much less with Van Til, who was only about a year old at the time that Vos wrote these words.

Despite this apparent reticence, Vos might be called an early formulator of neo-Calvinist absolute personalism. As mentioned previously, his progress in the field of biblical theology was clearly underwritten by a fruitful if unexplained cooperation of absoluteness and historical relationship, and Vos's doctrines of history, covenant, religion, knowledge, kingdom, church, and eschatology—and so on—bear this out. Furthermore, the same polemical concerns found in Bavinck's discussion of absolute personalism did evoke several pointed statements from Vos, statements that make much more sense in light of Bavinck's (concurrent) and Van Til's (subsequent) work on the theme in question.

"Almost the whole of modern philosophy claims," Vos says, that "infinity and personal existence exclude each other."[19] He observes that "this claim is based on the idea that an 'I' cannot exist without a 'not-I' and that the nature of infinity excludes such an opposite."[20] Vos was wary of the influence of modern

---

16. Vos, *RD*, 1:15.

17. One such statement from Bavinck is this: "Thanks to revelation, it is certain, first of all, that God is a person, a conscious and freely willing being, not confined to the world but exalted high above it" (Bavinck, *RD*, 1:30). It is not clear that Bavinck here affirms unipersonality, nor, however, can that possibility be eliminated with certainty. Van Til, for his part, leaves no doubt. Thus, in retrospect, whether or not Bavinck meant to say so, unipersonality had begun to play a role in his thinking.

18. And Vos published enthusiastic reviews of volumes 1 and 2, making no mention of absolute personalism or unipersonality. His reviews were published in *The Presbyterian and Reformed Review* in 1896 and 1899. The reviews, as John Bolt points out, pleased Bavinck. See John Bolt, "Bavinck Tributes," *Bavinck Review* 3 (2012): 180–2.

19. Vos, *RD*, 1:15.

20. Vos, *RD*, 1:15.

psychology,[21] and he opens several lines of response. First he denies that relational opposition gives rise to personality. "Thou" does not evoke subjective self-awareness, but depends upon it. Consciousness of the other presupposes self-consciousness, not the other way around: "personal consciousness is not caused by the consciousness of another outside us, but completely the reverse; the former makes the latter possible. Only where there is personal consciousness can one distinguish something else from one's self."[22]

If this is true of human personality, how much more of the divine. And applied to the Trinity, the necessity of self-consciousness for relational opposition hints at consubstantiality and co-equality within the Godhead, in which personal differences, or relations of opposition, are predicated upon the indivisibility of the divine essence, which requires the full and self-sufficient deity of the persons. The Son must be God of himself in order to understand himself as begotten of the Father; otherwise, eternal generation is an act of creation ex nihilo. The Son is not God by virtue of eternal generation; "God by virtue of" is incoherent; but neither is he Son because he is God. The second person is both Son and God.

Vos's response to the modern line concludes with this:

Within God's being itself there is a distinction that should explain completely how there can be consciousness of personal existence in God apart from other things. The Father is indeed conscious not to be the Son, and the Son not to be the Father, and the Holy Spirit not to be the Father and not to be the Son. And these three do not limit each other but together are the one, infinite God.[23]

Vos says, in other words, that orthodox Trinitarianism signals the infinite mutuality of absoluteness and personality that modern philosophy believed impossible. Where modern philosophy assumed that personality implied limitation, and that therefore absoluteness is necessarily impersonal, historic trinitarian theology claims to be a conspicuous exception to the rule (and thus, one would think, a challenge to the rule). The persons in the Godhead are each the one, self-same fullness of the being of God, and thus are subject to no limitation. The divine personality of the first, second, and third persons is thrice unqualified, but numerically one. If relations of opposition do not entail division of the divine

---

21. Herman Bavinck published a great deal on psychology, and his nephew Johan Herman Bavinck was something of an expert in religious psychology. Van Til, too, published on the topic.

22. Vos, *RD*, 1:15. He then adds: "That in us, human beings, consciousness of personality is certainly awakened and developed by contact with the world outside us, but that we may not make this a rule for God. He is wholly independent from all that is outside Him" (Vos, *RD*, 1:15–16). In sum: human personality precedes consciousness of another, but it is "awakened and developed" by such contact. Independence is featured here; all the more, then, is independence a feature of divine personality.

23. Vos, *RD*, 1:16.

being (partialism), then distinction and absoluteness are equally ultimate, and tri-personality is absolute unity; divine personality is absolute. Vos thus rejects speculative (philosophical) unipersonality and, more or less, prepares for Van Til's unipersonalism.

It is noteworthy, then, that Vos locates distinction "within God's being." Since, without implying partialism, distinction resides in the singular divine being, neither the numerical nor the metaphysical unity of God may be affirmed independent of essential difference. There is in this sense no "oneness" in the Christian God that is not also, irreducibly, "threeness." Vos here intends to undercut accidental personality in the Godhead, and so he says that God's personality is independent of other things, self-sufficient and uncaused, because the relations indicative of God's personality are relations between three persons each no less than the others essentially and eternally God. Put yet another way, Vos draws into organic interdependence the polemical sensitivity and the constructive trinitarian instincts of Bavinck's absolute personalism and equal ultimacy of unity and diversity in the Godhead, and the two together thus leave the necessary components in place for Van Til's creative apologetics and even for his claim that "God is one person."

Van Til

Unipersonality is indeed a high point of Van Til's absolute personalism. As Vos has done, Van Til wishes to bring unity and difference into the greatest possible proximity, and repeatedly to affirm that the three gives way to the one and the one to the three. No trinitarian would deny this. Van Til's particular ambition is to preclude bottomless apophaticism as regards the divine essence. He desires, in a polemical mode, to distinguish the unity of the triune God from abstract notions of unity—impersonal, abstract, deified but ineffable oneness—which by equivocation pollute confessional theology and ensnare biblical interpretation in various dualisms or antinomies. It is his view that impersonal or abstract deity prowls the field of theological construction.

Van Til says, somewhat opaquely, that "absolute numerical identity should be opposed to specific or generic unity."[24] By this he means that the unity of the tri-personal Godhead is reducible neither to specific unity, as in tri-theism, three united under a single species, nor to generic unity, as in partialism, a reduction of the full deity of persons. That is, classical Trinitarianism requires more than both unity and diversity—more than both "essence and attributes," on the one hand, and "tri-personality," on the other. The three persons are each God; and the three persons are each the same God; so they are both metaphysically one and numerically one in the fullness of divine personality. Van Til thus insists upon the perfect and ultimate oneness and identity of the three persons in God. This requires that the essence subsist in difference no less than in unity, so that affirmation of unity, numerical or metaphysical, is affirmation also of difference. The two notions

---

24. Van Til, *IST*, 341.

are not merely concurrent or artificially juxtaposed or haphazardly simultaneous—also this, also that—but mutually informative and interdependent. Put differently, Van Til (with Bavinck and with modern philosophy) denies that there is oneness as such, absoluteness as such. Rather, there is only oneness-in-difference, absolute personality self-expressed.[25] There can be no impersonal divine essence; the essence is exhaustively personal; that is, God is one person.

Van Til attempts to explain this by a detailed comparison of two relations: that between essence and attributes, and that between essence and persons. "In a similar manner," he says, "we have noticed how theologians insist that each of the persons of the Godhead is coterminous with the being of the Godhead."[26] And just as it is denied that "the distinctions of the attributes are merely nominal," it is also denied that "the distinctions of the persons are merely nominal."[27] He writes:

> We have noted how each attribute is coextensive with the being of God. We are compelled to maintain this in order to avoid the notion of an uninterpreted being of some sort. In other words, we are bound to maintain the identity of the attributes of God with the being of God in order to avoid the specter of brute fact.[28]

Each attribute is mapped according to the full circumference, as it were, of the divine being; God, with no remainder, is each of his attributes, so that there is no attribute that characterizes God only partially. There are problems with putting it this way, but in some sense it may be said that God is identical to or identifiable with each of his attributes. This relationship is, however, in Van Til's view, not symmetrical. That is, Van Til is not here deifying properties in a Platonic manner, in which properties are self-existent just as God is. In that case, "God is good" and "good is God" would be mutually implicatory. Rather, Van Til is reiterating the classical understanding of divine attributes, attributes of a unique and metaphysically simple being. In this case, what is God's will is good for the simple fact that it is God's; the creature has no recourse beyond the divine personality.

Put negatively, if God's knowledge were delimited by his will, God would not have exhaustive knowledge of his own being. There would be darkness in the being of God even for God, darkness and mystery rather than the light of perfect self-knowledge, with particular reference to God's will. In however small a measure, arbitrariness is then introduced into divine self-knowledge and thus into revelation, since God is not a wholly trustworthy source of information regarding his own being or his own will. Consequently, every theological datum must be qualified

---

25. Hegel is in the background here. See Shao Kai Tseng, *G. W. F. Hegel* (Phillipsburg, NJ: P&R, 2019), 46–50.
26. Van Til, *IST*, 363–4.
27. Van Til, *IST*, 363–4.
28. Van Til, *IST*, 363.

as provisional or hypothetical or subject to change or correction. The authority of Scripture dissolves and religion is a human invention most purely expressed in silence, mysticism, not knowing. Indeed, the Creator–creature relation itself is at stake. If God's knowledge is not coterminous with his being, not only for man but even for God a measure of indetermination appears, and it comes at the price of omniscience and omnipotence, and by implication the incommunicable attributes in toto. And in moral terms: if the connection between the moral nature of God and the revealed will of God is insecure, ethics and the moral fabric of religious fellowship, of human experience in general, begins to unravel. Moral adjudication must defer to intuition or consensus and God is rendered powerless, a mere moral curiosity.

The unity of God is an absolute rule, in other words, in the explanation of the attributes; but the distinction or diversity of the attributes is no less important, since without real distinction the attributes are all identical, their differences merely linguistic, their designations only word games, and the being of God again slips into ineffable darkness.[29] Van Til insists that the attributes truly characterize the absolute God, and that each attribute characterizes God in his fullness. Unity and diversity are both ultimate. He believes that the way to maintain the equal ultimacy of unity and diversity is to give unity a clear kataphatic articulation in the form of unipersonality. For Van Til, therefore, the tetragrammaton as the quintessential expression of self-existence must indicate this; the "I am" is personal, singular, self-objectification. It cannot but mean "I am a person."

And now the second relation. "In a similar manner," he says, "each of the persons of the Godhead is coterminous with the being of the Godhead."[30] Unipersonality means equal ultimacy of essence and tri-personal existence:

> If, in God, being and essence are really coterminous, we have before us an absolute personality. There is then no distinction between absoluteness and personality. God does not merely have personality, but is absolute personality.[31]

And later:

> God's being presents an absolute numerical identity. And even within the ontological Trinity we must maintain that God is numerically one. He is one person. When we say that we believe in a personal God, we do not merely mean that we believe in a God to whom the adjective "personality" may be attached. God is not an essence that has personality; he is absolute personality.[32]

---

29. See Alvin Plantinga, *Does God Have a Nature?* (Milwaukee, WI: Marquette University, 1980).
30. Van Til, *IST*, 364.
31. Van Til, *IST*, 346.
32. Van Til, *IST*, 364.

As Christian dogmatics usually goes, discussion of essential attributes tends to major in unity, and then quickly backtracks to affirm difference, and thus—haphazardly, one observes—rescues meaning and the knowability of God. Discussion of Trinity dwells on tri-personality, affirms perichoresis, inseparability of operations, and the indivisibility of the divine essence. In both cases, equal ultimacy of unity and diversity receives less than its due—or so Van Til argues. Van Til insists upon "absolute cotermineity" and "the genuine significance of the distinctions," first for attributes and now for persons, so that a singular, essential, personal consciousness of God subsists in the distinctions that reside in the essence. Thomas Aquinas, for example, says that the distinctions constitutive of the persons are real distinctions in the essence. This is what Van Til means by the "equal ultimacy of unity and diversity." If there are real distinctions in the essence but the essence is undivided, then to deny personality, in the singular, of the essence is arbitrary.

If self-conscious persons are coterminous with essence, then God is wholly and exhaustively self-conscious just as he is wholly and exhaustively personal. Perhaps encouraged in this regard by Vos's reservations regarding modern psychology's definition of person as consciousness of the other, Van Til claims that "God is a one-conscious being, and yet he is also a tri-conscious being."[33] He means to affirm here that falling short of the equal ultimacy of one and three in the Godhead on any point signals a failure to give full voice to the absolute personalism of biblical religion. For Van Til, tri-consciousness and unipersonality thus represent simply the fact that God is. The "one person" is of course not a fourth person any more than the singular essence is an additional deity. "One person," in Van Til's view, is triune kataphaticism come into its own. And so as Christian theism thus requires, "we do assert that God, that is, the whole Godhead, is one person."[34]

It is not so much the novelty of this that is worthy of attention; the greater part of it is unoriginal. Both tri- and uniconsciousness are a matter of daily Christian speech and religious activity, and appear on every page, as it were, of biblical revelation, wherever the singular subject "God" appears. Jesus taught his disciples to pray to the Father (Mt. 6:9) in the name of the Son (Jn 14:13-14), and this is, according to Paul, with the assistance of the Spirit (Rom. 8). But Christians, with much of Scripture, often pray to "God," think about "God," and discuss together the will and work of "God." Unipersonality is implied as well in the doctrine of the inseparability of operations,[35] which is not merely a buffer against tri-theism but constructive affirmation of the full but self-identical deity of the persons and of the

---

33. Van Til, *IST*, 348.
34. Van Til, *IST*, 364, 363.
35. "When Scripture ascribes certain works specifically to the Father, others specifically to the Son, and still others specifically to the Holy Spirit, we are compelled to presuppose a genuine distinction within the Godhead back of that ascription. On the other hand, the work ascribed to any of the persons is the work of one absolute person" (Van Til, *IST*, 362).

fact that "God" is properly the subject of singular verbs—not because the persons are usually, as luck would have it, in agreement, but because they are one.

Nor does Van Til claim to have quantitatively increased our knowledge of God, or to have arrived at a complete definition of God. Rather, he believes that unipersonality is implied in classical Trinitarianism. He in fact claims that absolute personal self-consciousness is already implied in the doctrine of incomprehensibility: "As Christians we say that this," the doctrine of the Trinity, "is a mystery that is beyond our comprehension. It surely is. At the same time," he says, "this mysterious God is mysterious because he is, within himself, wholly rational"— that is, wholly self-known.[36] If in God, "considered apart from his relation to the world," "being and consciousness are coterminous," divine personality is eternally and sufficiently self-dependent.[37] Put negatively, if God were not "complete self-consciousness," "there would then be some vague undefined subject or substance not exhaustively predicated. It is therefore because of the fulness of the concrete self-existence of God that he is simple."[38]

As people today know all too well, humans cannot hide their identities because identities are connected to the world and to other humans. Personal identity is a familial, social, political, historical affair, and this connectivity renders humans discoverable to other humans. But God is who he is by virtue of the distinctions that reside irreducibly in his own being, so that unity and personality are equally ultimate, and God is truth and light unto himself. God is his own context. God may name himself and speak authoritatively about himself. Indicating the co-termineity of being and knowledge, and thus the perfection of divine self-knowledge, Van Til says that God is "the self-predicator."[39] The creature cannot discover God unless God makes himself discoverable; God can only be known by voluntary self-revelation; and divine self-revelation is therefore absolute and self-attesting.[40]

Edmond La Beaume Cherbonnier again serves as a helpful interlocutor. Cherbonnier defends the personality of the God of the Bible against the absolute of mystical religion and of philosophical abstraction. In point of fact, where Van Til (or J. H. Bavinck) might say "personalism," Cherbonnier says "anthropomorphism," taking the latter to indicate not a specific kind of God-talk but a personalized conception of God:

> By anthropomorphism I mean any theology that conceives of God in terms of those characteristics which are distinctively human: the capacity for discriminating judgment, the exercise of responsible decision and choice, the

---

36. Van Til, *IST*, 364.
37. Van Til, *IST*, 364.
38. Van Til, *IST*, 341.
39. Van Til, *IST*, 336.
40. "For better or for worse the Protestant apologist is committed to the doctrine of Scripture as the infallibly inspired final revelation of God to man" (Van Til, *CA*, 136).

ability to carry out long-range purposes. Such a God is appropriately (and literally) described in the language of personal pronouns and transitive verbs, such as "possess," "love," "judge," "promise," "forgive," and the like.[41]

Cherbonnier is especially concerned to identify and exorcise impersonalism and abstraction from religious or theological thought, and in this sense his concerns are similar to Van Til's. It is sometimes suggested, he writes, "that only those who believe in a personal God are liable to project themselves into their beliefs."[42] On the contrary, says Cherbonnier, personalists "hold no monopoly on this tendency. The worshipper of tribal totems (or of philosophical abstractions) is equally susceptible."[43] Van Til has labored to make the same objection: abstraction is univocism; the god of speculation, who is named by the creature, is finite. Only a basic receptivity to revelation—as opposed to creativity—enables true, doxological confession of the absolute God. Cherbonnier sees the univocism of philosophical abstraction come into its own in non-Christian religions: "Anthropomorphism is the guarantee that the individual worshipper will never confuse himself with the object of his worship. In the moment of ecstasy, on the contrary, when the mystic's separate personality is left behind, there remains nothing to distinguish him from God. Hence the esoteric teaching that in the moment of trance, 'I am God.'"[44]

Next, Cherbonnier points out the incoherence of going "beyond" personality, the tendency of speculative theology to look down with disdain, from the lofty realm of pure contemplation of the infinite, on the anthropomorphic god of popular religion. Cherbonnier responds:

> How is the allegedly "supra-personal" distinguished from the merely *sub*-personal? Unless this question can be answered, advocates of the "supra-personal" may fairly be likened to a person crossing the north pole. He believes himself to be going farther and farther north, when in fact he has begun to go south again. Devotees of the "supra-personal" likewise fancy themselves to have discovered a more exalted term for God. The burden of proof rests with them, however, to show that they have not unwittingly reverted to the sub-personal. Until they do, one may conclude that the category of the personal is the north pole of human thought.[45]

41. E. LaB. Cherbonnier, "The Logic of Biblical Anthropomorphism," *Harvard Theological Review* 55, no. 3 (1962): 187.
42. Cherbonnier, "Logic of Biblical Anthropomorphism," 188–9.
43. Cherbonnier, "Logic of Biblical Anthropomorphism," 188–9.
44. Cherbonnier, "Logic of Biblical Anthropomorphism," 198, citing the *Brihad-Aranyaka Upanishad*, 1.4.10, exemplifying the Hindu notion that the Atman, the self, is the Brahman, the all.
45. Cherbonnier, "Logic of Biblical Anthropomorphism," 189–90. Strikingly similar is Herman Bavinck's remark that "personality … is the most developed and rich and glorious system there is." Bavinck, "The Pros and Cons of a Dogmatic System," *Bavinck Review* 5 (2014): 92.

There are hints here once again of the unhappy interdependence, noted by J. H. Bavinck, of absoluteness and personality in human religious consciousness and non-Christian religion. The religious search simply cannot stay put there at the northernmost point; a moment's contemplation or the slightest indulgence of a desire to know God entails abandonment of the illusion of pure absoluteness. Religion is relation, and relation requires person. Cherbonnier in this sense diagnoses the ills of mysticism in much the same way that Van Til and the Bavincks have done.

Cherbonnier also articulates the constructive and corrective value of personalism in ways conducive to Van Til's approach. He notes that personalism is the fact that God has identity and that the word "God" has a real referent. By virtue of personalism, therefore, God can be known, addressed, contemplated, and worshipped in truth; and by virtue, therefore, of personalism, God can be known, addressed, contemplated, and worshipped falsely. In other words, religious particularism benefits in no way from speculative theology but only from personalism: "Precisely because God is anthropomorphic, with an unmistakable personal identity, He could not be represented by a bull or a baal or a solar disc. To worship Him under any other name than his own is to mistake his identity. To do it deliberately is to forsake Him."[46]

Impersonalism, by contrast, is conducive to all manner of religious creativity and thus to parity and pluralism. "The impersonal, even when declared to be unknowable, is, in the last analysis, subject to human manipulation, even manufacture. It serves as a passive screen for the projection of Freudian fantasies ... the mystic ultimately finds out the mystery."[47]

In this sense, while the claim that "God is one person" does attempt modest dogmatic advance, it is uttered initially in a defensive mode. It is designed to establish the strongest possible defense against impersonalism, to preclude idolatry and speculation, and to preserve truth in religion. "God is one person," to put it another way, means that "God is particular." "It is therefore misleading for a Christian to speak of the 'scandal of particularity.' 'Particularity' is only a 'scandal' within the mystical worldview, where God is the 'Infinite All.' In the biblical worldview, on the contrary, 'particularity' is, if anything, an honorific term, for God himself is a 'particular'—a particular *Person*."[48]

Hermeneutics and Fearless Anthropomorphism

Van Til sees himself not as an innovator, but as having attempted only to draw attention to the features of classical Trinitarianism, which he considers particularly promising for contemporary apologetics and for greater unity of dogmatics as

---

46. Cherbonnier, "Logic of Biblical Anthropomorphism," 194.
47. Cherbonnier, "Logic of Biblical Anthropomorphism," 204.
48. Cherbonnier, "Logic of Biblical Anthropomorphism," 194.

a whole. One such application of absolute personalism, appearing frequently in Van Til's work, is to theological method, involving biblical hermeneutics as well. The equal ultimacy of unity and diversity, he says, signals the difference between a negative theology weighed down by abstraction and a positive theology that seeks to name and know God according to the structure of a general and special revelatory pairing.

To explain this, Van Til contrasts two methods of articulating the incommunicable attributes, infinity in particular. The first is to "take the notions of time and of space, and subtract such characteristics as succession or continuity from them in order to reach the notions of eternity and omnipresence."[49] This method, he says, confuses negation with abstraction, and leads not to "the fulness of the being of God" but "to pure emptiness."[50] The reason it does this, in his view, is that the psychological starting point and the subject of experience are not qualified as derivative (created), so God is not presupposed. A river never runs higher than its source. Minus the presupposition that the creature is the analogue of the Creator and that, therefore, creaturely knowledge is reconstructive of the thoughts of God—that is, without a proper human self-understanding in light of the doctrine of creation—the stuff of creaturely thought and experience is taken as original or brute (uninterpreted), rather than as originating in the mind of God and given, by God, as the context for religious communion with the one who is. In this case, theological predication is not receptive and analogical but original and thus univocal. Man rather than God is self-existent and self-defined. Here God is not first the self-predicator, but first predicated by the creature. As a result, equivocation transpires between description of God and definition, and the infinity of God, thus articulated, becomes God's temporal irrelevance. God is not the fulness of temporality but the antithesis of temporal existence.

For a second, corrected method of negation, "we need the indescribable fulness of the being of God as the presupposition of our notions of time and space."[51] This is, Van Til will emphasize, to reverse the procedure just described; God is now the first fact, as it were, so that "the creation idea, the creation of the world by an absolutely self-sufficient God," is self-consciously presupposed in the thinking of the creature.[52] Experience is understood as creaturely, as derivative, and as analogous to a self-sufficient divine original. "He who planted the ear, does he not hear? He who formed the eye, does he not see?" (Ps. 94:9). This way, when, following the method of negation, familiar limitations are removed, there is still something left—the self-conscious fulness of God. By thus presupposing the creation of the world by the absolute personal God, "the way of negation is then, at the same time, the way of affirmation."[53] One might say that, on Van Til's

---

49. Van Til, *IST*, 335.
50. Van Til, *IST*, 335.
51. Van Til, *IST*, 335.
52. Van Til and Berkhof, *Foundations of Christian Education*, 84.
53. Van Til, *IST*, 335.

presuppositional method, theology follows special revelation seeking to rediscover the precondition of its own possibility.

Biblical hermeneutics, accommodation, and, in particular, the question of anthropomorphism, come into view. Van Til says that "we begin our thought about the infinity of God by insisting that the fulness of the being of God is back of the active fulness and variety in the spatio-temporal world," and that "Scripture leads us in this respect."[54] In fact, Scripture presents us with something of a challenge in that it "has no hesitation in speaking anthropomorphically of God" in the sense that it "ascribes all manner of activity to him."[55] The abundant anthropomorphism of Scripture, in other words, forces this methodological question. Since, says Van Til, "of this activity we cannot think otherwise than spatially and temporally … we are face to face with the choice either of thinking of God as altogether like unto ourselves, or of thinking ourselves the finite analogues of the fulness of his being."[56] Since we cannot take this first option "without wiping out the difference between Creator and creature," says Van Til, "we are compelled to do the latter."[57]

That is: "Everything with respect to God is on the plane of the absolute, while everything with respect to man is derivative."[58] Van Til's repeated affirmation that "God is the original and we are the derivatives"[59] means not that all created (biblical) characterizations of God must be construed as projection—the creature mistaking his own mutability for a mutability of God[60]—but rather that creatures, being derivative, lack epistemic rank to qualify or second-guess the word of the absolute God. The creature must take note of the structure of revelation, that in special revelation God names himself in creaturely terms but that these names have not arisen originally from creaturely use or religious reflection; they were first given by God. All human cognitive and contextual repertoire, every image of which human language is capable, has divine origin and already reveals God. "Thus God is not named according to what is found in the creature, except God has first named the creature according to what is in himself. The only reason why it appears as though God is named according to what is found in the creature is that, as creatures, we must psychologically begin with ourselves in our knowledge of anything."[61]

Put differently, God does not discover a self-sufficient human community and then introduce himself according to their understanding, utilizing the native thought patterns he happens upon. Rather, God creates the image-bearer already knowing and experiencing God's own self-presentation, so that when God

---

54. Van Til, *IST*, 336.
55. Van Til, *IST*, 336.
56. Van Til, *IST*, 336.
57. Van Til, *IST*, 336.
58. Van Til, *IST*, 327.
59. Van Til, *IST*, 326.
60. Not an uncommon hermeneutical option.
61. Van Til, *IST*, 323.

introduces himself, he introduces himself as already known. God presupposes creaturely knowledge of himself when he speaks to the creature. The creature thinks its own thoughts, but the creature's thoughts always already issue from a theologically saturated self-understanding, or there would be no thoughts at all. It is thus that "our attempts to say something about God then have back of them the original fact that God has said something about himself."[62] In sum: God first describes himself to the creature in the things that have been made; and then in special revelation God presents himself to his people in objectified form.

So Van Til thinks of createdness as revelatory analogous derivation and infers a biblical hermeneutic open to anthropomorphic realism. Van Til argues that biblical depictions of divine character and action are not merely creaturely record of divine revelatory activity but creaturely record divinely inspired, divinely sanctioned. In Scripture, man speaks about God, but the inspiration of Scripture means that in Scripture God speaks about God. This means that Scripture does not naïvely and recklessly portray an immutable God doing this and that, having this or that character trait; in Scripture, the immutable God tells the creature that he, the immutable God, is doing this and that. This revelatory self-objectification of special revelation signals the sphere of redemptive fellowship with the absolute God which by Vos and Van Til is often designated "covenant." It is, therefore, implied in the redemptive relationship that image-bearers exercise "a fearless anthropomorphism based on the doctrine of the ontological trinity" in their interpretation of the written record of the historical works of the absolute God.[63]

Does God have unactualized potentiality? Van Til holds to the classical incommunicable attributes and denies that God has unactualized potentiality. One reason, though not the only one, for a negative answer here is that the question of unactualized potentiality expresses classical or Thomistic (or late medieval) metaphysics. The predominant view is that in classical or Thomistic metaphysics it is denied that in the divine being there is unactualized potentiality because it is believed that to affirm unactualized potentiality would compromise simplicity, amounting to wholesale abandonment of the incommunicable attributes.[64] So, in terms of historic orthodoxy, or wherever Thomas's terminology has set the terms of theological discourse, it is and ought to be—for the sake of historic orthodoxy— denied that there is unactualized potentiality in the divine being. Bavinck, Vos, and Van Til do not disappoint here; each is in step with historic orthodoxy on this point and with regard to this language.

But of course such denial appears to imply that God eternally and unchangeably is whatever he could be, that in the being of God the possible and the actual are indistinguishable. This has been called "modal collapse."[65] More relevant

62. Van Til, *IST*, 324.
63. Van Til, *CGG*, 111.
64. See James E. Dolezal, *God without Parts: Divine Simplicity and the Metaphysics of God's Absoluteness* (Eugene, OR: Pickwick, 2011).
65. See, for example, J. P. Moreland and William Lane Craig, *Philosophical Foundations for a Christian Worldview* (Downers Grove, IL: InterVarsity Press, 2003); R. T. Mullins,

presently: the classical articulation of simplicity[66] has been thought to entail a number of hermeneutical restrictions. One such restriction pertains to the relation of God, and the works of God, to history. A classical articulation of simplicity tends to require evasive hermeneutical maneuvers whenever Scripture represents God as involved in the historical realm of human experience. What Christians are accustomed to thinking of as historical acts of God—those acts of God depicted in Scripture—are in fact not historical in the sense in which Christians are accustomed to think, in the sense in which the ordinary reader of Scripture might assume, or the ordinary meaning of the text. Since God is eternal, all of God's acts are eternal; God cannot act temporally. Temporality is inimical to the divine being, so the thought goes. So in one way or another—and there are numerous options—those divine acts that appear to creatures, including the writers of Scripture, as historical, are not—at least not without requisite metaphysical qualification. What creatures witness are the temporal effects of eternal acts. A similar restriction, or a refraction of the same, has to do with impassibility. Interpretation of biblical portrayals of God affected by creatures must reckon with the fact that God cannot undergo, or have, passions at all. God may represent himself in Scripture as though he did in fact have passions, or was in fact affected by human activity. One is caught between a particular metaphysic of the incommunicable attributes and the plain meaning of the text. And so on. Van Til believes that these restrictions are the hermeneutical byproducts of exaggerated apophaticism, and by virtue of that apophaticism also of equivocation. Here "eternal," "immutable," and "impassible" tend rather toward silence than toward the affirmation, the conviction, that God is.

Notice, furthermore, that the divine acts in question must include all *opera ad extra*, everything God does save the immanent personal processions within the divine life. Everything that God does relative to whatever is not identical to his own being is called into question. So, included are creating, self-revealing, and entering into covenant with creation principally through a relationship with the image-bearer. And these are the divine acts presupposed in theological knowledge. So, if such acts are eternal in the very same way that the being of God is itself eternal, if divine acts partake of the same ontology as the divine being and there is no modal distinction between God and the acts of God, then either God is wholly known or not known at all. Even this: "The self-existent God has created and revealed himself so that he can be known" is a theological statement with dubious methodological credentials because the classical metaphysic disallows attribution

---

"Simply Impossible: A Case against Divine Simplicity," *Journal of Reformed Theology* 7, no. 2 (2013): 181–203; Klaas J. Kraay, "Theism and Modal Collapse," *American Philosophical Quarterly* 48, no. 4 (2011): 361–72. For a response, see Christopher Tomaszewski, "Collapsing the Modal Collapse Argument: On an Invalid Argument against Divine Simplicity," *Analysis* 79, no. 2 (2019): 275–84.

66. "Classical" is criminally generic; one should doubt that there is such a thing. Nonetheless, the term is used in this way, and tends to signal the thought of Thomas Aquinas.

of any act or character to a non-revealed God. God is his revelation, or "God" is a religious speech act which fails to refer.

Theologians have acknowledged and debated at length the problem of anthropomorphism as a subset or special instance of accommodation in revelation. Gen. 6:6 and Mal. 3:6 are common test cases for the relationship between the relevant classical categories and biblical interpretation. In Van Til's view, revelation as such is at stake—Scripture as a whole, not just a few egregiously anthropomorphic statements—and if revelation then "the creation idea," too, hangs in the balance, since there is no creation apart from revelation, and no revelation apart from creation. As we have seen, creation is divine revelatory self-giving. But on the classical model, "God self-reveals" is on shaky ground. A divine act of self-revelation is incoherent, since it presupposes a subject who moves unnecessarily (changes) from hidden to revealed. The creature may only know the revealed subject, but he cannot know the subject as revealed; in the end, the classical model that was designed to protect the purity of divine being and act appears to render deity unknowable. There can be, as Bavinck has said, no fellowship with God on this model. On the classical model the names of God uttered by creatures cannot refer; they are tossed into unknowable darkness; there is no *sensus divinitatis* or natural Creator–creature relationship, just the echoes of the religious chatter of a finite creature reverberating in his own mind. Or so Van Til appears to claim.

Vern Poythress describes similar hermeneutical fallout of a false notion of divine transcendence. He says that such an error "can enter even after someone has affirmed the transcendence of God using the Creator-creature distinction."[67] Poythress illustrates:

> So someone—let us call her Donna—imagines God doing the same thing. And indeed, there is an analogy. But the analogy is only partial. Donna cannot actually become an observer of God, on his own level, in the same way that she can become an observer of a human father. But she can try to imagine it, and then fall into the temptation of trying to figure out just what God is leaving out, compressing, and simplifying in the process of speaking to "child-like" human beings. Donna's speculation about what God is really doing may then function as a more ultimate authority than Scripture. Scripture only has the qualified authority of being for the child-like. And Donna?—Donna has become godlike.[68]

Poythress says that Donna has effectively revived a gnostic and unbiblical notion of transcendence along with its accompanying hermeneutic. In doing so, he says, "Donna tries to transcend our human limitations in order to watch God over his shoulder, so to speak, and thereby to know the ways in which she can and cannot receive Scripture at full value."[69] Donna's trouble with the text

---

67. Vern Poythress, "Rethinking Accommodation in Revelation," *Westminster Theological Journal* 76, no. 1 (2014): 146.
68. Poythress, "Rethinking Accommodation," 146.
69. Poythress, "Rethinking Accommodation," 146–7.

of Scripture is indicative of a deeper theological trouble. She has adopted a notion of transcendence that cannot tolerate anthropomorphism and therefore leaves her in a difficult relationship with the text of Scripture. Poythress says that even though hermeneutical difficulties may be subtle and theologically well explained, the fact is that Donna has taken a "new seat of authority" relative to Scripture, one constituted by her "personal vision of how God practices father-like condescension."[70] That vision "trumps the authority of Scripture itself."[71] How far this undoing of the authority and clarity of Scripture is carried is incidental. Donna's theology has restructured hermeneutics and theological method so that revelation has lost its authority. The Bible may accompany her metaphysics but, when in conflict, Scripture gives way.

Poythress explores a complementary error in which a second fictional character, Joe, adopts a false notion of divine immanence. Joe, says Poythress, affirms the full authority of Scripture and of the incomprehensibility of God, which highlights the necessity and authority of divine revelation, but the way that he handles Scripture runs afoul of this confession. Joe is hermeneutically heavy-handed; he insists on rationalizing every bit of biblical data. "He thinks that (in principle) he can master Scripture, precisely because it is accommodated to us and therefore falls within the sphere of human control."[72] Joe, in other words, "reasons that, unlike God himself, Scripture as accommodated language must be completely subject to human ideas of rationality."[73] Hermeneutically, the effects are similar. Joe will try theological hermeneutics like he is shopping for new shoes—until he finds one that, for now, makes maximal "sense" of the text of Scripture. Poythress is concerned that Joe, inadvertently, is involved in an unhealthy kind of theological creativity, the rule for which is not obedience but intellectual satisfaction, or theoretical functionality. Poythress proposes an alternative: "God's immanence implies in the sphere of epistemology that he makes himself known to us, both in general revelation and in Scripture."[74]

Wary perhaps of modal collapse and of surrendering the relational symmetry of true religion to self-referential metaphysics, Vos asks: "Is God's power limited by the reality of what exists?" He answers: "No, this would be a pantheistic thought. God is able to do more than He actually does."[75] The significance of this statement is rendered apparent by comparison with the classical model. With such a statement Vos affirms that God can do more and other than he has done, that God lacks nothing but can do infinitely more than he has done, that the actual world is not deducible from the divine being. It is Van Til's view that the classical metaphysic simply cannot hold these predicates together—that eternally God is and that

---

70. Poythress, "Rethinking Accommodation," 147.
71. Poythress, "Rethinking Accommodation," 147.
72. Poythress, "Rethinking Accommodation," 147.
73. Poythress, "Rethinking Accommodation," 147.
74. Poythress, "Rethinking Accommodation," 147.
75. Vos, *RD*, 1:36. See also Van Til, *IST*, 392.

eternally God can. Pure act and personality, in other words, are to neo-Aristotelian classical metaphysics as absoluteness and personality are to the Platonist or the Idealist or the modern metaphysician. When Van Til says "absolute person" he says both "pure act" and "potentiality." But by adopting modern language he at once honors the tradition that forbids such affirmation and enjoys his freedom from secondary sources and of conscience. In other words, effectively, Van Til affirms both pure act and unactualized potentiality even though the historical credentials of this language render demurral heterodox. Van Til is aware that the language of absolute person critically and constructively engages the tradition, but he also knows that if he will speak constructively to the tradition he must adopt new language. Classical thought patterns are in knots. So, while saying something relatively new, or while attempting to make a point that honors but does more than repeat the tradition, Van Til—and Herman and J. H. Bavinck as well—adopts new language. In this sense, it is evident that Van Til should be understood as attempting constructively to engage the tradition with regard to the Creator–creature relation and theological hermeneutics of creaturely experience and self-understanding.[76] In fact he believes that the classical doctrine of God, that conviction of the divine self-existence dating to Augustine, is precisely that which draws out attention to the plain meaning of the biblical text and enjoins regular reassessment of the metaphysical machinery of biblical interpretation.

Fearless Anthropomorphism and Reformed Tradition

These hermeneutical issues represent ground well-trod by Reformed writers. Richard A. Muller writes:

> The Reformers and their scholastic followers all recognized that God must in some way condescend or accommodate himself to human ways of knowing in order to reveal himself. This *accommodatio* occurs in the use of human words and concepts for the communication of the law and gospel, but it in no way implies the loss of truth or the lessening of scriptural authority.[77]

Accommodation, then, for the Reformed in particular, is the general term for the idea that revelation is somehow designed by God to enable effective communication with the creature. God cannot speak to man as he, God, speaks to himself. Revelation reflects, necessarily, the ontological distinction between God and the creature, and is therefore a function of the divine act of creation.

---

76. Van Til argues that his fearless anthropomorphism and theology of history restore important emphases of John Calvin obscured by Abraham Kuyper, Herman Bavinck, and Herman Hepp. He looks to Calvin's debate with Albertus Pighius. See Van Til, *CGG*, 34–113.

77. Richard A. Muller, *Dictionary of Latin and Greek Theological Terms: Drawn Principally from Protestant Scholastic Theology* (Grand Rapids, MI: Baker, 1986), 19.

And as Muller indicates, authority and trustworthiness hang in the balance. It is not uncommon, for example, to construe accommodation as God's free use of erroneous human beliefs or as God's use of dispensable didactic forms to convey enduring religious or moral principles. Kenton Sparks, for example, describes accommodation as "God's adoption in inscripturation of the human audience's finite and fallen perspective. Its underlying conceptual assumption is that in many cases God does not correct our mistaken human viewpoints but merely assumes them in order to communicate with us."[78] Nor is Sparks's view novel. René Descartes had claimed that God could be directly dishonest in Scripture, making use of *"verbale aliquod mendacium."*[79] Benedict Spinoza also took the doctrine to an extreme, abandoning the authority of Scripture altogether. He said of Holy Scripture that "every man now has the duty to accommodate it [the text of Scripture] to his own beliefs (*eandem suis opinionibus accommodare*), so as thus to accept it without any misgivings or doubts."[80] The Socinians of the seventeenth century "argued that only by employing misconceptions was God able to communicate superior knowledge to a less-than-superior audience."[81] The Socinian influence struck close to home for the Reformed in the work of Jean-Alphonse, son of Francis, Turretini, who was during his day "the most prominent theologian of the Genevan Academy."[82] Historians Martin Klauber and Glenn Sunshine summarize Turretini's thinking as follows:

> Socinus's rationalistic approach to apologetics was part and parcel of his overall theological method. Although Socinus argued for biblical authority, in practice he placed Scripture below reason as a means of determining truth. Part of the reason for this was that he denied that the fall marred man's ability to reason. In addition, he contended that revelation can reach us only through our reason, since it is given in rational terms and categories. It follows that nothing in revelation can be contrary to reason; anything in Scripture that reason finds unacceptable or contradictory cannot be true.[83]

78. Kenton L. Sparks, *God's Word in Human Words: An Evangelical Appropriation of Critical Biblical Scholarship* (Grand Rapids, MI: Baker, 2008), 230–1.

79. René Descartes, *Oeuvres de Descartes*, ed. Charles Adam and Paul Tannery, 12 vols. (Paris: Cerf, 1897–1957), 7:142–3; quoted in Arnold Huijgen, *Divine Accommodation in John Calvin's Theology* (Göttingen: Vandenhoeck & Ruprecht, 2011), 30 n.92.

80. Benedict Spinoza, *Tractatus Theologico-Politicus*, trans. Samuel Shirley (Leiden: Brill, 1989), 14.178.34; quoted in Huijgen, *Divine Accommodation*, 32.

81. Hoon J. Lee, *The Biblical Accommodation Debate in Germany: Interpretation and the Enlightenment* (Cham, Switzerland: Palgrave Macmillan, 2017), 212.

82. Martin I. Klauber and Glenn S. Sunshine, "Jean-Alphone Turretini on Biblical Accommodation: Calvinist or Socinian?," *Calvin Theological Journal* 25, no. 1 (1990): 8.

83. Klauber and Sunshine, "Jean-Alphonse Turretini," 13. See Richard A. Muller, *Holy Scripture: The Cognitive Foundation of Theology*, vol. 2 of *Post-Reformation Reformed Dogmatics: The Rise and Development of Reformed Orthodoxy, ca. 1520 to ca. 1725*, 2nd ed. (Grand Rapids, MI: Baker Academic, 2003), 303–10.

Through all this, and into the twentieth century, Calvin's view of accommodation has served as a benchmark for Reformed theologians. Or, more precisely, the principles that he sought to maintain are still represented by the language of "Calvin's theology of accommodation," while Calvin himself has come under scrutiny for allegedly failing to maintain those principles. "Calvinist accommodation" is, in other words, something of a Reformed ideal, while Calvin himself highlights both the importance of getting it right and, it turns out, the many challenges of doing so. For establishing a historic, Reformed context for Van Til's fearless anthropomorphism, therefore, Calvin's and contemporary Calvinist thought serve well, and for this we look to Arnold Huijgen.

Huijgen reconstructs Calvin's theology of accommodation within its historical context, and then tests its viability against Calvin's own goals. In fact he finds Calvin falling short at important points, as shall be noted below. And Huijgen's interests are not exclusively historical and descriptive. He draws Calvin's thought into the contemporary setting by reflecting on relevant modern developments and by reintroducing Calvin's priorities as a challenge to contemporary theology.

Huijgen points out that linguistic and analytic reflection on the nature of theological predication and religious language—"Godtalk," so-called—is a modern undertaking. Calvin himself did not feel beholden to the terms of these discussions, which are so familiar to contemporary readers. Instead, Calvin's concerns are of a relational or religious or, one may say, covenantal sort. Huijgen notes, with Cornelius van der Kooi, that "Calvin is more concerned about a reliable soteriology than about a doctrine of God free from tensions."[84] More to the point, "coming from a modern perspective, we have to note that Calvin does not provide a theory of religious language, and the possibility of God-talk."[85]

But the fact that Calvin is not available for anachronistic retrieval in this sense is not due to the sheer freshness of modern inquiry. Modern questions regarding the knowability of God would be in many ways nothing new under the sun—Descartes, Spinoza, and the Socinians, among others, as noted, had already laid the ground work. So the issues, even for the late twentieth century, were more or less already clear. Calvin's position *contra* these challenges, it should be noted, constitutes a methodological distinctive—not disagreement in this point or that, but a clarification of the nature of theology. The initiative and origin of theology, Calvin insists, are divine; theology and true religion have their inception in a movement of God toward the creature, not in a movement of the creature toward the supernatural. Theology expresses divine summons not human experiment. Against the backdrop of the Socinian approach to accommodation, says Huijgen, Calvin "pictures the reverse movement: God employs human language to reveal Himself. Biblical language is no expression of experiences of God dressed in

---

84. Huijgen, *Divine Accommodation*, 283. See Cornelius van der Kooi, *As in a Mirror: Calvin and Barth on Knowing God: A Dyptych*, trans. Donald Mader (Leiden: Brill, 2005).

85. Huijgen, *Divine Accommodation*, 271.

human language, which may conform to the reality of God, but it is the way God presents Himself to human [sic] who otherwise cannot grasp Him."[86]

To be clear, the Socinian view is portrayed this way as well; it is, to be sure, God who makes use of human language and ideas. But the Socinian view portrays God using human language and ideas that encumber with his purposes, and thus compromise his meaning. God can find no adequate means to communicate; he is forced to work with what he finds in the world, faulty and unreliable as it is. Revelation is always, on all accounts, subject to misinterpretation, but the Socinian view denies God control over his own self-expression. He does not have the colors he wants; he has to paint in the dark; like Beethoven in his later years, God does not actually know how the final product will actually sound. So even correct interpretation is an elusive concept. Calvin's view does not reject the idea that God contends with human weakness and confusion, but Calvin incorporates it into a broader view of the data of creation. According to the doctrines of creation and general revelation, the structures and data of creation were originally good; presently they are inhospitable to special revelation only because they are under the influence of the suppressive unholiness of sinful humans.

When, for example, God in Scripture calls himself "father," the Socinian view would allow the reader to note that human fathers are fallible, disloyal, selfish, even abusive, and to draw the conclusion that the biblical designation of God as father must be—because God is good and God is perfect love—only a vague approximation that cannot be taken too literally. God, says the Socinian view, is not "father" but fatherly goodness, but also mother, or parent, or grandparent, or tender if impersonal presence—life itself or the universe itself.

Calvin's view distinguishes common and familiar use of terms from a good original use, noting that experience shows us corrupted and suppressive notions parasitic on the good originals. When God calls himself "father," the reader faces in Scripture an authoritative representation of fatherly goodness against which a common, human, fallible fatherhood may be evaluated. More directly: God created fathers good, loving, and godly; then he approaches man in sin and misery—sinful fathers and children of imperfect men—and invites him to cry, with the perfect Son, "abba, Father." Huijgen writes: "God has to speak our language, because if He would speak His own language, no one would understand Him. God's employment of human language as such is an accommodation, which guarantees the reliability of revelation: as far as we are able to bear, God Himself comes to us in the words He uses."[87] "Calvin does not start from our human words to assess the solidity of God's Words, but rather starts at the other end: God's Word is firmer than any human word."[88]

The importance of this methodological qualification can hardly be overstated. Calvin is demarcating the difference between human subjective experience as

---

86. Huijgen, *Divine Accommodation*, 271.
87. Huijgen, *Divine Accommodation*, 271.
88. Huijgen, *Divine Accommodation*, 272.

the precondition for receiving revelation and human subjective experience as the result of divine self-revelation. The latter notion is among the telltale indications of Calvinist thought. Before addressing this in more detail, however, a bigger picture of Calvin's theology of accommodation is needed.

Institutes 1.1—Method and Relationality in Calvin

Huijgen in fact traces accommodation to the opening of the *Institutes* and uncovers there not a memorable theological slogan—though it surely is this!—but an opening announcement of a structural principle that will guide Calvin's approach to theological formulation and biblical exegesis. *Institutes* 1.1 presents the Delphic oracle of Calvinist theological reflection:

> Nearly all the wisdom we possess, that is to say, true and sound wisdom, consists of two parts: the knowledge of God and of ourselves. But, while joined by many bonds, which one precedes and brings forth the other is not easy to discern. In the first place, no one can look upon himself without immediately turning his thoughts to the contemplation of God, in whom he "lives and moves."[89]

Huijgen, accordingly, emphasizes the tremendous importance of the analyticity of knowledge of the self and knowledge of God for Calvin and for Calvinism. He writes:

> The famous opening sentence of the *Institutes* indicates the primacy of relationality and mediation in Calvin's understanding of accommodation. … The relation between God and humans is primary for any theological knowledge: humans are placed before God. So, when God accommodates, He does not hand over a set of truths, an external datum, that humans need to use as a puzzle to find their way to their Creator, but, rather the relation between God and humans is presupposed.[90]

That is, when God takes up, as Muller says, "human words and concepts," he (God) is not trying to introduce into human experience notions erstwhile unknown. If that were the case, God would be in the impossible situation of having to use a known language to evoke knowledge of utterly unknown things—precisely

---

89. John Calvin, *Institutes of the Christian Religion*, ed. John T. McNeill, trans. Ford Lewis Battles (Philadelphia: Westminster Press, 1960), 1.1.1.

90. Huijgen, *Divine Accommodation*, 294. As would become characteristic of Reformed theology: "the Reformed conception of Christian theology is fundamentally a relational enterprise, determined by and determinative of the divine-human relationship." Willem Van Asselt, "The Fundamental Nature of Theology: Archetypcal and Ectypcal Theology in Seventeenth-Century Reformed Thought," *Westminster Theological Journal* 64, no. 2 (2002): 324.

the script for modern religious pluralism. For Calvin, relation (logically) precedes revelation; or revelation is a function of a relation already in place, of a relation that is indistinguishable from creaturely life and creaturely consciousness as such. As a result, "the limitation of accommodated revelation results in reduction to the actual relation between God and humans, and functions in an anti-speculative way."[91] In other words, if revelation presupposes relation, revelation objectifies a God already implicitly known (relationally), and revelation cannot proceed beyond the boundaries of that relation. The creature may know only the God who already knows the creature. So there is a natural and necessary correlation between the God who is already known and the God who invites the creature to know himself (God's self) further. Theology is thus basically practical and relational. Speculation is then not pious wonder or meditative self-subjection, which of course are commended in Scripture, but pointless, directionless theoretical monologue and religious echo. "Most notably," Huijgen continues, "the correlation of the knowledge of God, and the knowledge of ourselves, focuses theology, and reduces its task in comparison to scholastic forms of theology."[92] And the main point is this: "For true theology is useful, and edifying, because she stays within the bounds of the knowledge of God and of ourselves. In that sense, the first sentence of the *Institutes* is programmatic."[93]

Huijgen attempts to capture Calvin's understanding of accommodation with an image of multiple concentric circles. Relational intimacy is maximized in the middle and decreases moving outward. Degrees of accommodation are represented as inversely proportional to relational intimacy. So, maximal intimacy, at the center, requires minimal accommodation. Where the relation is less direct, as represented by the circles further from the center, accommodation increases to compensate. And all movement is toward the center. Beginning from the largest circle, increasingly narrowing circles indicate incremental progress toward the consummate, relational center.

Accommodation, in other words, as Huijgen understands Calvin, presupposes covenant relation and serves eschatological relation. Accommodation is basically the character or means of a relational overture designed to achieve greater intimacy in the form and through the means of historical relation. Accommodation is not, by contrast, an unfit means or mismatched form or crude and clumsy mechanism that revelation must reckon with if God will hope to communicate with the creature. Accommodation is not, to put it differently, forced upon God, the price of admission, if God wishes to convey something to a creature who, to the surprise and dismay of his maker, is essentially deaf to divine communication. Rather, God has created both the creature and his environment so that the creature already knows God, and accommodation is a notion designed to highlight the relational condescension of God for the sake of the personal edification of the creature in relationship with God. Like an orphaned child who finally meets his biological

---

91. Huijgen, *Divine Accommodation*, 295.
92. Huijgen, *Divine Accommodation*, 295.
93. Huijgen, *Divine Accommodation*, 295.

parents, the sinner meets in special revelation a God he in the fabric of his being already knows and now can get to know better. Accommodation is something like a pedagogy or covenant curriculum geared toward the singular goal of personal, relational fruition of God.

Huijgen identifies, furthermore, a trinitarian economy in Calvin's theology of accommodation:

> The various accommodations have their place in a distinct circle, near to the center, or further away, but they are all governed by the Spirit's intention to lead inward. This operation of the Spirit is inherently bound to the central idea of Christ's mediatorial office, which serves a very broad function in Calvin's thought. Christ the Mediator reaches out, by His Spirit, through accommodation in means both universal, and more intimate, to lead His people to the knowledge of Himself.[94]

According to Huijgen, Calvin's view is that accommodation is by Christ and for the sake of Christ. Although the creature meets first the Spirit, the Spirit's activity is on behalf of the Son. The Spirit is sent by the Son to bear witness to the Son, or to draw attention to the Son, to draw people toward the Son. And the Son, furthermore, is the sole mediator between creatures and the Father. So, as Huijgen understands Calvin, in accommodation the Son sends the Spirit to draw creatures in the Son to the Father. Within the Godhead, the Son is the only person who is both the origin of another person (the Spirit) and who also has his personal origin in another (the Father). This in a manner of speaking puts the Son in the center of the Trinity. Likewise, here in Calvin's understanding of accommodation, the Son is central. Although the Spirit may be said to be the agent in accommodated encounter, the Spirit takes his charter from the Son and serves on behalf of the Son. Although the Father may be said to be the telos of accommodated encounter, the Father may be approached and known only in the Son.

Huijgen takes the famous opening of the *Institutes*, in which Calvin declares an unsearchable interdependence of knowledge of God and knowledge of the self, as programmatic for Calvin not only for his doctrine of accommodation, but for his theology entirely: "for Calvin the entire character of the knowledge of God and of theology is at stake. Knowing God is not a matter of discursive reason reaching higher than the skies, but the other way around: God, who dwells in inapproachable light, has come near in Christ."[95] That opening statement of the interdependence and reciprocity of self-knowledge and knowledge of God, says Huijgen, proves to be a basic rule: biblical revelation articulates the always and already actual relation between God and man. Biblical anthropology therefore is already in-reference-to-God; it is a theological or theocentric anthropology. This basic relationality is not initiated by revelation but exposed and objectified by revelation. More

---

94. Huijgen, *Divine Accommodation*, 306.
95. Huijgen, *Divine Accommodation*, 269–70.

importantly, the doctrine of God conveyed in Scripture is a self-portrait of God in relation. Scripture presents God and man in mutual relationship, and it is the task of biblical revelation to present God as he has presented himself to man.

For Huijgen, this signals two important themes in Calvin's thought and exegesis. The first is an aversion to speculation, in which wandering and wondering beyond what is revealed is discouraged.[96] Calvin often warns against a lust for illicit knowledge and the allure of speculation.[97] But the point is the doctrine of God: Scripture will not underwrite an independent and speculative expedition, philosophical or meditative, in search of the unrevealed God. The Scripture indeed speaks of the God "behind revelation," in the sense that from within relation and revelation, God teaches about his hidden nature. While no one has ascended into heaven, Jesus has descended from heaven; the Spirit descends from heaven in the form of a dove; and the voice of the Father comes from heaven (Jn 1:32; 3:13; 12:28) into the realm of human experience. The creature may therefore say that "God dwells in heaven," but only because God has come down to underwrite that confession. Revelation in relation is the only vindication of theological predication involving the God who has self-revealed, the only warrant for a distinction between revelation and the God who is revealed.

The second theme is the practical end or reason for biblical revelation. For Calvin, whatever God has revealed he has revealed for our edification theocentrically understood, for religious practical purposes, for fruition of God. Theological information for the satisfaction of a cold curiosity is nowhere to be seen; knowledge is never an end in itself in that speculative sense. Scripture does not serve such purposes. Huijgen writes: "Calvin intends to keep his 'doctrine' of Scripture within the realm of his axiom of the knowledge of God and the knowledge of ourselves. Scripture teaches us who God is, and who we are, in mutual relation; no more, no less."[98]

So it turns out that Muller's description—accommodated revelation is God's "use of human words and concepts"—only scratches the surface of the Calvinist conception.[99] The Calvinist point of view is that revelation is accommodation and

---

96. On these themes in Calvin's exegesis, see Richard C. Gamble, "'Brevitas et Facilitas': Toward an Understanding of Calvin's Hermeneutic," *Westminster Theological Journal* 47, no. 1 (1985): 1–17; Gamble, "Exposition and Method in Calvin," *Westminster Theological Journal* 49 (1987): 153–65; Myung Jun Ahn, "The Influences on Calvin's Hermeneutics and the Development of His Method," *HTS Teologiese Studies/Theological Studies* 55, no. 1 (1999): 228–39; Ahn, "The Ideal of *Brevitas et Facilitas*: The Theological Hermeneutics of John Calvin," *Skrif en Kerk/Verbum et Ecclesia* 20, no. 2 (1999): 270–81; Ahn, "*Brevitas et Facilitas*: A Study of a Vital Aspect in the Theological Hermeneutics of John Calvin" (PhD diss., University of Pretoria, 1998).

97. A notable example is *Institutes*, 1.13, on the Trinity.

98. Huijgen, *Divine Accommodation*, 311.

99. Muller distinguishes the Calvinist view from the Socinian when he says that, in Calvinist thought, accommodation does not entail the loss of truth or of biblical authority (*Dictionary of Latin and Greek Theological Terms*, 19).

that creation itself is revelation. More precisely, the Calvinist view is that revelation is a twofold accommodation. The first is general or creational, and this revelation is a divine self-revelation that constitutes creaturely subjective experience, so that for the creature to register experience as a self-conscious subject is for a created being to be in relation to God. The uncompelled, creative movement of God toward the self-conscious creature brings that creature out of nothing into a realm of subjective experience, a subjective realm indistinguishable from experience of the objective and self-defined but self-expressed (accommodated) God. The second accommodation is the special, eschatological self-objectification of God for the sake of a teleological covenant relationship in which the bearer of the divine image is invited to consummate enjoyment of the divine original. And the second presupposes the first.

Calvin as Imperfect Calvinist

Calvin's theology of accommodation appears to fall short of his own ideals. Reflecting upon Calvin's lackluster performance in this regard will highlight where and how Bavinck, Vos, and Van Til have sought to honor their predecessor. Absolute personalism, and unipersonality in particular, may be thought of as their best attempt at maximizing a balance between accommodation and biblical truth and authority—precisely where, according to Huijgen, Calvin himself disappoints.

For Calvin, the personal nature of revelation and revelation's relational context signal the trustworthiness of the written Word of God. Huijgen is concerned that these features of Calvin's theology of accommodation are compromised when a speculative expression of the creation idea, and of the Creator–creature distinction in particular, troubles Calvin's interpretation of biblical passages that portray God as changing or having emotions. A speculative metaphysic gives way to inconsistent and at times indefensible exegesis and compromise of the authority and trustworthiness of revelation. Hindsight, Huijgen suggests, has helped expose these troubles: "Whereas Calvin could," in his day, "find additional support in common sense metaphysical presuppositions, this support has lost its *prima facie* plausibility."[100]

Note, for example, Calvin's commentary on Jon. 3:10, in which the Lord has threatened judgment upon Nineveh but then extends mercy:

> Now as to what Jonah adds, *that God was led to repent*, it is a mode of speaking that ought to be sufficiently known to us. Strictly speaking, no repentance can belong to God: and it ought not to be ascribed to his secret and hidden counsel. God then is in himself ever the same, and consistent with himself; but he is said to repent, when a regard is had to the comprehension of men: for as we conceive God to be angry, whenever he summons us to his tribunal, and shows to us our sins; so also we conceive him to be placable, when he offers the hope

---

100. Huijgen, *Divine Accommodation*, 317.

of pardon. But it is according to our perceptions that there is any change, when God forgets his wrath, as though he had put on a new character. As then we cannot otherwise be terrified, that we may be humbled before God and repent, except he sets forth before us his wrath, the Scripture accommodates itself to the grossness of our understanding. But, on the other hand, we cannot confidently call on God, unless we feel assured that he is placable. We hence see that some kind of change appears to us, whenever God either threatens or gives hope of pardon and reconciliation: and to this must be referred this mode of speaking which Jonah adopts, when he says, that God repented.

We hence see that there is a twofold view of God,—as he sets himself forth in his word,—and as he is as to his hidden counsel. With regard to his secret counsel, I have already said that God is always like himself, and is subject to none of our feelings: but with regard to the teaching of his word, it is accommodated to our capacities. God is now angry with us, and then, as though he were pacified, he offers pardon, and is propitious to us. Such is the repentance of God.

Let us then remember that it proceeds from his word, that God is said to repent; for the Ninevites could form no other opinion but that it was God's decree that they were to be destroyed,—how so? because he had so testified by his word. But when they rose up to an assurance of deliverance, they then found that a change had taken place, that is, according to the knowledge of their own faith: and the feelings both of fear and of joy proceeded from the word: for when God denounced his wrath, it was necessary for the wretched men to be terrified; but when he invited them to a state of safety by proposing reconciliation to them, he then put on a new character; and thus they ascribed a new feeling to God. This is the meaning.[101]

It is difficult to distinguish this from the Socinian notion of accommodation. Calvin states clearly that God uses theological falsehoods to represent himself and even that the soteric crisis, when creatures contemplate repentance before an angry God, depends acutely upon those premeditated misrepresentations.

At least three difficulties may be identified. First, Calvin appears to transgress his own theology of accommodation. Personalism is reduced to revelational decoy and the trustworthiness of revelation is severely qualified. Second, unless Calvin will distinguish accommodated portions of Scripture from unaccommodated portions, the Socinian principle of God's using fallible or mistaken forms of human thought or speech should be consistently applied, so that if the immutable God "to whom no repentance can belong" is also the God of the Bible, that same immutability will also be divine accommodation to erroneous forms of thought for perlocutionary religious purpose. An unknown god is mutable or immutable—no one knows—but presents himself as mutable in order to evoke piety in his followers. Third, as this passage stands, if only the immutable, infinite God can be the self-named God

---

101. John Calvin, *Jonah, Micah, Nahum*, vol. 3 of *Commentaries on the Minor Prophets*, trans. John Owen (Grand Rapids, MI: Baker Book House, n.d.), 115–16, Lecture 79 on Jon. 3:10.

whose revelation is self-attesting—authoritative and trustworthy—then there is a troubling mismatch here between the doctrine of God Calvin affirms here and the doctrine of God implied in his hermeneutic. To straighten this out, there appear to be two options: adjust the doctrine of God to the hermeneutic, which means to introduce a basic rule of agnosticism; or adjust the hermeneutic to the doctrine of God, and restore the authority of the plain meaning of the text.

Aside from that, there may be another way to understand Jonah's preaching and God's dealing with Nineveh. It would seem that in Paul and in the Pentateuch, the law itself implicitly bears the perlocutionary intention of drawing its hearers to repentance, even to Christ. This is Calvin's first use of the law. This connection between law and gospel is an excellent instance of properly grounded perlocutionary intention. God's design is to bring about repentance and to draw sinners to Christ. His chosen means of accomplishing this is through exposing and aggravating sin by the giving and propagating of the law (Rom. 5; Gal. 3). The author of Hebrews makes this clear when he points out the absurdity of atoning for human sin with the sacrifice of animals (Heb. 9–10). The law is moral truth itself, given for Israel. Though true in that moral sense, it is nonetheless provisional, and not an end in itself, nor intended as a self-sufficient means to salvation by works (Rom. 3). So it has a subordinate function but not in a sense that diminishes its sincerity or (moral) truth value. The Scripture confirms that Jesus preached the gospel (Lk. 20:1), but his early preaching appears to have taken this indirect route, focusing on the single imperative, "repent" (Mt. 4:17). With that bigger picture in mind, when Jonah is sent to preach the wrath of God, this is, effectively, in a perlocutionary fashion, to preach the gospel. To repent means to acknowledge God is the immovable personal standard and one's unqualified unworthiness in comparison. Repentance is a natural and necessary precursor to pleading for divine mercy; pleading for divine mercy is the flip side of repentance. If to repent is to inhale, to call upon the mercy of God is to exhale. To call upon the name of Christ as the "handle" for such mercy is, in a sense, a matter of historical detail. Though his name is only known from the time of his earthly ministry and mediatorial accomplishment at Calvary, he is the substance of mercy all along.

Notice the book of Jonah features the prophet's disdain for the generosity of God; in other words, Jonah has received from the Lord a task that exposes Jonah's presumption, and by extension the presumption of Israel who is ever prone to forget that the law is given to uphold the promise to Abraham, and that the promise was that through Abraham all the nations of the world—not only Israel—would be blessed. Jonah should have understood, in other words, that the gospel is for all nations, and that this is precisely the rationale for his calling. The point is not consequential here, but it may be that the problem of divine change in Jonah is not quite so severe as is sometimes—and here by Calvin—supposed. It is worth noting, accordingly, that Calvin had at his disposal a richer approach to this problem. And if so, his estimation of the problem of divine mercy is overdone and his response hasty. He appears to have overreacted, betraying a peculiar sensitivity to texts which irked his metaphysical sensibilities.

Be that as it may, Huijgen identifies the same problems as those noted above. He says of Calvin's thoughts here that "Calvin rather pays the price of insufficient certainty that God's words are unequivocally true, than ascribing change of whatever kind to God."[102] He also notices that Calvin applies the rule of revelatory duplicitousness arbitrarily: "The question is how Calvin can distinguish between figurative, and non-figurative language. He provides no criteria"—except that, evidently, "his implicit criterion obviously is the axiom that change belongs to the creaturely realm, and unchangeability to God's realm."[103] The problem, says Huijgen, "is not that Calvin regards certain descriptions as accommodated to human understanding," but that his selection of which passages are accommodated in a non-realist sense is biblically indefensible, and in fact exacts a high hermeneutical price.[104] Calvin "does not consistently regard *all* Biblical texts as accommodated," as he should do, so long as he remains without defensible criteria of selection.[105] Again, Calvin's criteria—unexplained but inferred from his exegetical habits—damage the trustworthiness of Scripture, personalism, and hermeneutical plausibility. So the criteria ought to be disregarded. Arbitrariness must be removed from the exegetical household such that "not only the Biblical description of God's repentance is accommodated to our understanding, but also the Biblical description of God's unchangeability."[106]

Huijgen calls this "an assimilation of the distinction between Creator, and creature," the application of the creation idea to biblical hermeneutics, "but in a form that is obviously defined by metaphysical presuppositions."[107] It should be noted that when Huijgen here says "metaphysical presuppositions," he means speculative metaphysics imposed upon Scripture, as opposed to a metaphysical framework excavated, as it were, from Scripture itself and then utilized as interpretive grid, Scripture interpreting Scripture. "But all in all, the way Calvin uses the idea of God's unchangeability as hermeneutical key to texts that suggest God's changing plans, is unwarranted."[108]

Metaphysical presuppositions, in other words, at times weaken conspicuously Calvin's exegesis. Calvin "knows that God does not change, so all apparent changes are analyzed as not conforming to God. ... Rather, Calvin ascribes change to an intended perlocutionary effect."[109] That is, Calvin believes that where Scripture appears to represent change in God, Scripture is teaching falsehood for effect, in order to bring about a specific attitude or action.

---

102. Huijgen, *Divine Accommodation*, 274.
103. Huijgen, *Divine Accommodation*, 275.
104. Huijgen, *Divine Accommodation*, 288.
105. Huijgen, *Divine Accommodation*, 288.
106. Huijgen, *Divine Accommodation*, 288.
107. Huijgen, *Divine Accommodation*, 275.
108. Huijgen, *Divine Accommodation*, 275.
109. Huijgen, *Divine Accommodation*, 288.

Similarly, where Scripture attributes emotion to God, Huijgen sees numerous problems with Calvin's exegesis. Calvin appears to reason as follows: metaphysics prevents us taking such texts at face value (such texts cannot bear propositional theological truth); therefore, such texts must have only perlocutionary value (they are not given for knowledge but for action or effect). Huijgen cries foul. Perlocutionary force depends upon content and meaning; if the content or meaning of a proposition is denied, perlocutionary value is forfeited. He claims that perlocutionary interpretation evacuated of truth compromises not only trustworthiness but personalism as well:

> With respect to emotions, Calvin resorts to an impersonal rather than a personal understanding. He lays all emphasis on the perlocutionary force of the expression. … But how can the perlocutionary force stay, and even be enforced, when the expression is emptied of its content, and loosened from reality? This approach leads away from religious certainty, and certainly from a personal character of revelation.[110]

The net effect is inconsistency on Calvin's part: "In this sense, Calvin can be criticized based on his own theological standpoints."[111] In sum, according to Huijgen,

> Three observations must be made. First, Calvin's metaphysical presupposition of a hierarchy of being again shines through. For sensual apperception presupposes corporeality, which receives a lower ontological rank than incorporeality. Emotions, like materiality, belong to a lower mode of being. Secondly, Calvin neatly distinguishes between emotions and love, but this distinction, in this form, seems untenable to the present author. Calvin in fact pictures God's immutability as His not undergoing anything in reaction to His creation, but this makes many Biblical texts difficult, if not impossible, to understand—as shows from Calvin's often forced exegesis. Moreover, Calvin does not draw a consequence from the incarnation to God's love. Rather, he precisely ascribes all human emotions and passions to Christ's human nature. In the strict sense, this would prohibit any conclusion from Christ's suffering to who God is—while the Scriptures state that the love of the Father is expressed in the gift of His Son (John 3:16). Thirdly, not only with respect to the personal character of revelation, to which the former two point [sic] related, but also with respect to religious certainty, Calvin's approach shows serious flaws.[112]

---

110. Huijgen, *Divine Accommodation*, 277.
111. Huijgen, *Divine Accommodation*, 288.
112. Huijgen, *Divine Accommodation*, 279.

Van Til and Calvinist Accommodation

In general, one gets the overwhelming impression that Van Til's interests line up with Calvin's. Van Til's investment in Calvin's methodological reversal of Socinian hermeneutics is clear, for example, in his idea of analogy, which appears to be little more than a restatement of the traditional archetype/ectype theory of the origin of theology.[113] Additionally, his approach to apologetics is, for better or for worse, committed to the presupposition of Christian theism. Atheism, he says, presupposes Christian theism, and when defending Christian theism, Christians should not be ashamed to assume its truth. It is likewise clear that Van Til operates within the theological sphere articulated in that opening of Calvin's *Institutes*. Van Til believes that image-bearers always already know God by virtue of being image of God, and that this knowledge is not cognitive representation but personal acquaintance constitutive of human, image-bearing personality. Since it is impossible to conceive of human consciousness extracted from relationship with God, a human being cannot truly know himself until he acknowledges the one true God. Thus, after the fall, repentance and true knowledge of God are inseparable.

Huijgen says that the Calvinist trajectory with regard to accommodation holds clearly to three priorities, in light of which, as noted above, Calvin from time to time disappoints. The three priorities are personalism in revelation, the trustworthiness of Scripture, and hermeneutical (exegetical) plausibility.[114]

Van Til published no commentaries, and in fact he expressed regret that he had not put more exegetical work into print.[115] On the question of hermeneutical plausibility, in other words, he produced little argumentation. There does seem, however, to have been in the ensuing years a substantial response among biblical scholars to the interpretive oddities attendant to so-called classical theism. Open Theism is a case in point, in the sense that its impetus was exegetical rather than philosophical. Open Theism was, and still is, an attempt to restore the theological credentials throughout the *loci* of dogmatic formulation of the plain meaning of the text of Scripture. American evangelicalism proved, for the most part, inhospitable to Open Theism because it, Open Theism, appeared to play fast and loose with the doctrine of God. The Theological Interpretation of Scripture, a project devoted to rethinking the theological underpinnings of biblical interpretation, proved far more effective at bringing evangelical theology and the

---

113. See Van Asselt, "The Fundamental Meaning of Theology: Archetypal and Ectypal Theology in Seventeeth-Century Reformed Thought," *Westminster Theological Journal* 64 (2002): 319–35; Nathan D. Shannon, "Junius and Van Til on Natural Knowledge of God," *Westminster Theological Journal* 82, no. 2 (2020): 279–300.

114. These are Huijgen's criteria for a viable theology of accommodation. See *Divine Accommodation*, 43.

115. See *Jerusalem and Athens: Critical Discussions on the Theology and Apologetics of Cornelius Van Til*, ed. E. R. Geehan (Nutley, NJ: P&R, 1971), 204. See also Richard B. Gaffin Jr., "Some Epistemological Reflections on 1 Cor 2:6–16," *Westminster Theological Journal* 57, no. 1 (1995): 103–24.

theological perspective on hermeneutics into fruitful conversation. Together Open Theism and the Theological Interpretation of Scripture demonstrate a pervasive dissatisfaction with the state of the union between classical metaphysics and biblical interpretation. This suggests that Van Til, though hidden away in the Orthodox Presbyterian Church and Dutch neo-Calvinism, that feisty pocket of it in southeastern Pennsylvania, and continuously occupied with in-house polemics, was ahead of the game.

For Van Til as for Calvin, personalism and the trustworthiness and authority of Scripture are intertwined. Van Til affirms with requisite tenacity the classical absoluteness of the being of God, and he affirms the two-tiered epistemological layout for the interpretation of revelation. He affirms, in other words, the distinction between God's knowledge of God and the creature's knowledge of God, between the infinite perfection of God and divine action, on the one hand, and the accommodated revelation of God on the other:

> There is no fact that man meets in any of his investigation where the face of God does not confront him. On the other hand, in this way it is possible to see that the knowledge of God and the knowledge of man coincide at no point in the sense that, in his awareness of [sic] meaning of anything, in his mental grasp or understanding of anything, man is at each point dependent upon a prior act of unchangeable understanding and revelation on the part of God. The form of revelation of God to man must come to man in accordance with his creaturely limitations. God's thought with respect to anything is a unit. Yet it pertains to a multiplicity of objects. But man can think of that unit as involving a number of items only in the form of succession. So Scripture speaks of God as though he were thinking his thoughts step by step. All revelation is anthropomorphic. When God reveals himself to man, he reveals something of the fulness of his being. In God's mind any bit of information that he gives to man is set in the fulness of his one supreme act of self-affirmation.[116]

But Van Til infers from the same divine absoluteness an injunction to honor the plain meaning of the text:

> A fearless anthropomorphism based on the doctrine of the ontological trinity, rather than abstract reasoning on the basis of metaphysical and epistemological correlativism, should control our concepts all along the line. ... We shall not fear to be boldly anthropomorphic because, to begin with, we have, in our doctrines of the ontological trinity and temporal creation, cut ourselves loose once and for all from correlativism between God and man.[117]

---

116. Van Til, *IST*, 270. See also Van Til and Berkhof, *Foundations of Christian Education*, 84–7.
117. Van Til, *CGG*, 111.

Ontological absoluteness entails self-attestation and the perspicuity of Scripture—Scripture interpreting Scripture.[118] The self-existence of the primary author of the Bible, therefore, disallows a metaphysical canon within the canon as that which haunted Calvin's exegesis. In this sense the Creator–creature distinction feeds Van Til's view of revelation and the interpretation of revelation. But the Creature–creature distinction is only a partial account of the situation.

Van Til believes that God has not necessarily self-objectified as the self-existent God. This, that God-revealed bears witness to God-not-revealed, is in itself something of a conundrum. Van Til appears to understand it as follows. "God" is a term that denotes the incommunicable attributes—the infinite and simple divine essence. The term never denotes another or a lesser God. So the question is, how does Van Til explain this transfer of the ontological uniqueness of God eternal to the self-attestation of verbal revelation? How can created media bear the relational presence of deity? How does Van Til substantiate the union of personality in revelation with the divine authority of revelation? He turns, if predictably, to the incarnation, both to unite and to distinguish personality and deity. The Son, Van Til might have said, himself stands upon the earth in the flesh—he self-objectifies not only for humanity but as human—and takes to himself the divine name, signaling unqualified transcendence: "Before Abraham was, I AM." The real-time utterance of this statement by the Son enfleshed captures the revelational and relational significance of the incarnation, and since Christ himself is the organism of redemption and redemptive revelation, it signals as the fullest expression of the implicit structure of accommodated revelation. "Scripture teaches that there is no being, and can be no being, who is a mixture of the ingredients of eternity and temporality … and not even Christ is a mixture of the two."[119] Christ is not a mixture of the two, but he is their personal union. "In the incarnation," for the sake of the divine ontology, "the church has been anxious to maintain, Christ's personality remained divine; it was human nature, not a human person, that he assumed when he became incarnate."[120] The accommodation of Scripture to human readers, writes Vern Poythress, "is an additional feature, not a subtraction from the fullness of divine meaning."[121] Poythress continues:

> It is said concerning the incarnation of Christ, "Remaining what he was, he became what he was not." Remaining God, Christ took on human nature, which he did not have before. This pattern concerns him who is the eternal Word and now the incarnate Word. By analogy, the word of God, remaining what it was according to the divine plan from all eternity, became what it was not when God said, "Let there be light," and called light into being. It became an utterance

---

118. Conspicuously absent here is the doctrine of inspiration as Van Til learned it from B. B. Warfield.
119. Van Til, *CTE*, 39.
120. Van Til, *CTE*, 39.
121. Poythress, "Rethinking Accommodation in Revelation," 155.

going forth at a specific time in the history of the world. Likewise, the word of God, remaining the divine word that it was according to the divine plan understood from the foundation of the world in the co-inherence of the persons of the Trinity, became what it was not when God caused it to be written in an autographic text as an addition to the canon. Every such text suits the time and place and circumstances and human intermediaries who are present as contexts in which it newly comes. God's speech is always coherent with the contexts that he himself specifies by his speech governing the universe (Heb 1:3). That is the real meaning of accommodation.[122]

The person of the Son, as second person of the Trinity, represents the capacity, native to the eternal life of God, for the incarnation of the Son. According to Augustine's rule, missions *ad extra* display the processions *ad intra*. Therefore the eternal personality of the Son, and by implication of the whole Godhead, vindicates a self-attesting revelational personalism and require, in Van Til's view at least, a fearless anthropomorphism.[123]

For Calvin, too, as for Van Til, the problem of keeping transcendence and immanence together is of no less concern than keeping them apart, and Calvin, too, takes his cue from Chalcedon: "Paradoxical though it may sound, Calvin intends to keep God's exaltedness and His nearness together. ... God's various accommodations in the external world ... entirely depend on Christ's mediatorial office. In this context, the so-called *extra calvinisticum* ... safeguards God's exaltedness with His nearness in the accommodated means."[124] For Calvin, too, says Huijgen, "the personal character of revelation ... is ultimately based in the quintessential accommodation: the incarnation," where absoluteness and personality, infinite and eternal, self-declare as the only way to the Father.[125]

---

122. Poythress, "Rethinking Accommodation in Revelation," 155.

123. And yet, Van Til does not abandon classical theism to actualism; he does not anthropomorphize the divine being:

> If we begin all our thinking by presupposing the self-predicating God, we need not claim and cannot claim that we shall, for instance, understand, that is, conceptualize, the relation of time to eternity. In fact, we then know in advance that we cannot understand that relation. We are bound to speak of God in temporal language. And we know that time categories, when applied to God, must be thought of as merely analogous of the full richness of his internal being. (*IST*, 339)

And Van Til is unequivocally opposed to ontological diminution of God at the point of creation (see, for example, *IST*, 320).

124. Huijgen, *Divine Accommodation*, 270.

125. Huijgen, *Divine Accommodation*, 318. Shao Kai Tseng finds the same in Vos, and believes that the incarnation, and the *extra Calvinisticum* in particular, is the key to Vos's critical appreciation of Hegel. See Tseng, *G. W. F. Hegel*, 77–86.

Conclusion

Secondary discussion of Van Til's hermeneutic of anthropomorphic realism has been scarce.[126] The reason for this may be that for one reason or another it does not deserve attention. Or it may be that Van Til's prose rendered it difficult to access, or that he left it undeveloped and so there is not much to access. Indeed, the reader feels that Van Til's work here is unfinished. He devotes endless resources to method, epistemic structure, and somewhat obscure arguments connecting the doctrine of God to the nature of revelation to biblical interpretation, very often, in bold and sweeping claims, all at once.

This chapter has demonstrated that the neo-Calvinist ensemble of moment here has taken seriously the task of searching out the theological implications—the fuller doctrinal organism, one might say—of the relationship between absolute personalism and human self-understanding. Evidently, Bavinck, Vos, and Van Til were aware that without revisiting the whole of what Van Til calls "the creation idea," encompassing divine ontology and the Creator–creature relation, their theocentric ethics and theology of history would lack an essential framework. In other words, the claims that "God is man's ultimate environment," that pre-fall obedience bears the moral virtue of consistency with the known expectations of an absolute other, and that the Fall is self-conscious transgression of the very moral character of God self-expressed within the sphere of human experience—all this is either vindicated by locating its possibility in the eternal life of God or it is reduced to religious poetry of a peculiarly self-assured style. The Bavincks, Vos, and Van Til took up the challenge.

The absolute personalism that, as Johan Bavinck argues, everywhere haunts human religious consciousness, is both, as Bavinck and Van Til believe, a faithful republication of classical Trinitarianism and the introduction of a theism, which can sustain their demanding explorations of the creation idea. The notion of absolute person on the one hand represents the fullest expression of Christian theistic personalism, and on the other, signals a bedrock account for the theocentrism of their accounts of moral self-understanding and experience, history, and, finally, of theological truth. This chapter has highlighted Van Til's further reduction of the distance between Trinity and absolute person by his christological account of accommodation. The absolute Christ is the absolute person given among men, and as the personal organism of historical revelation and redemption, Christ himself is key to human experience of God and to theological expression.

Van Til and Vos are responsible for key aspects of this story. The silence of commentators, however, suggests that considered individually, their writings hide it too well. Indeed, it appears that the lion's share of the work articulating

---

126. With the notable exception of K. Scott Oliphint, *God with Us: Divine Condescension and the Attributes of God* (Wheaton, IL: Crossway, 2011). See also Oliphint's foreword to *CGG*, vii–xliv. Also relevant is Jason B. Hunt, *Cornelius Van Til's Doctrine of God and Its Relevance for Contemporary Hermeneutics* (Eugene, OR: Wipf & Stock, 2019).

a christological account for the self-expression of God as the precondition and substance of human moral experience—and subsequently as the presupposition of human religious expression—is not found in the works of either Vos or Van Til, but rather in the major works of Herman Bavinck, where even there it lies scattered and disjointed. Chapter 5, accordingly, introduces the role of the incarnation in Bavinck's understanding of both theological system and of human experience, of the whole of the creation idea.

Chapter 5

BAVINCK ON THE UNIQUENESS OF THE INCARNATION

No account of God exists in created reality by any reason except by this theology of Christ.

—Franciscus Junius

Divine ontology and the relation of God to all that is not God are major themes of twentieth-century Protestant theology. One thinks first of Karl Barth and Jürgen Moltmann, and on the Lutheran side only the name of Wolfhart Pannenberg resounds with comparable gravitas. Few expect mention of neo-Calvinist Herman Bavinck here, but the primary reason for his scarcity may only be that he did not make a point of it.

This chapter is motivated in part by a conviction that Bavinck deserves to be named among those modern theologians who scrutinized classical inheritance on the topics of ontology and relation and who produced an exceptionally compelling response. Accordingly, one might hope that due attention to Bavinck's contribution will begin to open new and fascinating avenues of dialogue among these giants of modern thought on a number of important issues ranging from divine ontology to accommodation and anthropomorphism to the relationship between means and grace and so on.

In Bavinck's case one way to advance such inquiry is through a study of the place of the incarnation—as the defining instance of ontological asymmetry and contact—in his theology, asking, for example, to what extent the incarnation is restricted to the mediation of Christ beginning with the conception in the womb of Mary, or in what sense the incarnation is not utterly unique to the life of Jesus but is implicated elsewhere—in method, Trinity, creation, revelation, and the history of redemption.

For the growing field of Bavinck studies, the relevance of such a study is first of all methodological, having primarily to do with the place of Christology in Bavinck's theological system. But as it is centrally located in a methodological sense, Christology neither can be nor is, as Bavinck's readers discover, thus restricted in the primary literature to methodological discussions. That is: Bavinck claims that Christology wields influence over his dogmatics as a whole, and one indeed finds this claim vindicated throughout the primary sources. Thus the difficulty of the task before us: within Bavinck's work the uniqueness of the incarnation is both extremely important and yet not easily indexed.

As I shall demonstrate in what follows, the primary rationale that Bavinck provides for the centrality of Christology in dogmatics is the centrality of Christ in Scripture, where Scripture is the material source for dogmatics. Method mimics the structure of its object in this sense, so that the presence of Christ throughout Scripture will determine the range of the influence of Christology on the scope of dogmatics. As a methodological rule, Bavinck would have it that our knowledge of God and of the works of God is "according to Christ" to the extent that Christ is present in Scripture. And it is possible to say that Christ is all of Scripture.

In what follows, I demonstrate these claims from Bavinck's methodological reflections and then from relevant dogmatic material. The implication is that, for Bavinck, Christ vindicates dogmatics as such, so that even where Christ is not the primary subject matter, the Son incarnate nonetheless serves as a kind of methodological precondition or prolegomena or truthmaker, if one allows, for theological predication throughout the dogmatics, even as a principle of regenerate knowing. These reflections on Christology in Bavinck's theological system will help to position Bavinck's thought on Creator–creature ontology and relation alongside that of other influential theologians of the twentieth century. One may have supposed, for example, that Barth is christological in his ontology while neo-Calvinism, remaining loyal to classical theism, has allowed Christology to influence only the doctrines of revelation and Scripture (biblical theology). I contend that this paradigm lacks depth in that it fails to do justice to the role of the incarnation in the theology of Bavinck, which, as shall presently be observed, in fact is far more expansive.

System and the Structure of Dogmatics

A young Herman Bavinck was invited to address an audience of pastors in August of 1881. Having defended his thesis on the ethics of Zwingli the previous year, Bavinck was twenty-six at the time, and would take up his first academic post the year coming. As he explains in the opening of his lecture, on that occasion he had been asked to "introduce ... the subject of the pros and cons of a dogmatic system."[1] Bavinck titled his remarks accordingly but argued that "a dogmatic system," generally considered, "has no cons, but only pros."[2] He went on to argue that a rising distrust of theological system as "narrow-minded rigidity," as "cold and formalistic," was itself "simply the proof of ignorance."[3] "After all, everything that exists is systematic."[4]

---

1. Herman Bavinck, "The Pros and Cons of a Dogmatic System," trans. Nelson D. Kloosterman, *Bavinck Review* 5 (2014): 90.
2. Bavinck, "Pros and Cons," 96, 100.
3. Bavinck, "Pros and Cons," 90, 92.
4. Bavinck, "Pros and Cons," 90.

Bavinck in fact argues that a notion of system is necessary for, and thus implied in, the pursuit of knowledge and therefore in science itself.[5] A person pursues knowledge assuming that a system precedes his pursuit, in order that difference may be discerned, and thus knowledge gained, against the backdrop of a more basic unity. This assumption, that an objective system precedes and vindicates the pursuit of knowledge, validates science as a modest but genuinely descriptive undertaking.[6] Science is thus equipped to say true and useful things about the world.

He then proposes a definition. "Dogmatics," Bavinck says, "is nothing other than the scientific description of the confession of the church."[7] An ambiguity must be acknowledged regarding this notion of "church." If the idea is an actual congregation and what it confesses, then systematic theology's task is to systematize the actual beliefs of that loosely delineated group; systematic theology is in this scenario descriptive and anthropological. It reports religion. On the other hand, if "church" refers in a somewhat idealized sense to the people for whom special revelation is intended, then systematic theology is envisioned as a compendium of the data of Scripture, not of what a people confess but rather what they should confess.

One may suppose that Bavinck's view is neither of these. By "church" here is meant a people self-consciously gathered around Scripture as their confessional bedrock and striving to confess what they find it to be teaching. Systematic theology is the confession of an actual people, but also of an actual people striving for an ideal embodied in Scripture. There will always be a tension, therefore, between Scripture and a given systematic endeavor; Scripture encourages but will always also resist the systematic undertaking.[8] Bavinck, in other words, recognizes

---

5. Bavinck, "Pros and Cons," 93.
6. Bavinck writes:

> Thus, a scientific system may be nothing other than a reproduction in words, a translation into language, a description, a reflection in our consciousness, of the system present in things themselves. Science does not have to create and to fantasize, but only to describe what exists. We contemplate what God has thought eternally beforehand and has given embodied form in the creation. (Bavinck, "Pros and Cons," 93)

On organism and diversity in unity, see James P. Eglinton, *Trinity and Organism: Towards a New Reading of Bavinck's Organic Motif* (Edinburgh: T&T Clark, 2012), 67–8. Eglinton focuses on Bavinck's *Christelijke Wereldbeschouwing* of 1904 (translated as *Christian Worldview*, trans. and ed. James P. Eglinton, Nathaniel Gray Sutanto, and Cory Brock (Wheaton, IL: Crossway, 2019)). Evidently, Bavinck's mind was busy with the theological potential of the organic motif much earlier.

7. Bavinck, "Pros and Cons," 94.
8. On this, see Richard B. Gaffin, "Systematic Theology and Biblical Theology," *Westminster Theological Journal* 38, no. 2 (1976): 281–99.

the precariousness of the systematic undertaking but understands it nonetheless to be enjoined by Scripture and underwritten by Scripture.

It becomes apparent as Bavinck proceeds that he intends by this wording first to distinguish dogmatics from its source—Scripture—and then to highlight the ecclesiastical responsibilities of a dogmatic system.[9] Such a system must "satisfy our religious and moral needs," and thus "prove itself to our heart," but it must no less "prove itself as truth to our understanding as well."[10] He thus highlights a unity of the practical and theoretical as dual features commending a dogmatic system, both of which serve to reflect or demonstrate—"prove" is Bavinck's notion of choice—"the reasonableness" and "the genuinely scientific nature, of Christianity."[11] This system-vindication must be achieved primarily, he argues, by demonstrating internal coherence and unity.[12] He writes:

> Now, it is the difficult but nonetheless glorious task of dogmatics to prove to the mind that the confession of the church is reasonable in the highest sense of the word. But then the primary requirement for our thinking mind is that the church's dogmas do not stand disconnected alongside one another, but they must be contained within one another; that together they constitute an unbreakable whole, an organic unity, a true and complete system.[13]

Bavinck here claims that vindication of an apologetic sort and internal self-realization require of the Christian faith the same task: the discovery and display of the material (organic) unity of its subject matter—in this case, of biblical revelation. One concludes that apologetics and the development of a dogmatic system are distinct but inseparable. Bavinck says that there is and must be a single organizing notion,[14] and that this singular, unifying principle will be that which appoints to all the parts their respective places within the system and which realizes itself in each of the parts.[15] In this sense, objectively speaking, dogmatics

---

9. See Bavinck, "Pros and Cons," 98–9.
10. Bavinck, "Pros and Cons," 95.
11. Bavinck, Pros and Cons," 95.
12. Bruce Pass notes that "Bavinck and many other nineteenth-century theologians under the sway of German idealism were interested not merely in accounting for what the Reformers wrote but in penetrating the 'representation' of their writings to the 'idea' that governed them." Bruce R. Pass, "The Question of Central Dogma in Herman Bavinck," *Calvin Theological Journal* 53, no. 1 (2018): 36.
13. Bavinck, "Pros and Cons," 95.
14. "In order, then, to obtain a dogmatic system, before everything else the principium must be uncovered (not introduced to or forced upon dogmatics), from which the entire system as it were is constructed and can without violence and force be deduced." "The truly pure principium of the dogmatic system is but one and can be only one" (Bavinck, "Pros and Cons," 95, 96).
15. "The only true principle of the dogmatic system is the one that appoints to every single truth its unique place within the organic whole ... in that manner unfolds organically

seeks to reproduce the objective unity of revelation by first identifying a unifying or organic principle.

The discovery of the unifying principle and subsequent development of a dogmatic system according to it are not for Bavinck the imposition of a naturalistic scientific procedure onto the data of Christianity. Christianity does not have to satisfy a non-Christian standard of rational integrity or reasonability; it must fully express its own internal capacity. Again, vindication and self-realization coincide here. Bavinck intends to demonstrate the inferiority of the mechanical, evolutionary worldview by developing Christian self-understanding according to Christianity's own native principle.

Noteworthy is that Bavinck has already, at a young age and in a brief lecture,[16] demonstrated a multifaceted apologetic strategy that is in practice not distinct from but continuous with constructive dogmatics as expository of Scripture.[17] He

on all sides in the multiplicity of truth in order again to be brought organically into the truth itself" (Bavinck, "Pros and Cons," 96).

16. See James Eglinton and Michael Bräutigam, "Scientific Theology? Herman Bavinck and Adolf Schlatter on the Place of Theology in the University," *Journal of Reformed Theology* 7 (2013): 27–50 (esp. 39–42) for historical background to Bavinck's view of theology as a science. In the Netherlands, hostility to theology as a legitimate academic discipline began as early as the mid-nineteenth century and took hold in the Higher Education Act of 1876. Thus, "Bavinck entered the sphere of higher education just as the secularisation of the academy came into full force" (p. 40). Eglinton and Bräutigam focus on "Godgeleerdheid en godsdienstwetenschap," which Bavinck published in 1892 (translated as "Theology and Religious Studies," in *Essays on Religion, Science, and Society*, ed. John Bolt, trans. Harry Boonstra and Gerrit Sheeres (Grand Rapids, MI: Baker Academic, 2008)). Bavinck's thought on these topics is shown to be fast maturing already in the "Pros and Cons" lecture of 1881. He seems already aware that the marginalization of theology will lead to the fragmentation of the academy, a claim he makes directly in the later publication. Eglinton and Bräutigam also note that "Bavinck … displays a strong aversion to the 'head for science, heart for theology' dualism so commonplace in his day" (p. 41).

17. Eglinton and Bräutigam explain Bavinck's apologetic as they find it in the *Reformed Dogmatics*: "Bavinck … challenged the positivist definition of science," and his "argument is directed at the impossibility of knowledge without metaphysics. … His idea … is to meet anti-theological scientists on their own terms and highlight that their worldview nonetheless depends on that which they deny: metaphysics." And yet "Bavinck is not engaging in natural theology. … Having claimed that the universe cannot be coherently viewed without metaphysics, Bavinck would have the reader then turn to the self-revelation of the Triune God" ("Scientific Theology?," 46). A recent study of Bavinck's apologetic method puts it this way: "Herein is the force of Bavinck's apologetic: it is only by a revelatory epistemology that begins with the triune God, as he has revealed himself in Scripture, that any adequate knowledge of the creation can be arrived at without sacrificing its unity for its diversity or its diversity for its unity." Daniel Ragusa, "The Trinity at the Center of Thought and Life: Herman Bavinck's Organic Apologetic," *Mid-America Journal of Theology* 28 (2017): 150. Ragusa argues that "Bavinck's organic ontology, which holds

opens his lecture with a defense of organism or system ad absurdum: one rejects system as difference-in-unity at the cost of coherence. No system, no knowledge. But he also offers positive argumentation: the highest form of system (organism) is personality, and the highest personality is the triune God.[18] Science as such proceeds assuming that (God-created) system precedes it and unifies its material source; dogmatic science proceeds on the confession that the triune God precedes it, and that divine, personal unity has been translated through divine works into the Spirit-inspired record of those divine works.

So, how is the dogmatician to identify the principium of his system? He must do so inductively by attempting to reproduce the inner, implicit logic of the material source. One must not impose upon the material source a contrived system, "for then it [the system] would be nothing more than a Procrustean bed."[19] Rather, "such a system with its own principium must always be derived from the material itself. The dogmatician does not have to invent or devise the system and the principium; … let him attempt to arrive at the discovery of what … comprises the constitutive, governing basic idea, the innermost driving force, the hidden stirrings, the deepest root."[20] In sum, a dogmatic system should "supply us with a correct insight into the organism of Holy Scripture. Thereby the true unity within those many and various revealed truths will become visible to us for the first time. Order will be provided in that apparent confusion, unity and system among that colorful variety," so that above all a "dogmatic system leads us to know God and to revere God."[21] A dogmatic system, in other words, aims to represent the organism of revelation by identifying its singular organic principle, the very principle that provides revelation with its structural unity and economy. By drawing that principle into the light of understanding, a dogmatic system optimizes its value as secondary elucidation of revelation.

Christology and Dogmatic System

It is worth noting that Bavinck was methodologically self-aware and therefore explicit on these matters, since disappointment with notions of "central dogmas"

---

that the archetypal unity-in-diversity of the triune God of Scripture necessitates an ectypal unity-in-diversity in the creation, provides the theological foundation for his apologetic" (pp. 150–1). Similarly, Eglinton notes that "the created order is marked by simultaneous unity and diversity" (*Trinity and Organism*, 67). Yet Eglinton also argues that "unity precedes diversity" (p. 68). It may be that "unity" in one instance indicates the singular co-equal deity of the persons, while in another use it indicates the numerical singularity of God (monotheism).

18. Bavinck, "Pros and Cons," 92.
19. Bavinck, "Pros and Cons," 96.
20. Bavinck, "Pros and Cons," 96–7.
21. Bavinck, "Pros and Cons," 101.

and Christocentrism has been registered by Reformed scholars.[22] Bruce Pass, undeterred, has published a study of the structural importance of Christology, as "central dogma" no less, within Bavinck's theology.[23] Pass proposes three sequential stages in the development of Bavinck's thinking on the question of central dogma. In the earlier stage, Pass argues, Bavinck focuses on the knowledge of God; a second stage shows Bavinck's dogmatic-structural interest split between the knowledge of God and Christology; in a third stage, the organizing principle of dogmatics is Christology.[24] But Bavinck's transition to this third stage stalled. Pass notes that "the later Bavinck ... concludes ... that Christology can and should function as the starting point of a dogmatic system," but that "Bavinck did not seek to integrate this new standpoint in his revision of *Reformed Dogmatics*."[25]

Bavinck does at one point appear to offer a clue as to why he did not feel pressured to restructure the dogmatics, and what he says in this regard illuminates the relationship between the doctrines of God and Christ. In *Our Reasonable Faith*, having addressed prolegomena, revelation, and Scripture, Bavinck turns to discuss the doctrine of God.[26] He opens this discussion acknowledging that "we can develop the rich content of this revelation in various ways," and he then proceeds to discuss two such approaches, one represented by the Heidelberg Catechism and the other by the Belgic Confession ("the Reformed *Confession of Faith*").[27] The former opens with a confession of comfort, conviction, and assurance, in the

---

22. Richard A. Muller, "A Note on 'Christocentrism' and the Imprudent Use of Such Terminology," *Westminster Theological Journal* 68, no. 2 (2006): 253–60; Cornelius Venema, "Covenant and Election in the Theology of Herman Bavinck," *Mid-America Journal of Theology* 19 (2008): 69 n.1.

23. By depending on Bavinck's "Pros and Cons," I have traded a simpler notion of "principium" for Pass's cluster of governing notions (starting point, middle point, and central dogma); cf. Pass, "Question of Central Dogma." James Eglinton also mentions "Bavinck's ultimate christocentrism" (*Trinity and Organism*, 115).

24. Pass writes:

> In the first stage, the knowledge of God constitutes a dogmatic system's central dogma as well as its starting point and midpoint. In the second stage, Bavinck identifies the knowledge of God as comprising the system's central dogma and starting point, yet Christology is identified as the system's midpoint. In the third stage, Christology is identified as the central dogma, starting point, and midpoint of a dogmatic system. (Pass, "Question of Central Dogma," 39)

25. Pass, "Question of Central Dogma," 49, 50. The first edition of the *Reformed Dogmatics* was published in 1895–1901, and a second, revised edition in 1906–11.

26. Originally titled *Magnalia Dei*, Bavinck's *Our Reasonable Faith: A Survey of Christian Doctrine* was intended to be a less academic presentation of the content of the *Reformed Dogmatics*. It was published in 1909, as the second revision of the *Reformed Dogmatics* was underway.

27. Bavinck, *ORF*, 128, 129.

first-person singular, signaling a confession of the faith of a person's heart and of the content of that revelation, which he has taken up into himself. The Heidelberg Catechism is unforgettably personal, heartfelt, tender, and practical. The primary benefit of this approach is that "it relates the truth immediately to the whole of Christian life ... and in its approach to every doctrine points out directly what is its value for the mind and heart."[28]

Alternatively, we may also "let the development of our confession be determined by the questions which are directed to us about it."[29] This approach attempts "to trace out what order is objectively present in the truths of the faith themselves, how these are related to each other, and what the governing principle of them all is. This is the order," Bavinck says, "followed in the Reformed *Confession of Faith*."[30] The Belgic Confession opens with corporate confession: "We all believe in our hearts." It therefore comes across as more personable, if that matters, than, say, the Augsburg or Westminster Confession. Belgic Confession Article 1, however, focuses first on the incommunicable attributes of God—certainly a beginning, but not a soteric, experiential entry point.

These two methods are of course not in conflict but "complement and balance each other."[31] By which Bavinck means: "The doctrine of God is at the same time a doctrine of the eternal salvation of souls, and the second of these also includes the first. The knowledge of God in the face of Jesus Christ His Son, this is eternal life."[32]

The conclusion to be drawn is that Bavinck, if one must say the later Bavinck, believes that these two approaches, the one subjective and the other objective, the one beginning with the applied principle of regenerate confession and the other with the self-existent principle of being, are mutually implicatory. Methodologically speaking there is no choice to be made here. Hans Burger has said, "Bavinck is a trinitarian theologian, but also a Christocentric thinker."[33] And so says Bavinck, on the opening page of his *God and Creation*: "The knowledge of God-in-Christ, after all, is life itself."[34]

Incarnation and the Trinity

Bavinck argues that the incarnation is possible because God is Trinity.[35] This is to make two distinguishable but interdependent points. First, the incarnation

---

28. Bavinck, *ORF*, 128.
29. Bavinck, *ORF*, 129.
30. Bavinck, *ORF*, 129.
31. Bavinck, *ORF*, 129.
32. Bavinck, *ORF*, 130.
33. Hans Burger, *Being in Christ: A Biblical and Systematic Investigation in a Reformed Perspective* (Eugene, OR: Wipf & Stock, 2009), 89.
34. Bavinck, *RD*, 2:29.
35. The titles of subsequent sections are borrowed from Bavinck, *RD*, 3:274–86, "The Centrality of the Incarnation."

indicates the triunity of God. In this sense theology reasons from revelation or incarnation, *ad extra*, to the works or nature of God *ad intra*, from mission to procession and thus from Jesus to Trinity. And second, that the being of God is such that the incarnation is possible though not necessary. This means that Trinity, or eternal generation representatively, is necessary for the incarnation; but once eternal generation is understood as a natural work of God *ad intra*, one observes that the former necessity is not reciprocated; eternal generation does not require the incarnation. Eternal generation implicates no non-divine thing, but it signals the divine capacity for the calling of things out of non-being.

The point for Bavinck is that the incarnation indicates the triune, personal life of God. So Bavinck says that divine self-union with another, or self-communication to another within the divine ontology, as the necessary character of God as God, is the precursor, or pattern and precondition, of the personal, non-necessary incarnation of God first in creation and then in the incarnation and re-creation. For Bavinck, in other words, divine self-communication is original to the triune being of God (the immanent processions of Son and Spirit) and is expressed *ad extra*, non-necessarily, in creation and in the incarnation of the Son.

Of the incarnation he says that "only the theistic and trinitarian confession of God's characteristic essence opens the possibility for the fact of the incarnation."[36] This is because Trinity displays the fact that "God remains who he is and can yet communicate himself to others. ... In a word, the Trinity makes possible the existence of a mediator who himself participates both in the divine and human nature and thus unites God and humans."[37]

One recalls at this point Bruce Pass's question regarding a lack of conviction on Bavinck's part as to the centrality of Christology in his dogmatic system. Here we see, as Bavinck indicates in *Our Reasonable Faith*, that Christology and the knowledge of God are interdependent. When one considers the hypostatic union one considers the triunity of God as both the doctrinal implication and the self-existent precondition of the incarnation as an act of the Son only (or particularly), in distinction from the Father and the Spirit.[38] So "the incarnation," says Bavinck, "has its presupposition and foundation in the Trinitarian being of God."[39]

---

36. Bavinck, *RD*, 3:275.
37. Bavinck, *RD*, 3:275.
38. Eglinton writes:

> However, while Bavinck allows the Son of God, in his incarnation, to become, he does not on this basis extend becoming to the Father or the Holy Spirit. The one divine essence remains immutable. ... As Bavinck maintains the classical immanent and economic trinitarian categories, he does not apply Christ's being-in-action, a factor he ties to Christ's incarnation and mediatorship, to the Father or the Spirit. (Eglinton, *Trinity and Organism*, 127)

39. Bavinck, *RD*, 3:274.

Bavinck's emphasis is not, however, on the metaphysics of immanent procession, but on the personal life that trinitarian theology is at pains to articulate. "In the first place, the doctrine of the Trinity makes God known to us as the truly living God."[40] Bavinck explains this as striking a balance between Deism and pantheism, or between monism and polytheism. Turning outward in the polemical mode, Bavinck writes:

> Deism creates as vast gulf between God and his creatures, cancels out their mutual relatedness, and reduces God to an abstract entity, a pure being, to mere monotonous and uniform existence. It satisfies neither the mind nor the heart and is therefore the death of religion. Pantheism, though it brings God nearer to us, equates him with the created world, erases the boundary line between the Creator and the creature, robs God of any being or life of his own, thus totally undermining religion. But the Christian doctrine of the Trinity makes God known as essentially distinct from the world, yet having a blessed life of his own.[41]

But this must first, before engaging in apologetics, be understood theologically:

> [The] creation cannot be conceived as mere happenstance, nor as the outcome of divine self-development. It must have its foundation in God, yet not be a phase in the process of his inner life. How can these two concerns be satisfied if not by the confession of a triune God? The life of God is divinely rich: it is fecund; it implies action, productivity. The doctrine of the Trinity, accordingly, speaks of the generation of the Son and the procession of the Spirit. Both of these acts are essentially distinct from the work of creation: the former are immanent relations, while the latter is work *ad extra*. The former are sufficient in themselves: God does not need the creation. He is life, blessedness, glory in himself. Still, the creation is most intimately connected with this fecundity. ... The doctrine of the Trinity ... tells us that God *can* reveal himself in an absolute sense to the Son and the Spirit, and hence, in a relative sense also to the world.[42]

He concludes: "God is a plenitude of life."[43] So here Bavinck highlights the apologetic import of the doctrine of the Trinity that, as he sees it, involves embracing the absoluteness of God and the personality of God equally. Personality is thus the key to Christian theism in this apologetic sense because it is, in a dogmatic sense, the doctrine of God in its fullest self-expression. Triune personality trumps the explanatory resources of philosophical counterfeits because it is in fact the marrow of the one, true, revealed religion. That true religion, true theism, is revealed in

---

40. Bavinck, *RD*, 2:331.
41. Bavinck, *RD*, 2:331.
42. Bavinck, *RD*, 2:332.
43. Bavinck, *RD*, 3:331.

creation and therefore unavoidably presupposed in all alternative accounts of being and meaning, even those openly hostile to Christianity. Here we may observe once again Bavinck's apologetic method: "alternative" theologies or theories of reality are varieties of deformation of that which is given in general revelation but which is known truly for what it is, the self-expression of the triune God, only through special revelation.[44] "The moment we step outside the domain of this special revelation in Scripture, we find that in all religious and philosophical systems the unity of the personality and absoluteness of God is broken."[45] Divine triune personalism is then, to borrow Daniel Strange's term, "subversive fulfillment" of the theological other.[46]

For Bavinck, the absolute personality of God distinguishes the Christian God from a false god either incapable of religious relation or itself constituted by that relation. So in the Trinity we find divine personality as the principle or possibility of divine action relative to creatures. That personality is triune of course, but Bavinck's emphasis falls here not upon "person" as the principle of individuation within the divine unity. Because God acts in one sense as a single agent, Bavinck will speak of the personality of God in a singular sense: "Thanks to that revelation, it is certain, first of all, that God is a person, a conscious and freely willing being, not confined to the world but exalted high above it."[47] The point is not that God is one person in the same sense that he is three persons, but that "God is a personal being, self-existent, with a life, consciousness, and will of his own,"[48] and that tri-personality is not annexed to impersonal unity; rather, God is as God acts, free and conscious. "Certainly, all God's works *ad extra* are undivided and common to all three persons. Prominent in these works, therefore, is the oneness of God rather than the distinction of the persons."[49] Self-revelation is a condescension or self-limitation, or relational self-contextualization, of which God as God is

---

44. Clearly for Bavinck nature reveals God as Trinity, but recognition of Trinity is possible only with the help of special revelation. See Bavinck, *RD*, 2:330. I have given the impression here that "outside the circle of special revelation" one finds only general revelation. This is not, however, the view of Herman Bavinck, Johan Herman Bavinck, or Van Til. It is perhaps better to say that the sphere or domain of special revelation is not the extent of the reach or influence of special revelation but the sphere of the regenerative and/or ecclesiastical activation of the redemptive impulse of special revelation. The sphere is where special revelation is the governing principle of deed and confession. See Strange on what he calls "remnantal revelation." Daniel Strange, *Their Rock Is Not Like Our Rock: A Theology of Religions* (Grand Rapids, MI: Zondervan, 2014), 95–120.

45. Bavinck, *RD*, 2:34.

46. Strange, *Their Rock Is Not Like Our Rock*, 237–73.

47. Bavinck, *RD*, 2:30. On absolute personalism in J. H. Bavinck, see Nathan D. Shannon, "Religions and the Doctrine of God: Comparing J. H. Bavinck and Cherbonnier," *Torch Trinity Journal* 23, no. 2 (2020): 29–66.

48. Bavinck, *RD*, 2:33.

49. Bavinck, *RD*, 2:330.

somehow capable; Bavinck's view is that the biblical explanation of this mystery is the absolute personality of God: "The same God who in his revelation limits himself, as it were, to certain specific places, times, and persons is at the same time infinitely exalted above the whole realm of nature and every creature."[50] "Or to put it in modern theological language, in Scripture the personality and the absoluteness of God go hand in hand."[51] Absoluteness and personality are, as Bavinck sees it, the incarnation's primary metaphysical declaration. In this sense the question of continuity with the incarnation is reversed. The incarnation as a divine work *ad extra* and thus non-necessary is the fullest expression and demonstration of the absolute personality of God. The incarnation as personalism consummately expressed is self-presented as the only way of truly conceiving of God.

There is a second sense in which divine personality features in Bavinck's understanding of the incarnation, again with an eye toward distinguishing Christian theism from pantheism. Bavinck sees this especially in the Reformed emphasis on the incarnation of the person of the Son as opposed to an incarnation of the divine nature.[52] "Patripassianism," he says, crouching at the door when this distinction is unappreciated, "is inherent in all pantheistic systems, especially that of Hegel, Schelling, Hartmann ... who conceive the absolute not as *being* but as *becoming* and who allow the divine to pour itself out in the world and to finitize itself."[53] He continues: "In that case the world and humanity with all its sorrow and misery is a moment in the life of God, and the history of revelation is the history of God's suffering."[54] Here again Bavinck emphasizes the role of divine personality in the self-expression of God as God. Personality is that by which God acts not necessarily as God, without, that is, ontological diminution. Trinity expressed in the incarnation thus affords incarnational or accommodated predication "of God" that does no violence to the incommunicable attributes but rather affirms them: "against every tendency to mix the two natures—they [the Reformed] emphasized that the person of the Son, in whom the divine nature existed in a manner of its own, had assumed human nature."[55] "The incarnation was prepared from eternity; it does not rest in the essence of God but in the person. It is not a necessity as in pantheism, but neither is it arbitrary or accidental as in Pelagianism."[56]

Elsewhere Bavinck connects creation and redemption explicitly with the personal union of divine and creaturely attributes. In his Stone Lectures he writes:

---

50. Bavinck, *RD*, 2:33.

51. Bavinck, *RD*, 2:34.

52. "It is also important ... to maintain that not the divine nature as such but specifically the person of the Son became human" (Bavinck, *RD*, 3:275).

53. Bavinck, *RD*, 3:275.

54. Bavinck, *RD*, 3:275.

55. Bavinck, *RD*, 3:275. Bavinck cites the sixth Synod of Toledo (p. 276).

56. Bavinck, *RD*, 3:277.

The world itself rests on revelation; revelation is the presupposition, the foundation ... the secret ... of all that exists in all its forms. ... In every moment of time beats the pulse of eternity; every point in space is filled with the omnipresence of God; the finite is supported by the infinite, all becoming is rooted in being. Together with all created things, that special revelation which comes to us in the Person of Christ is built on these presuppositions. The foundations of creation and redemption are the same.[57]

One thus observes that for Bavinck, *ad extra* as such, the full scope of God's relation to that which is not God, displays not the ineffability of abstract deity nor the conundrum of non-necessary divine action but the majesty and mystery of divine personality. The incarnation is both the fullest non-necessary expression of divine personality and, therefore, the primary theological confession of a Christian dogmatics, even of a Christian worldview. To look at it another way, Bavinck then would as Barth does understand natural theology as either a contradiction in terms or idolatry. Bavinck's ecumenical manner and broad use of sources[58] may obscure somewhat this orientation but would not contradict it.

Incarnation and Creation

Bavinck says that "the incarnation ... has its presupposition and preparation in the creation."[59] "Specifically, the creation of humans in God's image is a supposition and preparation for the incarnation of God."[60] This notion of "preparation" for the incarnation takes two distinguishable forms in Bavinck, one with reference to creation and the other with reference to redemption, or to the unity of historically progressive redemptive revelation (biblical theology).[61] The second of these is addressed below. The first, creation as preparation for the incarnation, finds an interesting supplement in Bavinck: the idea that the incarnation is yet preparation for a further, final, consummate incarnation of God. This eschatological trajectory brings into view Bavinck's idea that a kind of covenantal Creator–creature relation

---

57. Bavinck, *PoR*, 24. See Nathan D. Shannon, "Ontology and Revelation in Bavinck's Stone Lectures," *Scottish Journal of Theology* 73, no. 2 (2020): 112–25.

58. See Nathaniel Gray Sutanto, "Confessional, International, and Cosmopolitan: Herman Bavinck's Neo-Calvinistic and Protestant Vision of the Catholicity of the Church," *Journal of Reformed Theology* 12 (2018): 22–39; Cory Brock and Nathaniel Gray Sutanto, "Herman Bavinck's Reformed Eclecticism: On Catholicity, Consciousness and Theological Epistemology," *Scottish Journal of Theology* 70, no. 3 (2017): 310–32.

59. Bavinck, *RD*, 3:277.

60. Bavinck, *RD*, 3:277.

61. Bavinck in fact refers to Trinity, creation, and the history of revelation as three preparations for the incarnation (*RD*, 3:280).

is not restricted to formalized arrangements such as the covenant of works but is the "natural" or created situation as such.

Bavinck affirms an ontological distinction between the Creator and the creature. God and the creature, he says, are two but not numerically. They cannot be enumerated as instances of a single kind. And yet, "man ... *is* akin to God; man is his image, his son, his offspring."[62] This similarity indicates to Bavinck that the incarnation of the Son in the fullness of time has in terms of Creator–creature relation already been provided for:

> Thus the incarnation of God is a possibility. ... When God creates humans in his image and dwells and works with his Spirit in them, exerts influence on their heart and head, speaks to them, and makes himself known to them and understood by them, that is an act of condescension and accommodation to his creature, an anthropomorphizing of God and so, in a sense and to that extent, a humanization of God.[63]

He concludes: "Given with and in creation is the possibility of revelation and also of incarnation."[64] It is worth noting that in Bavinck's reasoning creation and revelation are closely associated. At significant points he uses the terms more or less interchangeably as signaling precedent for the incarnation:

> If God was able to create (and could reveal himself to) beings essentially distinct from him, then he must also be able to become man. For while the incarnation is certainly different from all revelation, it is also akin to it: it is its climax, crown, and completion. All revelation tends toward and groups itself around the incarnation as the highest, richest, and most perfect act of self-revelation. Generation, creation, and incarnation are closely related, even if the latter ones do not necessarily flow from the preceding.[65]

Creation, therefore, is a revelatory incarnation of God that does not presuppose redemption but signals the realization of a relational determination of God. Creatureliness as such presupposes a revelatory, relational self-giving of the Creator.[66]

---

62. Bavinck, *RD*, 3:277.
63. Bavinck, *RD*, 3:277.
64. Bavinck, *RD*, 3:277.
65. Bavinck, *RD*, 3:278. "Creation is the initial act and foundation of all divine revelation" (*RD*, 2:407).
66. "God, accordingly, from all eternity, conceived finite creatures and gave them existence within the necessary boundaries of time and space. In those creatures, therefore, he has, as it were, limited his eternal thoughts and infinite power. Specifically, the creation of humans in God's image is a supposition and preparation for the incarnation of God" (*RD*, 3:277). So observes Eglinton: "For Bavinck, God cannot practice self-disclosure at a

In his study of Bavinck's use of the organic motif, James Eglinton devotes sequential chapters to the doctrines of God and general revelation. In between these, Eglinton pauses to point out that before one moves on from the doctrine of God in order "to explore Bavinck's doctrine of general revelation ... before this takes place, a conceptual bridge between the doctrines of God and creation must be built: how do the Creator and the creation meet?"[67] Eglinton here suggests that conceptually something "bridges the gap" between God and revelation, or to put it another way, that revelation implies creation that requires something more than the doctrine of God alone.[68] Standard insertions here include the doctrines of the will and knowledge of God or, in historic Reformed thought, the doctrine of the decree. Eglinton instead focuses on "various ontic categories applied by Bavinck to God, Creation, humanity and the incarnate Christ."[69] "Evidently, within this triniform organic worldview there is also a consequent understanding of being and becoming."[70] In other words, Bavinck articulates an ontology he takes to be implied in the revealed content of Christian faith, something implied in everything touching upon Creator–creature relation and distinction. In the course of this discussion Eglinton identifies an important difference between the theologies of Bavinck and Barth:

> Bavinck formulates a divine ontology in line with the *extra-Calvinisticum*. This points towards a significant diversion between ... neo-Calvinism and neo-Orthodoxy. In the latter, Barth held election closely to divine ontology. In the former, Bavinck posits that God's ontology is separate from election. According to Bavinck, God does not will the ultimate ontic reality, himself, to be. Thus while God's will proves determinative for all else, his ontology nonetheless remains separate.[71]

Here Eglinton points to something very significant: Bavinck allows a distinction between the being and the will of God. Eglinton emphasizes the relevant difference on this point between Bavinck and Barth, but classical Thomism is similarly loathe to alienate the being from the will of God. Where Barth denies epistemic access to God prior to or apart from election, where election stands for God in the execution

---

distance. God must either 'inhabit' his revelation ... or he must refrain from self-disclosure altogether" (Eglinton, *Trinity and Organism*, 144).

67. Eglinton, *Trinity and Organism*, 114.

68. "When Bavinck speaks of the fundamental ontological distinction between God and the cosmos, this is not the totality of his doctrines of God or divine knowability ... his God is the Trinity whose ontological being is outwardly manifested in revelations and works" (Eglinton, *Trinity and Organism*, 122; he cites *RD*, 2:318).

69. Eglinton, *Trinity and Organism*, 114.

70. Eglinton, *Trinity and Organism*, 115 (see 117–18).

71. Eglinton, *Trinity and Organism*, 120.

of his eternal will, Aquinas resists a notion of the will of God distinguishable from the divine being as such. The divine acts that represent actualizations of the eternal will of God therefore represent a hermeneutical problem for Thomas. Eglinton suggests that between the immutable being of God and mutable creaturely ontology Bavinck affirms a free, nonessential movement of the will of God, maintaining that while God does not become Creator[72] and in no way changes he nonetheless nonessentially wills independently of his being.

As noted, Eglinton suggests that Bavinck approaches the doctrine of God along the lines of the *extra-Calvinisticum* in which the omnipresence of the Son of God is in a harmonious relationship with the spatio-temporal humility of the Son's incarnate presence. The point of the doctrine, for Calvin, is to maintain the full and immutable deity of the divine nature despite its being united inseparably in the person to the human nature. The Son is still God while he walks the earth as man. The mediatorial work of the incarnate Son, his humiliation and subsequent exaltation in the flesh, may thus be attributed to the second person of the Trinity without implying diminution of the fullness of the divine nature; not even omnipresence is compromised. If the finite cannot contain the infinite, and the natures remain unconfused and each retains its own properties, then the spatial presence of Jesus of Nazareth though predicated of the person of the Son of God does not compromise incommunicable attributes. "The Son is here; not there" and "the Son is omnipresent, no less there than here," may both be true of the person of the Son, the first according to the human and the second according to the divine nature. Such predications, in fact, are meaningless without the incommunicable attributes.

Eglinton appears to suggest that Bavinck "bridges the gap" between God and creation as follows: the God who is and does not change eternally wills to create in time, if not temporally to become Creator, and to limit his own thoughts in created, revelatory self-expression while remaining unchangeably who he is. Deferring to Chalcedon suggests that the triune God after the manner of the incarnation takes to himself a non-necessary relation, or enters into a Creator–creature relationship, in something like the way the Son became flesh. One might say that eternally but not necessarily God is Creator but also that there is a sense in which God is not Creator until he creates; God, when he creates, becomes Creator, just as the Son, eternally the mediator of the covenant, and thus eternally *incarnandus*, is not incarnate until his conception in the womb of Mary.

Eglinton notes that, as Bavinck sees things, the divine being as such cannot account for creation nor for the relational precondition, which creation displays.

---

72. Bavinck writes:

> Eternal is also the act of creating as an act of God. … For God did not *become* Creator. … Rather, he is the eternal Creator, and as Creator he was the Eternal One, and as the Eternal One he created. The creation therefore brought about no change in God; it did not emanate from him and is no part of his being. He is unchangeably the same eternal God. (Bavinck, *RD*, 2:429)

He says that Bavinck embraces this difficulty when he affirms, *pace* neo-Orthodoxy, that there is God and then there is the electing God, that the divine nature as such cannot account for creation, revelation, or redemption, nor can these or any non-necessary works of God account for or produce the divine nature. Eglinton also rehearses Bavinck's reiteration of the classical understanding of the Creator–creature relation, that eternity posits time, and so on, but not the reverse. Classical iterations of this asymmetry are usually designed to fortify asymmetry. If eternity posits time, time therefore reveals eternity because time—createdness—cannot account for itself either metaphysically or conceptually. Bavinck certainly stands by this, but adds relational symmetry, arguing that the incarnation is a personal self-manifestation of the asymmetrical relationship. The *extra-Calvinisticum* is in this context shorthand for the mystery of deity as such—eternal and immutable by definition and yet personal and voluntarily self-revealed. Deity and immanence in cooperation address the creature, from within creation.

Christian theism is therefore distinguished even perhaps defined by a self-revelatory relational establishment that we understand as God creating the world:

> From the very first moment, true religion distinguishes itself from all other religions by the fact that it construes the relation between God and the world, including man, as that between the Creator and his creature. ... No right relation to God is conceivable apart from this.[73]

Christian theism founded upon the incommunicable attributes nonetheless displays a Creator–creature relatedness of such profundity that it precedes and makes possible creaturely reflection upon that relation—and it makes possible human moral experience. Creation for Bavinck is Creator–creature relation. Cornelius Venema has seen fit to defer to the notion of covenant at this point: "Bavinck argues that the idea of covenant corresponds to the nature of man as a moral and rational creation. ... The beauty of the covenant is that it provides a framework within which a fully personal and responsible engagement may transpire between God and human beings."[74] This is simply to give a name to Bavinck's view of the original state of the human creature and the creature's original context:

> We cannot understand or imagine humanity without God ... human beings always and everywhere stand in some relation to God. ... The human person, therefore, has to be viewed theologically, and also in ethics. Morality ... finds its principle and standard in the relation in which a human being stands to God.[75]

---

73. Bavinck, *RD*, 2:407.
74. Cornelis Venema, "Covenant and Election in the Theology of Herman Bavinck," *Mid-America Journal of Theology* 19 (2008): 82.
75. Bavinck, *RE*, 40.

Bavinck rejects a distinction between a moral relation to nature and a religious relation to God, an unhelpful suggestion he attributes to Schleiermacher.[76] Rather: "Religion is therefore not a piece of life, but life itself. Our entire life must be serving God."[77] For Bavinck, "covenant" refers to the historical covenants of works and grace and to those theistic encounters in the lives of the patriarchs, prophets, priests, and kings of Israel. But more basically, "covenant" is the relational fabric of the human situation as a self-conscious bearer of the divine image:

> For according to its essence, religion is nothing less than fellowship with God, the most deep, inward, and tender fellowship that can be imagined and understood second only to the fellowship between the three persons of the Godhead and the fellowship between the two natures of Christ. That is what Scripture expresses in its beautiful doctrine of the covenant. For the covenant refers to that act of God whereby God places man as His image in relationship to Himself and causes him to dwell continually in His fellowship. That fellowship is more intimate and tender than the fellowship between husband and wife, between the vine and its branches, between a foundation and its superstructure. Scripture can hardly find words or metaphors sufficiently powerful and clear to make us understand something of that fellowship.[78]

Incarnation and Revelation

The point here is not biblical theology or a biblico-literary Christocentricism. Contemporary evangelical biblical scholars consider the claim that "Christ is in all of Scripture."[79] This tentative, inductive approach falls short of the neo-Calvinist dogmatic conviction that Christ *is* all of Scripture, that special revelation is a soterically efficacious expression and extension of the grace of God in Christ. The Bible is not a book about Jesus; rather, the organism of Scripture is Christ himself.[80] While exegetical demonstration of this conviction was under development in Michigan and New Jersey,[81] Bavinck at Kampen and later at Amsterdam had developed a doctrine of historical revelation appreciative not merely of the soteric unity of the Bible but of its relational and, one may surely say, covenantal organism.

---

76. Bavinck, *RE*, 40.
77. Bavinck, *RE*, 74.
78. Herman Bavinck, *Saved by Grace: The Holy Spirit's Work in Calling and Regeneration*, ed. J. Mark Beach, trans. Nelson D. Kloosterman (Grand Rapids, MI: Reformation Heritage, 2008), 25.
79. "Christ in all of Scripture" was the theme for the 2019 meeting of the Evangelical Theological Society.
80. See, for example, Vos, *RHBI*, 12.
81. Vos, *BT*.

In his Stone Lectures of 1908, published as *Philosophy of Revelation*, Bavinck develops within an apologetic context a notion of revelation's self-evident self-awareness. He argues, on the offensive, that the evaluation of systems should be twofold: on the basis of their capacity to account for the diversity-in-unity of experience and on the basis of their capacity to account for that explanatory capacity; a system should be able to explain but also to explain itself. Bavinck argues that the triunity of God is the only basis upon which the unity and diversity of experience is intelligible and that the Christian system displays conspicuously the principle of its organism, Christ the Son enfleshed. The person of the Son incarnate bears this explanatory value for the Christian faith as a whole because and only because the incarnation is the fullest expression of the relational substructure of both creation and redemption.

Throughout the lectures Bavinck characterizes competing systems as failing to balance unity and diversity; each tends either toward unity at the expense of diversity or the reverse. In this sense he is bold to characterize unbelieving or non-Christian thought as such along precisely these lines and his conviction regarding the futility of all such systems is striking: "Whoever within the world tries to reduce unity to multiformity, being to becoming, spirit to matter, man to nature, or the reverse, always plays false with the other half of the distinction."[82] "Much, therefore, will have to be done before the modern, pantheistic or materialistic, worldview shall have conquered the old theistic one. Indeed ... it may safely be added that this will never happen."[83] The triunity of God means for Bavinck that neither the unity nor diversity of the divine being is reducible to the other. For this reason even the numerically singular decree of God, foreordaining whatsoever comes to pass, does not undermine but rather vindicates the diversity of human experience: "But unity, true unity, a unity which does not destroy differentiation but rather includes and enfolds it, may come and can come only when the entire world is conceived as the product of wisdom and power which reveal God's eternal plan."[84]

Bavinck therefore sees increased doctrinal organism (unity) as a foremost virtue of dogmatics and also as apologetic vindication of Christian theism.[85] In this sense it is a matter not only of native integrity but also of polemical stamina that Christian thought develop not mechanically but organically from within, not by aggregation from without but by self-cultivation according to native principles. Method, accordingly, must articulate a system's self-understanding. "The philosophy of revelation," the Christian notion of revelation, that is, "must take its start from its object, from revelation," so that "its idea," one's conception of revelation, "cannot be construed a priori."[86] Bavinck sees only one possibility

---

82. Bavinck, *PoR*, 88.
83. Bavinck, *PoR*, 17.
84. Bavinck, *PoR*, 79.
85. Hans Burger has suggested cultural motivations for Bavinck's thinking so thoroughly through a trinitarian or christological view of creation. See Burger, *Being in Christ*, 88.
86. Bavinck, *PoR*, 23.

for Christian self-understanding, that "there comes to us out of history such a revelation, shining by its own light; and then it tells us, not only what its content is but also how it comes into existence."[87]

For Bavinck the singular shining light of revelation is Christ. The light of Christ extends outward, illuminating the full scope of revelation, in such a way that not only soteric, religious, or moral claims take Christian form but the prelapsarian order, general revelation, and eschatology, too, are to be understood in the light of the hypostatic union of being and becoming:

> Revelation, while having its center [*middenpunt*] in the Person of Christ, in its periphery extends to the uttermost ends of creation. It does not stand isolated in nature and history, does not resemble an island in the ocean, nor a drop of oil upon water. ... In every moment of time beats the pulse of eternity; every point in space is filled with the omnipresence of God; the finite is supported by the infinite, all becoming is rooted in being. Together with all created things, that special revelation which comes to us in the Person of Christ is built on these presuppositions. The foundations of creation and redemption are the same. The logos who became flesh is the same by whom all things were made. ... General revelation leads to special revelation, and special revelation points back to general revelation. The one calls for the other, and without it remains imperfect and unintelligible.[88]

Bavinck claims that "the groundwork for the incarnation first had to be laid in the preceding history," but even this wording in fact understates his view of revelation-historical precedent for the incarnation.[89] He does not, that is, hold to something like a deistic view of history as that sphere of creaturely experience into which God has inserted self-manifestation with increasing intensity, clarity, or frequency—and violence to the natural order—as temporal distance to the

---

87. Bavinck, *PoR*, 23.
88. Bavinck, *PoR*, 24–5. Also:

> The incarnation of God is the central fact in special revelation, the fact that sheds light upon its whole domain. Already in creation God made himself like human beings when he created them in his image. But in re-creation he became human and entered totally into our nature and situation. In a sense God's becoming human starts already immediately after the fall, inasmuch in his special revelation God reached back deeply into the life of the creation, linked up with the work of his own providence, and so ordered and led persons, situation, and events, indeed the entire history of a people, that he gradually came close to the human race and became ever more clearly knowable to it. But it reaches its culmination only in the person of Christ, who therefore constitutes the central content of the whole of special revelation. (*RD*, 1:344)

89. Bavinck, *RD*, 3:280.

incarnation decreased. Bavinck everywhere rejects what he calls a "mechanical" view of history as a series of inorganically related concatenations. And, in fact, this kind of deistic "interruption" is precisely what he is at pains to deny with reference to the incarnation. When Christ comes in the flesh, Bavinck argues, he is not upsetting metaphysical precedent or introducing an unforetold relational principle, but bringing to crisis-fruition a revelatory principle, which begins in one sense with creation itself, and in another with the first announcement of a redemptive gospel (Gen. 3:15), and which is provided for in the triunity of God.

Bavinck argues this by more or less rewording the Johannine prologue: "Just as the incarnation presupposes the generation [of the Son] and the creation [of humans in the image of God], so now there is added still another presupposition and preparation: revelation. It is especially John in his prologue who brings out for us this preparation for incarnation in a preceding history."[90] Bavinck's take on Jn 1:5 is noteworthy:

> Even after the fall, this revelation did not stop. On the contrary, the light of that Logos shone in the darkness and enlightened everyone coming into the world. He revealed himself particularly in Israel, which he had chosen for his own inheritance and led and blessed as Angel of the covenant. He came continually to his own. ... In that manner the Son prepared the whole world ... for his coming in the flesh.[91]

In this sense Bavinck inserts the entire history of special revelation in between Jn 1:5, in which darkness falls but does not overcome, and 1:6, in which the Baptist as the immediate forerunner to Christ is named. So Bavinck says: "It was the Son himself who thus immediately after the fall, as Logos and as Angel of the covenant, made the world of Gentiles and Jews ready for his coming."[92]

But here at precisely this point Bavinck reverts to creational, as opposed to revelational, precedent for the incarnation: "He was in the process of coming from the beginning of time and in the end came for good, by his incarnation making his home in humankind."[93] And in so doing he locates precedent for the incarnation in general revelation no less than in special: "The incarnation links up with the preceding revelation, both the general and the special. It stands and falls with them. ... Revelation, after all, is based on the same idea as the incarnation: on the communicability of God, both in his being to the Son (generation) and outside his being to creatures (creation)."[94]

The incarnation is the metaphysical first word of the *principium cognoscendi externum*. This means that the internal principle, the work of the Spirit, draws the

---

90. Bavinck, *RD*, 3:280.
91. Bavinck, *RD*, 3:280.
92. Bavinck, *RD*, 3:280.
93. Bavinck, *RD*, 3:280.
94. Bavinck, *RD*, 3:281.

sinner to confess the personal self-revelatory condescension of God as the precondition of doxological knowledge of God. Revelation in this sense is not discrete bits of information, which by adopting a positive doxastic attitude a sinner makes his or her own. Revelation is not—or not only—information the affirmation of which signals conversion. Revelation, typified in Scripture, is an objective state of personal communion, the creature with God in the Son.

Strong indication that the incarnation functions this way for Bavinck is the fact that he takes a personal union of two natures as vindicating biblical anthropomorphism: "Everywhere in Scripture, divine as well as human predicates are attributed to the same personal subject: divine and human existence, omnipresence and [geographical] limitation, eternity and time, creative omnipotence and creaturely weakness. What is this but the church's doctrine of the two natures united in one person?"[95] Here the church's confession of the hypostatic union vindicates realist readings of biblical humanizations of God not only in the four gospels but throughout the whole of Scripture. Chalcedon, as Eglinton suggests (noted above), permeates Bavinck's understanding of theological predication because Christ is the organism of revelation.

Of Old Testament theophanies Bavinck says: "These appearances do not presuppose God's corporeality ... but are perceptible signs by which his presence is made known, just as on Pentecost the Holy Spirit made himself known by wind and fire."[96] Interesting here is that Bavinck on the one hand does not identify the phenomena that signal divine presence with divine presence itself; but nor, on the other hand, does he take phenomena and presence to be mutually exclusive. Phenomena do not fabricate presence but rather indicate presence. The phenomena signal a real, special presence, but a presence that itself is non-phenomenal and in itself unobservable. Other interpreters will likewise make a point to say that the phenomena are not to be identified with God, and then infer from this dissociation that divine presence is only of a "manifested" kind, that the sign of divine presence has no real (theological) referent but reduces to a religious self-evocation on the part of God. Bavinck moves past this inference and affirms a presence signaled by Old Testament theophany akin to the presence of the Spirit at Pentecost. So he says of the *Malak* YHWH that it "is not an independent symbol nor a created angel but a true personal revelation and appearance of God, distinct from him ... and still one with him in name ... in power ... in redemption and blessing ... in adoration and honor."[97]

Bavinck says that Reformed theologians "rigorously maintained" the unity of the person of the Son but also, with reference both to the person and to the life experience of Christ, the rule that the finite cannot contain the infinite. "In that way," he says, "Reformed theology secured space for a purely human development of Christ, for a successive communication of gifts, and for a real distinction

---

95. Bavinck, *RD*, 3:298–9.
96. Bavinck, *RD*, 1:328.
97. Bavinck, *RD*, 1:329.

between humiliation and exaltation."[98] Bavinck says here that the combination of two elements—personal or hypostatic principle of union and the incomparability of divine and human natures—affords predication of development and distinction in the life experience of the Son of God. Here again the personality of Christology features and from this constitutive center permeates Christian understanding: "As it does in the doctrine of the Trinity, of humanity in the image of God, and of the covenants, so here in the doctrine of Christ as well, the Reformed idea of conscious personal life as the fullest and highest life comes dramatically to the fore."[99]

Bavinck rehearses historic Reformed emphasis on the agency of the person of the Son in the incarnation. Bavinck does not here refer to a substance-irrelevant appellation, "person not deity," but to divine personality in Trinity. He emphasizes conscious personal life in order to specify the relevant distinction between incarnation of the divine nature of the Son and incarnation of the divine Son. Incarnation of the divine nature is either inadequately personal, and therefore suggests a Christology inhospitable to the attributes and experiences of a created nature, or Nestorian, in which a union of two natures functions simply as the cooperation of two separate if equal personalities. By contrast, incarnation focusing on the person of the Son presents a self-conscious divine personality enfleshed. This means that the divine second person moves to take to himself both anthropomorphic predicates and the nature that vindicates them, not a docetic manifestation of incarnation, a relational sleight of hand evoking metaphysically naïve religiosity. Because divine personality, as opposed to a bare divine nature, "self-incarnates," the person of the Son "speaks" by metaphysical assumption that he is man—born, suffered, and died—before apostolic testimony and Scripture, by Spirit-inspiration, rehearse those predicates on behalf of the church. The hypostatic union precedes and vindicates New Testament theological predication. In the case of the Old Testament, the incarnation proper precedes logically, according to the logic of the covenant of grace, but also historically, since creation itself is a preparatory incarnation of God.

One thus observes the theologico-hermeneutical implications of Bavinck's conviction that the "center of that revelation is the person of Christ," and thus that "revelation, not as a doctrine, but as incarnation, can self-evidently be nothing other than history, i.e., occur at a certain time and be bound to a certain place. The incarnation is the unity of being (ἐγὼ εἰμί, John 8:58) and becoming (σὰρξ ἐγένετο, John 1:14)."[100]

As Bavinck argues for the surpassing explanatory capacity of the Christian worldview, so he commends in the "marketplace" of religions a doxological confession after the pattern of Christ himself as the announcement of a divine overture to man via condescension by way of covenant. "God has to come down from his lofty position, condescend to his creatures, impart, reveal, and give

---

98. Bavinck, *RD*, 3:258.
99. Bavinck, *RD*, 3:259.
100. Bavinck, *RD*, 1:379–80.

himself away to human beings," that this condescension is "nothing other than the description of a covenant," and that outside of biblical revelation "all peoples either pantheistically pull God down into what is creaturely, or deistically elevate him endlessly above it." Neither alternative may "arrive at true fellowship, at covenant, at genuine religion," "but Scripture insists on both: God is infinitely great and condescendingly good."[101]

Finally, it must also be noted that the incarnation in this way sets a pattern for eschatology, for covenant consummation, just as it does for creation. Bavinck understands Scripture as the literary instantiation of a revelation, which extends outward from Christ himself not only retrospectively—"Revelation follows this law [of organism]; re-creation is adapted to creation"[102]—but prospectively, toward consummate covenantal communion of God with and in creation. For all his emphasis upon the determinative influence of the incarnation for the Christian worldview, he will even say that the purpose of revelation transcends the redemptive accomplishment of Christ in the flesh. "The purpose of revelation is not Christ," he writes.[103] Though "Christ is the center and the means," the purpose of revelation, extending beyond redemptive accomplishment to application and finally to consummation, is "that God will again dwell in his creatures and reveal his glory in the cosmos," and notice that for Bavinck "this, too, is an incarnation of God."[104] Scripture "is the product of God's incarnation in Christ and in a sense its continuation, the way by which Christ makes his home in the church, the preparation of the way to the full indwelling of God. But in this indwelling, accordingly, it has its τέλος, its end and goal. ... Like the entire revelation, Scripture, too, is a passing act."[105]

In sum, we find in Bavinck three distinct levels or modal instances of self-communicative relation. The first is an orthodox doctrine of eternal generation as a natural and necessary, personal self-communication within the Godhead. God as such is a personal, self-imaging God. The second is the free and uncompelled triune decree and work of creation in which God grants existence to a world within but distinguished from his own being, the "distance" being ontological rather than geographical, patterned after the objects of his eternal but non-necessary creative mind and will. Here already Bavinck speaks of a humanization of God and of a Creator–creature relation forged by God in the Son, one which is free but nonetheless determined or decreed *ad intra*, and of which Bavinck speaks as constituting a historical, covenant relation. The third unfolds within the created,

---

101. Bavinck, *RD*, 2:569, 70.
102. Bavinck, *RD*, 1:380.
103. Bavinck, *RD*, 1:380.
104. Bavinck, *RD*, 1:380.
105. Bavinck, *RD*, 1:380–1. Richard B. Gaffin Jr., *God's Word in Servant Form: Abraham Kuyper and Herman Bavinck and the Doctrine of Scripture* (Jackson, MS: Reformed Academic, 2007), 56, points out that this association of the incarnation with the "servant form" of Scripture Bavinck has in common with Kuyper.

covenant context of the second, is determined or decreed eternally but unfolds nonetheless in historical-covenant response to the image-bearer's handling of the covenant of works. One observes a covenant modality such that the incarnation proper is unnecessary from the point of view of the covenant of works, but then, subsequently, necessary for the accomplishment of the covenant of grace, for the Christ as redemptive surety. "In the divine being he occupies the place between the Father and the Spirit, is by nature the Son and image of God, was mediator already in the first creation, and as Son could restore us to our position as children of God."[106]

Uniqueness of the Incarnation

Some scholars have been troubled by Bavinck's close association of creation with redemption. Hans Burger, for example, writes: "The Christological teleology of creation is in tension with the contingent, soteriological character of the incarnation. As a result the unique character of the incarnation as an answer to sin and guilt seems to disappear, although Bavinck does not want this."[107]

But this tension arises only if one fails to note the levels or distinctions examined above. So far as these distinctions are identified, the difficulty Burger identifies should subside. But methodological precision helps here as well. Bavinck understands trinitarian theology as a confession afforded by special revelation. God is triune and is revealed as such in general revelation. But the human confession of the triunity of God is a feature of the sphere of special revelation only. The variable here is human. Trinitarian theology thus emerges as methodologically or epistemically christological; one confesses the triunity of God in Christ and in him only. Now, if one confesses in this Christo-methodological manner the doctrines of God, creation, anthropology, the Fall, and the doctrine of sin, the danger that caught Burger's attention emerges. Christ himself is implicated in the Fall and the soteric uniqueness of the incarnation is compromised. But method thus deployed, it must be remembered, tracks with soteriology, with Heidelberg's subjective rather than with the Belgic Confession's objective. Bavinck's dogmatic system, as noted above, is a confession of the church as the sanctified people of God. That is, dogmatic confession epistemically speaking is native to the sphere of redemptive grace, even as it confesses a good creation originally without sin and a Holy God self-existent and eternal. Creation, the image of God, and the Fall into sin are not "christological" in the same sense that Christology is for the sake of the remaking of creation and humanity through the undoing of sin and wrath. All this is to highlight the second distinction above, and the redemptive uniqueness of the incarnation.

---

106. Bavinck, *RD*, 3:276.
107. Burger, *Being in Christ*, 93.

Bavinck is indeed at pains to defend the strictly soteric purpose of the incarnation.[108] He distances himself from what he says is a typically Roman Catholic notion of the necessity of the incarnation apart from sin, and at this point cites Calvin.[109] Calvin writes:

> I admit that in the first ordering of creation, while the state of nature was entire, he
>
> was appointed head of angels and men; for which reason Paul designates him "the first-born of every creature" (Col. 1:15). But since the whole Scripture proclaims that he was clothed with flesh in order to become a Redeemer, it is presumptuous to imagine any other cause or end.
>
> In fine, the only end which the Scripture uniformly assigns for the Son of God voluntarily assuming our nature, and even receiving it as a command from the Father, is, that he might propitiate the Father to us by becoming a victim.[110]

Deferring to Calvin, Bavinck identifies a principle of discontinuity, that the taking on of flesh, the incarnation proper, is for the purpose of redemption from sin and for that purpose only. In the sense that "creation itself is a revelation," "revelation and creation are not opposed to each other."[111] That is, revelation in Christ does "not just consist in a number of disconnected words and isolated facts but is one single historical and organic whole,"[112] not because creation and the Fall are decreed identically nor because the incarnation is implied in creation but because "the covenant of grace … links up with the creation order, and, reaching back to it, qualitatively and intensively incorporates the whole of creation into itself."[113] Bavinck is simply emphasizing here that missions reflect processions, that redemption is re-creation but not *ex nihilo*, and that "revelation … is always an act of grace," because "in it God condescends to meet his creature, a creature made in his image. All revelation is anthropomorphic, a kind of humanization of God."[114] And yet, for Bavinck, the uniqueness of the incarnation is primarily

---

108. As Burger appears to acknowledge: "In Bavinck's view incarnation is not necessary to perfect creation, but to remove sin" (*Being in Christ*, 92).

109. Bavinck, *RD*, 2:547–8.

110. John Calvin, *Institutes of the Christian Religion*, trans. Henry Beveridge (Edinburgh: Calvin Translation Society, 1846), 2.12.4. Calvin in fact says that the image of God of Gen. 1:26-7 is an image of the image of God who is the eternal Son. Eternal generation, in other words, signals an eternal and essential "imaging" of God that is the eternal template for the temporal, created imaging of God in the human creature (*Inst.*, 2.12.6).

111. Bavinck, *RD*, 1:361.

112. Bavinck, *RD*, 1:340.

113. Bavinck, *RD*, 3:231.

114. Bavinck, *RD*, 1:310.

redemptive-historical: whatever is necessary for the mediatorial humiliation and subsequent exaltation begins in the womb of Mary and not before.

Conclusion

The salient discovery of this chapter is a multilayered function of divine incarnation in Bavinck's thought. First, eternal generation, as a necessary act of God *ad intra*, is an eternal and immutable personal self-giving, a personal self-expression to another, constituting both affinity and difference with the other. This self-differentiating emanation signals an undiminishable capacity within the divine being for creation, for quantitatively increasing "being" without a diminution or attenuation of the uniqueness and immutability of deity. Strictly speaking, this is a misstatement since God and creation cannot be enumerated as members of a single class. God and creation are, strictly speaking, no more two than they are one. And this is precisely the point, that God is Creator eternally though not necessarily, while that non-necessity does not amount to actualized potential in the being of God because the appearance of created being can make no claims on deity. And eternal generation specifically is an eternal and immutable self-giving, a self-existent self-emanation, which signals the self-sufficiency of God which lies behind his being Creator. Eternal generation signals the fact that God can create ex nihilo, and that there are no external restraints on the forms which his creative works must take. Eternal generation signals the fact that God will remain as he is in the full glory and joy of eternal triune perfection whether he creates or does not. Eternal generation guards the orthodox modality of God as Creator: eternal but non-necessary and implicating no change in God. Eternal generation, in other words, is the necessary but insufficient condition for the creative divine will and actualization of creation. Only the triune God can create; God can create because he is triune.

The act of creating is, therefore, according to Bavinck, a non-necessary humanization or incarnation of God in the sense that in the act of creating, God, while remaining God, expresses himself not necessarily and meets the creature in a relational discourse suited to the created nature. Needless perhaps to say, God is not in any sense restrained or contained by the creation to which he has given being and which he sustains. Nonetheless, creation as act and product express eternal generation as ontological and relational precondition, respectively. Eternal generation is the capacity to will to create, and creation itself is a temporal relation of the God who has condescended for the sake of a relation, which is a relationship, with the creature.

Second, this divine humanization in the act and fact of creation provides for the incarnation proper, in the womb of Mary and forever thereafter. Creation prepares, necessarily but insufficiently, for the hypostatic union in the fullness of time. Bavinck appears, in fact, to suggest that as a humanization of God, creation itself—considered in its prelapsarian condition—anticipates a further humanization of God as the culmination of historical covenant relation. That is, there are undeveloped echoes and pregnant suggestions here and there that an incarnation of some kind would have occurred, fall or not, as the summation of an eschatological relationship between God and creation. This is not to say that a consummate, relational incarnation is implied in creation as such, but that from the point of view of creation at least two consummate relational alternatives are conceivable, one redemptive and one non-redemptive but no less consummate or eschatological. This much is speculative and remains unconfirmed in the primary sources. Be that as it may, it is clear that the incarnation in the womb of Mary is provided for in the humanization of God in creation but by no means required. Thus, again, as eternal generation is a necessary but insufficient condition for the possibility of divine humanization in creation, so creation is a necessary but insufficient condition for the possibility of the incarnation of the Son. There is thus in Bavinck a threefold divine self-giving in which each self-giving serves as necessary but insufficient condition for the next, and which culminates in Jesus Christ as the non-necessary, mediatorial self-giving of the personal substance of the Creator–creature relation itself.

This means that the uniqueness of the incarnation of the Son in the fullness of time must be revisited. Bavinck establishes striking precedent for the incarnation in creation and thus some form of metaphysical continuity. He does not, as might have proved imprudent, venture into the details of a classical metaphysical articulation of this continuity. The uniqueness of the incarnation does, however, as a consequence of this continuity, reappear with a markedly different emphasis. One is not led to ponder the sheer metaphysical peculiarity of the hypostatic union; instead, the redemptive and historical rationale for the incarnation now takes center stage. That is, the *why*—if not the *when*—of the incarnation now is unavoidably as important as the *what* of the incarnation. If creation in some sense already signals a humanization of God, then it becomes impossible to conceive of the hypostatic union apart from the Son's mediatorial function and from the historical moment of his appearing, the fullness of time as a moment of redemptive historical accomplishment—since this mediatorial fulfillment is the self-evident rationale for the incarnation as not necessarily expressive of the humanization of God in creation. The incarnation proper is indeed a metaphysical wonder; "metaphysical wonder" is, however, not the point. The point is gracious redemptive historical fulfillment for which the hypostatic union serves as the condition or manner of mediatorial assumption for the sake of eschatological relational consummation.

Put more directly: Bavinck sees three self-emanations of God. The first, eternal generation, is necessary and eternal but fully personal. Eternal generation makes creation possible but not necessary. The second, creation (act and object), is non-necessary and can make no demands on the divine being. Creation makes incarnation possible but not necessary. The third, the hypostatic union, is non-necessary or, better, gracious, makes no demands on the divine being, and expresses the divine self-imagings that precede it: eternal generation and creation.

Finally, Bavinck's christological sequence indicates a christological approach to the religious relation which, as has been argued throughout this study, constitutes the whole of the sphere of human experience. Religion, moral self-understanding, and theological predication are implicated. The christological approach to the religious relation constitutive of human self-understanding and experience shall be addressed in the sixth and final chapter of this study.

Chapter 6

CONCLUSION: MORAL EXPERIENCE AND
THE SON FORSAKEN

Therefore, let no one deceive you, when perchance you suffer annoyance from flies.

—Augustine

The foregoing five chapters attempt to reproduce a neo-Calvinist account of human moral experience. This sixth chapter condenses and rehearses the material from the preceding chapters, summarizes, and draws the study to a close.

Chapter 1 has examined the views of Herman Bavinck, Geerhardus Vos, and Cornelius Van Til on the broadest contextual matters relevant for understanding the probation of Gen. 2:17 as morally and religiously original and thus as prototypical for the human creature, as, in other words, constitutive of human experience as such. It is demonstrated, first of all, that these thinkers view Eden against a background of cosmic conflagration between God and fallen angels. Bavinck, Vos, and Van Til believe that biblical evidence of a prior angelic fall and the subversive, angelic influence in the garden in serpentine form indicate a cosmic framework for the Edenic probation within which creation itself is both the arena and the prize for a clash of two antithetical kingdoms, one of darkness and idolatry and the other of light and truth. And second, the probation itself is examined and shown to be, according to these writers, a highly controlled and concentrated covenant confrontation between God and his image-bearer, and designed for relational consummation by means of personal confirmation of the lordship of God. Relational eschatology is the subtext of original moral experience. This chapter argues that the probation—not the prohibition, but the probationary historical context for the prohibition—is already a primordial and prototypical instance of morally significant creaturely self-expression. Adam's conduct prior to the Fall and prior to the issuing of the prohibition (Gen. 2:17) is rightly dubbed "obedience." This is indicated by, among other things, not only moral mutability but also consciousness of that mutability and the inevitability of divine judicial response should transgression materialize. The probation is therefore instructive both ontologically and morally, since in it one observes not the origin of evil—according to Bavinck, Vos, and Van Til, strictly speaking evil has no origin—but the original, relational structure of human moral self-expression. This structure gives meaning to evil as such, and therefore signals, even before the Fall, the actuality of the relational preconditions for the transgression of the moral character of God self-given as moral norm for the creature. Chapter 1 argues that a transgressable self-expression of God as moral norm for the creature just is the fabric of original and prototypical human moral experience.

Chapter 2 focuses on Gen. 3:6, and argues that although the covenant of works provides an informative account of the significance of the transgression of Gen. 3:6, and therefore of the nature of sin and evil, these neo-Calvinists believe that the explanatory resources of the formalized covenant arrangement are at this point exhausted. For all that has been said about the nature of sin and evil, the possibility of sin—of creaturely transgression of divine law—is still no less obscure. The Westminster Confession of Faith (WCF) offers a way of locating that very lacuna. WCF 7.1 speaks generally of covenant condescension, claiming that although creatures naturally owe God obedience, there would be "no fruition" of God as the creature's "blessedness and reward" were it not for "voluntary condescension on God's part ... by way of covenant." Bavinck, Vos, and Van Til understand Eden in precisely the same terms. The original, natural, and prototypical state of affairs is that the image-bearer is always under obligation of obedience, and self-consciously so. So the original situation is exhaustively moral, or religious, or relational. It bears noting that the original situation betrays no ultimate separation of morality and religion, and that no human thought or action—because God fills time and space—is amoral. Thus God himself, not necessarily self-expressed, is the very fabric of human subjective experience as such. But then, in 7.2, the Westminster Confession says that "the first covenant made with man was a covenant of works." The Confession thus identifies moral experience with the covenant of works and with covenant eschatology. The neo-Calvinists have no reservations with this way of putting it, but their analysis is more specific. Bavinck, Vos, and Van Til give greater attention to a distinction between original and natural fruition of God and special, eschatological fruition of God. As regards the latter, the Confession says it all, as it were. But the Confession devotes indirect attention at best to the natural moral and religious situation. If "fruition of God as blessedness and reward" refers exclusively to special, eschatological covenant arrangement—the covenant of works—then the Confession has nothing to say, at least in chapter 7, about the original moral situation and the possibility of disobedience. If, however, there may be non-eschatological fruition of God, then one may imagine WCF 7.1.5 in which the natural moral situation and mutable original righteousness are explained in terms of the covenant condescension that is creation itself. Precisely here is where the neo-Calvinist account supplements harmoniously Reformed confessional heritage.

Accordingly, Chapter 2 of the present study examines the natural moral situation within which the covenant of works takes shape. Bavinck, Vos, and Van Til reject as Pelagian the idea of a nonmoral situation preceding the covenant arrangement; Adam was never without moral status before God and he was, from the first moment of self-consciousness, a moral character who understood himself as morally mutable and accountable to God. Natural morality is therefore covenant morality. Bavinck, Vos, and Van Til thus argue that the covenant of works enhances significantly but is markedly continuous with the natural moral fabric that precedes it. The implication is that human moral experience is not, most basically, a function of formal covenant arrangement but of a divine relational initiative which is logically prior to the prohibition, and which dates even to the design of the human creature, before the foundation of the world, as a corporate, covenant organism.

Chapters 1 and 2 thus propose a definition or account of the nature of evil as transgression of the moral character of God given both implicitly and explicitly as norm for the image-bearer. The covenant-moral substance of the natural situation prior to the covenant of works indicates that covenant theology, or the covenant of works in particular, cannot sustain a robust explanation of the possibility of evil, and that a more basic theology of that possibility is required. Bavinck and Vos insist that the mystery of a good character succumbing to temptation must and does remain unresolved. But they defer at this point, as the subsidiary nature of the confrontation in Eden leads one to expect, to the doctrine of God for an account of the actualization of a created, relational, moral mutability upon which the course of history and human moral experience depend. In other words, it becomes apparent at this point that, on a neo-Calvinist account, moral experience is direct experience of Creator–creature relationality, such that the human moral life is an expression of that relationality.

Chapter 3 takes up the task, as Van Til has put it, of "looking more steadfastly into the face of God."[1] That is, accepting the challenge, from Chapters 1 and 2, of accounting for the possibility of evil, one turns to the doctrine of God, where Bavinck and Van Til have developed the notion of absolute personality in order to highlight classical Trinitarianism's capacity for an account of a relational ontology up the task of substantiating creaturely moral experience theocentrically. Herman Bavinck, Johan Herman Bavinck, and Van Til have argued that creation, history, and moral meaning are possible only if God is both absolute and personal. They take the unipersonality of God to be implied by the equal ultimacy of unity and diversity in the Godhead—by the co-eternity of the persons and the inseparability of operations. But it is for their views of covenant and historical relationality that they deploy the language of God as "one person" or as "absolute personality." This chapter argues that Bavinck and Van Til are at pains to avoid two unbiblical dichotomies—absoluteness and personality, nature and grace—and to achieve greater doctrinal organicism by strengthening the integrity and interdependence of the doctrines of God and divine action. Chapters 1 and 2 demonstrate that for these writers, the unchangeable, unknowable God is himself the moral fabric of human moral experience. Chapter 3 presents the neo-Calvinist way of deferring the mystery of the possibility of theocentric moral accountability to the doctrine of God as divine or absolute personality. That is, Bavinck and Van Til account for

---

1. Van Til, *CGG*, 19.

meaningful historical contingency no less than for metaethical value in terms of the relational omnipresence of an absolute God.

Chapter 4 demonstrates the importance of absolute person for a Christian theistic account of the Creator–creature relation that fully personalizes the law of God that is known to the image-bearer implicitly, as the moral fabric of experience and history, and explicitly in the covenant of works and in redemptive special revelation. It is demonstrated, furthermore, that absolute person is viewed as classical Trinitarianism come into its own, and that, therefore, absolute person expresses Trinity and the capacity for Trinity to account for moral experience. Van Til's discussion of this is highlighted, along with his claim that absolute person in this way retrieves the theistic moral absoluteness of Augustine. Chapter 4 then engages Van Til's claim that absolute person suggests a theology of accommodation and therefore a hermeneutic of "fearless anthropomorphism," which he takes to be maximally faithful to classical theism and to Scripture as the self-attesting, verbal self-expression of God. Calvin's and a Calvinist theology of accommodation is analyzed in order to assess the Reformed pedigree of Van Til's approach to accommodation and anthropomorphism. It is argued that Van Til is more faithful to Calvin's theology of accommodation than Calvin himself, and that Van Til finds refuge from many challenges to accommodation in Chalcedonian Christology, as Vos, too, has at least suggested. This chapter demonstrates the role of absolute person in Bavinck, Vos, and Van Til's metaethics and the further value of absolute person in closing the distance between Trinity and religious experience.

Chapter 5 analyzes the role of the incarnation in Bavinck's theology. Bavinck argues that the relation of God to all that is not God may be conceived of as a three-tiered self-emanation of humanization of God: eternal generation, creation, and then the hypostatic union for the purpose of redemptive re-creation. A few features of this view are now especially noteworthy: Bavinck views creation as preparatory; its principles of absolute personalism and humanization are not necessarily but summarily expressed in the incarnation. There is an important reciprocity here: creation is a necessary precondition for the incarnation proper, so that the latter depends upon the former. At the same time, the relational theology explicative of creation is summarily expressed or comes into its own in the incarnation, so that creation as such is rightly understood only in light of the hypostatic union in which God as God is personally self-manifested. Eternal generation stands, mutatis mutandis, in a similar relation to the incarnation. The incarnation is in no sense implied in or required by eternal generation, while eternal generation is a necessary precondition for incarnation. And while eternal generation serves as that non-necessary precondition, it nonetheless is fully expressed only in the incarnation, so that apart from Christ no one can know the Father as the Father—as unbegotten one from whom the Son is eternally begotten. God cannot be known apart from Christ; all fruition of God as blessedness and reward is only in the Son.

Bavinck thus maintains, with historic Reformed theology, that the works of God *ad extra* are indivisible, but in his view the absolute personal God has moved toward that which is not himself primarily in the Son. For Bavinck and for Van

Til as well, therefore, the incarnation is the fullest display of a Creator–creature relation, which obtains beginning from within the eternal decree of God, from the first divine gesture toward all that is not himself. Human moral experience indicates that from the beginning God had condescended to establish a relation with the creature within which God himself, self-expressed as moral norm, would be subject to rejection. In the incarnation, the Son did not divest himself of power much less of nature; he divested himself of divine royal privilege relative to his own creatures. He assumed weakness and, in relational terms, transgressability, veiling but not renouncing deity.

Already in Gen. 3:6, in other words, the Son stands accused but offers no defense, and is handed over to be mocked and murdered. The uniqueness of the incarnation, on this account, is not primarily metaphysical but redemptive-historical. In terms of historical covenant relation, it may be said that the God the Son was first forsaken in Gen. 3:6, and that until Calvary, because a gracious Lord does not change, Israel is not consumed. Until the fullness of time, God has restrained both sin and his own wrath; that is, within the context of a covenant-relational history, God has exercised the divine mastery that belongs to his absolute nature in order to maintain enmity, both to uphold, ontologically, and to restrain, covenantally, the sinful forces that desired the defaming of his name. In the incarnation, only and exactly as divine sovereignty allows, God in the Son conquers the world by finally and conclusively succumbing to it. In the fullness of time, the wrath of God is revealed in the Son's being given over on the cross, where he is forsaken. In this sense, Bavinck and Van Til propose a covenant condescension of God in the Son, which begins with creation—in which creation has its beginning—and which serves as the precondition for moral and religious experience and as a relational logic of the mediatorial humiliation and crucifixion of Christ.

The original moment of human self-consciousness presupposes an assumption of creaturely weakness and the common infirmities thereof, by God in the Son, in which God is expressed as transgressable moral norm for the creature. Apart from this voluntary, divine, relational self-expression, moral experience is not possible. This voluntary, divine, relational self-expression is the stuff of human moral experience. In this sense the Son is first forsaken, despised, and rejected, when in Eden Eve took and ate and gave to her husband, and he, too, ate. This neo-Calvinist account of moral experience is thus basically christological and ultimately trinitarian.

BIBLIOGRAPHY

Ahn, Myung Jun. "Brevitas et facilitas: A Study of a Vital Aspect in the Theological Hermeneutics of John Calvin." PhD dissertation, University of Pretoria, 1998.
Ahn, Myung Jun. "The Ideal of Brevitas et Facilitas: The Theological Hermeneutics of John Calvin." *Skrif en Kerk/Verbum et Ecclesia* 20, no. 2 (1999): 270–81.
Ahn, Myung Jun. "The Influences on Calvin's Hermeneutics and the Development of His Method." *HTS Teologiese Studies/Theological Studies* 55, no. 1 (1999): 228–39.
Baird, James Douglas. "Analogical Knowledge: A Systematic Interpretation of Cornelius Van Til's Theological Epistemology." *Mid-America Journal of Theology* 26 (2015): 77–103.
Balserak, Jon. *Divinity Compromised: A Study of Divine Accommodation in the Thought of John Calvin*. Dordrecht: Springer, 2006.
Bavinck, Herman. *Our Reasonable Faith: A Survey of Christian Doctrine*. Translated by Henry Zylstra. Grand Rapids, MI: Eerdmans, 1956.
Bavinck, Herman. *Philosophy of Revelation: A New Annotated Edition*. Edited by Cory Brock and Nathaniel Gray Sutanto. Peabody, MA: Hendrickson, 2018.
Bavinck, Herman. "The Pros and Cons of a Dogmatic System." Translated by Nelson D. Kloosterman. *Bavinck Review* 5 (2014): 90–103.
Bavinck, Herman. *Reformed Dogmatics*. Edited by John Bolt. Translated by John Vriend. 4 Vols. Grand Rapids, MI: Baker Academic, 2003–8.
Bavinck, Herman. *Reformed Ethics: Created, Fallen, and Converted Humanity*. Edited by John Bolt. Grand Rapids, MI: Baker Academic, 2019.
Bavinck, Herman. *Saved by Grace: The Holy Spirit's Work in Calling and Regeneration*. Edited by J. Mark Beach. Translated by Nelson D. Kloosterman. Grand Rapids, MI: Reformation Heritage, 2008.
Bavinck, Herman. *Christian Worldview*. Translated and edited by Nathaniel Gray Sutanto, James Eglinton, and Cory C. Brock. Wheaton, IL: Crossway, 2019.
Bavinck, J. H. *Between the Beginning and the End: A Radical Kingdom Vision*. Translated by Bert Hielema. Grand Rapids, MI: Eerdmans, 2014.
Bavinck, J. H. *The Church Between Temple and Mosque: A Study of the Relationship between the Christian Faith and Other Religions*. Grand Rapids, MI: Eerdmans, 1981.
Bavinck, J. H. *Essays on Religion, Science, and Society*. Edited by John Bolt. Translated by Harry Boonstra and Gerrit Sheeres. Theology and Religious Studies. Grand Rapids, MI: Baker Academic, 2008.
Bavinck, J. H. "Human Religion in God's Eyes: A Study of Romans 1:18–32." *Scottish Bulletin of Evangelical Theology* 12 (1994): 44–52.
Bavinck, J. H. *An Introduction to the Science of Missions*. Translated by David H. Freeman. Phillipsburg, NJ: P&R, 1960.
Bolt, John. "Bavinck Tributes." *Bavinck Review* 3 (2012): 180–2.
Bolt, John. "An Opportunity Lost and Regained: Herman Bavinck on Revelation and Religion." *Mid-America Journal of Theology* 24 (2013): 81–96.

Brock, Cory. *Orthodox yet Modern: Herman Bavinck's Use of Friedrich Schleiermacher.* Bellingham, WA: Lexham, 2020.

Brock, Cory, and Nathaniel Gray Sutanto. "Herman Bavinck's Reformed Eclecticism: on Catholicity, Consciousness and Theological Epistemology." *Scottish Journal of Theology* 70, no. 3 (2017): 310–32.

Brown, Robert F. "The First Evil Will Must Be Incomprehensible: A Critique of Augustine." *Journal of the American Academy of Religion* 46, no. 3 (1978): 315–29.

Burger, Hans. *Being in Christ: A Biblical and Systematic Investigation in a Reformed Perspective.* Eugene, OR: Wipf & Stock, 2009.

Calvin, John. *Commentary on the First Book of Moses Called Genesis.* Translated by John King. Grand Rapids, MI: Christian Classics Ethereal Library, n.d.

Calvin, John. *Institutes of the Christian Religion.* Edited by John T. McNeill. Translated by Ford Lewis Battles. Philadelphia: Westminster Press, 1960.

Calvin, John. *Institutes of the Christian Religion.* Translated by Henry Beveridge. Edinburgh: Calvin Translation Society, 1846.

Calvin, John. *Jonah, Micah, Nahum.* Vol. 3 of *Commentaries on the Minor Prophets.* Translated by John Owen. Grand Rapids, MI: Christian Classics Ethereal Library, n.d.

Cary, Phillip. "Augustine on Evil." In *The Routledge Handbook on the Philosophy of Evil*, edited by Thomas Nys and Stephen de Wijze, 13–36. New York: Routledge, 2019.

Cherbonnier, E. LaB. "The Logic of Biblical Anthropomorphism." *Harvard Theological Review* 55, no. 3 (1962): 187–206.

Descartes, René. *Oeuvres de Descartes.* Edited by Charles Adam and Paul Tannery. 12 Vols. Paris: Cerf, 1897.

Doornbos, Gayle. "Herman Bavinck's Trinitarian Theology: The Ontological, Cosmological, and Soteriological Dimensions." PhD dissertation, University of St. Michael's College, 2019.

Dolezal, James E. *God without Parts: Divine Simplicity and the Metaphysics of God's Absoluteness.* Eugene, OR: Pickwick, 2011.

Edgar, William. "Geerhardus Vos and Culture." In *Resurrection and Eschatology: Theology in Service of the Church: Essays in Honor of Richard B. Gaffin Jr.*, edited by Lane G. Tipton and Jeffrey C. Waddington, 383–95. Phillipsburg, NJ: P&R, 2008.

Edgar, William. "Turn! Turn! Turn! Reformed Apologetics and the Cultural Dimension." In *Revelation and Reason: New Essays in Reformed Apologetics*, edited by K. Scott Oliphint and Lane G. Tipton, 242–57. Phillipsburg, NJ: P&R, 2007.

Eglinton, James. *Trinity and Organism: Towards a New Reading of Herman Bavinck's Organic Motif.* London: T&T Clark, 2011.

Eglinton, James, and Michael Bräutigam. "Scientific Theology? Herman Bavinck and Adolf Schlatter on the Place of Theology in the University." *Journal of Reformed Theology* 7 (2013): 27–50.

Eitel, Adam. "Trinity and History: Bavinck, Hegel, and Nineteenth Century Doctrines of God." In *Five Studies in the Thought of Herman Bavinck, A Creator of Modern Dutch Theology*, edited by John Bolt, 101–28. Lewiston, NY: Edwin Mellen Press, 2011.

Evans, G. R. *Augustine on Evil.* Cambridge: Cambridge University Press, 1982.

Frame, John M. "Divine Aseity and Apologetics." In *Revelation and Reason: New Essays in Reformed Apologetics*, edited by K. Scott Oliphint and Lane G. Tipton, 115–30. Phillipsburg, NJ: P&R, 2007.

Gaffin, Richard B., Jr. *God's Word in Servant Form: Abraham Kuyper and Herman Bavinck and the Doctrine of Scripture.* Jackson, MS: Reformed Academic, 2007.

Gaffin, Richard B., Jr. "Some Epistemological Reflections on 1 Cor 2:6–16." *Westminster Theological Journal* 57 (1995): 103–24.
Gaffin, Richard B., Jr. "Systematic Theology and Biblical Theology." *Westminster Theological Journal* 38, no. 3 (1976): 281–99.
Gamble, Richard C. "'Brevitas et Facilitas': Toward an Understanding of Calvin's Hermeneutic." *Westminster Theological Journal* 47, no. 1 (1985): 1–17.
Gamble, Richard C. "Exposition and Method in Calvin." *Westminster Theological Journal* 49, no. 1 (1987): 153–65.
Geehan, E. R., ed. *Jerusalem and Athens: Critical Discussions on the Theology and Apologetics of Cornelius Van Til.* Nutley, NJ: P&R, 1971.
Gilson, Etienne. *Introduction à l'étude de Saint Augustin.* Vol. 11, part 1. 3rd Ed. Paris: Librairie Philosophique J. Vrin, 1949.
Gleason, Ron. *Herman Bavinck: Pastor, Churchman, Statesman, and Theologian.* Phillipsburg, NJ: P&R, 2010.
Harinck, George. "The Religious Character of Modernism and the Modern Character of Religion: A Case Study of Herman Bavinck's Engagement with Modern Culture." *Scottish Bulletin of Evangelical Theology* 29 (2011): 60–77.
Huijgen, Arnold. *Divine Accommodation in John Calvin's Theology.* Göttingen: Vandenhoeck & Ruprecht, 2011.
Hunt, Jason B. *Cornelius Van Til's Doctrine of God and Its Relevance for Contemporary Hermeneutics.* Eugene, OR: Wipf & Stock, 2019.
Jong, Marinus de. "The Heart of the Academy: Herman Bavinck in Debate with Modernity on the Academy, Theology, and the Church." In *The Kuyper Center Review, Volume 5: Church and Academy,* edited by Gordon Graham, 62–75. Grand Rapids, MI: Eerdmans, 2015.
Klauber, Martin I., and Glenn S. Sunshine. "Jean-Alphone Turretini on Biblical Accommodation: Calvinist or Socinian?" *Calvin Theological Journal* 25, no. 1 (1990): 7–27.
Kooi, Cornelis van der. *As in a Mirror: Calvin and Barth on Knowing God: A Dyptych.* Translated by Donald Mader. Leiden: Brill, 2005.
Kraay, Klaas J. "Theism and Modal Collapse." *American Philosophical Quarterly* 48, no. 4 (2011): 361–72.
Lee, Hoon J. *The Biblical Accommodation Debate in Germany: Interpretation and the Enlightenment.* Cham, Switzerland: Palgrave Macmillan, 2017.
Lints, Richard. "Two Theologies or One? Warfield and Vos on the Nature of Theology." *Westminster Theological Journal* 54 (1992): 235–53.
Madsen, Truman G., ed. *Reflections on Mormonism: Judaeo-Christian Parallels.* Provo, UT: Religious Studies Center, 1978.
McCormack, Bruce L. "Revelation and History in Transfoundationalist Perspective: Karl Barth's Theological Epistemology in Conversation with a Schleiermacherian Tradition." *Journal of Religion* 78, no. 1 (1998): 18–37.
Meister, Chad. *Evil: A Guide for the Perplexed.* 2nd ed. London: Bloomsbury, 2018.
Meister, Chad, and James K. Dew Jr., eds. *God and the Problem of Evil: Five Views.* Downers Grove, IL: InterVarsity Press, 2017.
Moreland, J. P., and William Lane Craig. *Philosophical Foundations for a Christian Worldview.* Downers Grove, IL: InterVarsity Press, 2003.
Muller, Richard A. *Dictionary of Latin and Greek Theological Terms: Drawn Principally from Protestant Scholastic Theology.* Grand Rapids, MI: Baker, 1986.

Muller, Richard A. "A Note on 'Christocentrism' and the Imprudent Use of Such Terminology." *Westminster Theological Journal* 68 (2006): 253–60.

Muller, Richard A. *Holy Scripture: The Cognitive Foundation of Theology*. Vol. 2 of *Post-Reformation Reformed Dogmatics: The Rise and Development of Reformed Orthodoxy, ca. 1520 to ca. 1725*. 2nd ed. Grand Rapids, MI: Baker Academic, 2003.

Mullins, R. T. "Simply Impossible: A Case against Divine Simplicity." *Journal of Reformed Theology* 7 (2013): 181–203.

Niehaus, Jeffrey J. "An Argument against Theologically Constructed Covenants." *Journal of the Evangelical Theological Society* 50, no. 2 (2007): 259–73.

Niehaus, Jeffrey J. "Covenant: An Idea in the Mind of God." *Journal of the Evangelical Theological Society* 52, no. 2 (2009): 225–46.

Oliphint, K. Scott. "Cornelius Van Til and the Reformation of Christian Apologetics." In *Revelation and Reason: New Essays in Reformed Apologetics*, 255–93, edited by K. Scott Oliphint and Lane G. Tipton. Phillipsburg, NJ: P&R, 2007.

Oliphint, K. Scott. *God with Us: Divine Condescension and the Attributes of God*. Wheaton, IL: Crossway, 2011.

Pass, Bruce R. *The Heart of Dogmatics: Christology and Christocentrism in Herman Bavinck*. Göttingen: Vandenhoeck & Ruprecht, 2020.

Pass, Bruce R. "The Question of Central Dogma in Herman Bavinck." *Calvin Theological Journal* 53, no. 1 (2018): 33–63.

Petris, Paolo de. *Calvin's Theodicy and the Hiddenness of God: Calvin's Sermons on Job*. Bern: Peter Lang, 2012.

Plantinga, Alvin. *Does God Have a Nature?* Milwaukee, WI: Marquette University, 1980.

Poythress, Vern. "Rethinking Accommodation in Revelation." *Westminster Theological Journal* 76, no. 1 (2014): 143–56.

Ragusa, Daniel. "The Trinity at the Center of Thought and Life: Herman Bavinck's Organic Apologetic." *Mid-America Journal of Theology* 28 (2017): 149–75.

Rehman, Sebastian. "Theistic Metaphysics and Biblical Exegesis: Francis Turretin on the Concept of God." *Religious Studies* 38 (2001): 167–86.

Ridderbos, Herman N. *Paul: An Outline of His Theology*. Grand Rapids, MI: Eerdmans, 1975.

Shannon, Nathan D. "Herman and Johan Herman Bavinck on the Uniqueness of Christian Theism." *Mission Studies* 39, no. 1 (2022): 50–69.

Shannon, Nathan D. "Junius and Van Til on Natural Knowledge of God." *Westminster Theological Journal* 82, no. 2 (2020): 279–300.

Shannon, Nathan D. "Ontology and Revelation in Bavinck's Stone Lectures." *Scottish Journal of Theology* 73, no. 1 (2020): 112–25.

Shannon, Nathan D. "Religions and the Doctrine of God: Comparing J. H. Bavinck and Cherbonnier." *Torch Trinity Journal* 23, no. 2 (2020): 29–66.

Smyth, Newman. *Christian Ethics*. New York: C. Scribner's, 1892.

Sparks, Kenton L. *God's Word in Human Words: An Evangelical Appropriation of Critical Biblical Scholarship*. Grand Rapids, MI: Baker, 2008.

Spinoza, Benedict. *Tractatus Theologico-Politicus*. Translated by Samuel Shirley. Leiden: Brill, 1989.

Stek, John H. "'Covenant' Overload in Reformed Theology." *Calvin Theological Journal* 29, no. 1 (1994): 12–41.

Strange, Daniel. *Their Rock Is Not Like Our Rock: A Theology of Religions*. Grand Rapids, MI: Zondervan, 2015.

Suh, Chul Won. *The Creation-mediatorship of Jesus Christ: A Study in the Relation of the Incarnation and the Creation*. Amsterdam: Rodopi, 1982.

Sutanto, Nathaniel Gray. "Confessional, International, and Cosmopolitan: Herman Bavinck's Neo-Calvinistic and Protestant Vision of the Catholicity of the Church." *Journal of Reformed Theology* 12 (2018): 22–39.

Sutanto, Nathaniel Gray. *God and Knowledge: Herman Bavinck's Theological Epistemology.* London: Bloomsbury, 2020.

Sutanto, Nathaniel Gray. "Herman Bavinck on the Image of God and Original Sin." *International Journal of Systematic Theology* 18, no. 2 (2016): 174–90.

Tomaszewski, Christopher. "Collapsing the Modal Collapse Argument: On an Invalid Argument against Divine Simplicity." *Analysis* 79, no. 2 (2019): 275–84.

Tseng, Shao Kai. *Barth's Ontology and Sin and Grace: Variations on a Theme of Augustine.* New York: Routledge, 2019.

Tseng, Shao Kai. *G.W.F. Hegel.* Phillipsburg, NJ: P&R, 2018.

Tseng, Shao Kai. *Immanuel Kant.* Phillipsburg, NJ: P&R, 2020.

Van Asselt, Willem J. "The Fundamental Meaning of Theology: Archetypal and Ectypal Theology in Seventeeth-Century Reformed Thought." *Westminster Theological Journal* 64 (2002): 319–35.

Van Til, Cornelius. *The Case for Calvinism.* Phillipsburg, NJ: P&R, 1979.

Van Til, Cornelius. *Christian Apologetics.* Edited by William Edgar. 2nd ed. Phillipsburg, NJ: P&R, 2003.

Van Til, Cornelius. *Christian Theistic Ethics.* Phillipsburg, NJ: P&R, 1980.

Van Til, Cornelius. *Common Grace and the Gospel.* Edited by K. Scott Oliphint. 2nd ed. Phillipsburg, NJ: P&R, 2015.

Van Til, Cornelius. *The Defense of the Faith.* Edited by K. Scott Oliphint. 4th ed. Phillipsburg, NJ: P&R, 2008.

Van Til, Cornelius. "Evil and Theodicy." Unpublished paper, 1923. Westminster Theological Seminary Archives.

Van Til, Cornelius. *Introduction to Systematic Theology: Prolegomena and the Doctrines of Revelation, Scripture, and God.* Edited by William Edgar. 2nd Ed. Phillipsburg, NJ: P&R, 2007.

Van Til, Cornelius. "Nature and Scripture." In *The Infallible Word: A Symposium by the Members of the Faculty of Westminster Theological Seminary*, 255–93. Phillipsburg, NJ: P&R, 1946.

Van Til, Cornelius. *A Survey of Christian Epistemology.* Phillipsburg, NJ: P&R, 1969.

Van Til, Cornelius, and Louis Berkhof. *Foundations of Christian Education: Addresses to Christian Teachers.* Edited by Dennis E. Johnson. Phillipsburg, NJ: P&R, 1989.

Venema, Cornelis. "Covenant and Election in the Theology of Herman Bavinck." *Mid-America Journal of Theology* 19 (2008): 69–115.

Visser, Paul J. "Introduction: The Life and Thought of Johan Herman Bavinck (1895–1964)." In *The J. H. Bavinck Reader*, edited by John Bolt, James D. Bratt, and P. J. Visser, translated by James A. De Jong, 1–92. Grand Rapids, MI: Eerdmans, 2013.

Vorster, Nico. "The Augustinian Type of Theodicy: Is It Outdated?" *Journal of Reformed Theology* 5 (2011): 26–48.

Vos, Geerhardus. *Anthropology.* Vol. 2 of *Reformed Dogmatics.* Edited by Richard B. Gaffin Jr. Bellingham, WA: Lexham, 2013.

Vos, Geerhardus. *Biblical Theology: Old and New Testaments.* Carlisle, NJ: Banner of Truth, 1975.

Vos, Geerhardus. *Ecclesiology, Means of Grace, Eschatology.* Vol. 5 of *Reformed Dogmatics.* Edited by Richard B. Gaffin Jr. Bellingham, WA: Lexham, 2016.

Vos, Geerhardus. *The Eschatology of the Old Testament*. Edited by James T. Dennison Jr. Phillipsburg, NJ: P&R, 2001.

Vos, Geerhardus. *Pauline Eschatology*. Phillipsburg, NJ: P&R, 1979.

Vos, Geerhardus. *Redemptive History and Biblical Interpretation: The Shorter Writings of Geerhardus Vos*. Edited by Richard B. Gaffin Jr. Phillipsburg, NJ: P&R, 1980.

Vos, Geerhardus. *Self-Disclosure of Jesus: The Modern Debate about the Messianic Consciousness*. Edited by Johannes J. Vos. Phillipsburg, NJ: P&R, 2002.

Vos, Geerhardus. *The Teaching of Jesus Concerning the Kingdom of God and the Church*. Eugene, OR: Wipf & Stock, 1998.

Xu, Ximian. "Appreciative and Faithful? Karl Barth's Use of Herman Bavinck's View of God's Incomprehensibility." *Journal of Reformed Theology* 13 (2019): 26–46.

INDEX

absolute person xiii, 76, 101, 115, 117, 118, 121–5, 131 n.35, 141, 158, 194
absolute personalism 77, 95, 96, 99, 101, 103, 111–14, 119, 122–6, 128, 131, 135, 149, 158, 171 n.47
absolute personality xiii, 2, 77, 88, 89, 91, 96, 97 n.88, 101–3, 115, 118, 119, 129, 130, 171, 172, 193
accommodation 117, 136, 139–59, 161, 174, 194
ad extra 102, 138, 157, 169, 170–3, 194
ad intra 157, 169, 184
Adam 1, 10–12, 17, 18, 20–6, 28, 29, 32–5, 38–60, 62–75, 79, 82, 102, 106, 108–10, 112, 114, 122, 123, 191, 192
Adamic 38, 39, 57, 58, 70, 72, 74, 75
angels 3–9, 11–13, 17, 18, 35, 186, 191
anthropology 25, 31, 42, 43, 51 n.62, 59, 69–72, 79 n.4, 93, 147, 185
anthropomorphism 91, 99, 100, 117, 124, 132–4, 136, 137, 139–41, 143, 155, 157, 161, 182, 194
Aquinas, Thomas 131, 138 n.66, 176
aseity 77
Augustine ix–xiii, 33, 76, 94, 117, 119–21, 125 n.15, 141, 157, 194

Barth, Karl ix, 104 n.118, 123 n.12, 161, 162, 175
Belgic Confession 167, 168, 185
Bolt, John 94 n.74
Brock, Cory 113 n.155, 123 n.12, 124 n.13, 163 n.6, 173 n.58
Burger, Hans 168, 179 n.85, 185, 186 n.108

Calvin, John 25 n.102, 26 n.109, 56 n.95, 77, 90 n.52, 117, 141 n.76, 143–55, 157, 176, 186, 194
Calvinism xiii, 145
Chalcedon 15, 117, 157, 176, 182, 194
Cherbonnier, E. LaB. 99, 100, 101, 132, 133, 134, 171 n.47
Christ xii, 6 n.24, 7, 13, 15, 16, 17, 33, 57, 66, 67, 68, 70, 71, 72, 74, 75, 93, 98, 108, 114, 117, 147, 151, 156, 158, 161, 162, 167, 168, 173, 175, 178, 179, 180, 181, 182, 183, 184, 185, 186, 188, 194, 195

Christianity xii, 71, 101, 103, 113, 114, 120, 164, 165, 171
Christocentrism 167, 178
Christology 15, 104, 117, 161, 162, 166, 167, 169, 183, 185, 194
common grace 7, 63, 71 n.161
condescension 23 n.97, 35, 51, 76, 96, 103, 104, 105, 107, 108, 110, 111, 140, 146, 158 n.126, 171, 174, 182, 183, 184, 192, 195
consciousness ix, x, 6, 11 n.46, 14, 15, 18, 27, 30, 34, 35, 40, 44, 45, 73, 75, 76, 82, 86, 87, 90 n.52, 96 n.83, 101, 105, 106, 107, 110, 113 n.155, 115, 123, 127, 131, 132, 134, 146, 154, 158, 163 n.6, 171, 173 n.58, 191
creator-creature distinction 90, 102, 139, 149, 156

death 10, 15, 21, 24 n.99, 33, 34, 37, 41, 59, 62, 63, 64, 65, 71, 73, 74, 75, 83, 107, 109 n.133, 170
decree 18, 106, 112, 150, 175, 179, 184, 185, 186, 195
Descartes, René 103, 142, 143
dogmatics 3, 66, 77, 79 n.4, 95, 97 n.90, 98, 99, 101, 102, 104 n.120, 123 n.12, 125, 126, 131, 134, 142 n.83, 161, 162, 163, 164, 165, 167, 173, 179

eclecticism 113 n.155, 173 n.58
Eden/Edenic 1, 2, 3, 8, 9, 10, 11, 12, 13, 18, 19, 20, 22, 23, 25, 30, 31, 33, 34, 35, 38, 41, 46 n.37, 49, 51, 52, 54, 57, 72, 76, 98 n.95, 108 n.132, 191, 192, 193, 195
Eglinton, James P. 78 nn.2, 3, 97 n.90, 124 n.13, 163 n.6, 165 nn.16, 17, 167 n.23, 169 n.38, 174 n.66, 175, 176, 177, 182
epistemology 77, 83 n.20, 104 n.188, 113 n.151, 123 n.12, 140, 165 n.17, 173 n.58
eschatology 3, 16, 17, 19, 26, 27, 31, 32, 33, 34, 35, 46 n.37, 50 n.56, 63, 78 n.1, 106, 108, 114, 126, 180, 184, 191, 192
eternal generation 127, 169, 184, 186 n.110, 187, 188, 194
Eve 18, 20, 25, 28, 29, 40, 48, 49, 51 n.61, 55, 56, 57, 58, 67, 73, 81, 195
extra-Calvinisticum 175, 176, 177

Hegel, G. W. F. xiii n.17, 13 n.51, 78 n.2, 101, 102 n.14, 113, 129 n.25, 157 n.125, 172
Heidelberg Catechism 48 n.45, 167, 168, 185
Huijgen, Arnold 142 nn.79, 80, 143, 144, 145, 146, 147, 148, 149, 152, 153, 154, 157
humanization 174, 184, 186, 187, 188, 194
hypostatic union 194, 169, 180, 182, 183, 187, 188

idealism 78 n.2, 97, 126, 164 n.12
immutable/immutability xiii, 23 n.97, 33, 113, 137, 138, 150, 153, 169 n.38, 176, 177, 187
impassible/impassibility 138
incarnation 76, 153, 156, 157, 159, 161, 162, 168, 169, 172–4, 176, 177, 179–88, 194, 195

kingdom 2, 3, 9, 12–18, 32, 112, 126
Kuyper, Abraham 49, 59 n.107, 104 n.119, 124 n.14, 125 n.15, 141 n.76, 184 n.105

Logos 180, 181

monism 81, 100, 102, 170
Muller, Richard 141, 142, 145, 148, 167 n.22

natural theology xii, 165 n.17, 173

Oliphint, K. Scott 78, 158 n.126
original righteousness 24, 25, 28, 42, 46, 48–51, 53, 60, 65, 72 n.165, 108, 110, 192
organism 4, 6, 9, 10, 13, 16, 17, 38, 64, 68–70, 77, 79, 98, 156, 158, 163, 166, 178, 179, 182, 184, 193

Pass, Bruce 104 n.120, 164 n.12, 167, 169
Paul (the apostle) 4 n.13, 16, 29, 58, 63, 65, 78 n.2, 88 n.45, 131, 151, 186
Pauline 3, 48
Pelagianism 57, 172
perichoresis 131
Poythress, Vern 139, 140, 156, 157
presupposition 11, 20 , 45, 78, 83, 112, 135, 153, 154, 159, 169, 173, 181

prohibition 1, 2, 5, 8, 11, 19, 21, 23, 25, 26, 28, 30, 31, 35, 39–41, 46, 51, 53–9, 62, 73, 74, 107, 122, 191, 193
probation 10, 11, 19, 21, 23, 25, 26, 28, 30, 32, 39, 46, 54, 55, 73, 191

Ragusa, Daniel 165 n.17
revelation
  general 24, 140, 144, 171, 175, 180, 181, 185
  special xii, 21, 23, 32, 41, 91, 97, 111, 117, 124, 136, 137, 144, 147, 163, 171, 173, 178, 180, 181, 185, 194

Satan 3, 6, 7, 9–19, 26, 29, 30, 54, 93, 121, 122
self-communication 169, 184
self-existence 27, 130, 132, 141, 156
self-existent xiii, 12, 31 n.133, 45, 50, 77, 79, 81, 85, 86, 129, 135, 138, 156, 168, 169, 171, 185
simplicity 113, 137, 138
Sparks, Kenton 142
Strange, Daniel xii, 81 n.14, 95, 96 n.81, 171
Sutanto, Nathaniel Gray xiv, 68, 69, 110, 113 n.155, 123 n.12, 124 n.13, 163 n.6, 173 n.58

theological method 78 n.2, 125 n.15, 135, 140, 142
tree of life 31, 32, 71, 108, 109
tree of the knowledge of good and evil 1, 2, 11, 24–6, 28–32, 41, 43, 46, 51 n.61, 54–6, 75, 81, 106, 107, 109
Trinity 30, 34, 78, 87, 98–100, 115, 117, 119, 127, 130–2, 137, 147, 148 n.97, 155, 157, 158, 161, 165, 168–72, 173 n.61, 175 n.68, 176, 183, 194
Tseng, Shao Kai ix, xiii n.17, xiv, 13 n.51, 78, 79 n.4, 102 n.114, 129 n.25, 157 n.125

Urzeit x

Venema, Cornelius 167 n.22, 177

Westminster Standards 37, 48 n.45, 53 n.72, 168, 192

www.ingramcontent.com/pod-product-compliance
Lightning Source LLC
Chambersburg PA
CBHW062225300426
44115CB00012BA/2230